Peter Riley was born in Stockport in 1940. His education was at Stockport Grammar School, Pembroke College Cambridge, and the Universities of Sussex and Keele, and he has lived since in the south-east of England, Denmark, the Peak District, Cambridge, and Hebden Bridge. His first book of poetry was published in 1969. His poetry has always pursued the intersection of diurnal and exceptional experience, the commonplace and the potential, seeking to inhabit the route where language, on a loose rein, leads the author towards the unexpected recognition. It is also a poetry of result, personal, political, and historical, so it does not exhort and it does not decry: it stands witness. While much of it is a pure extension of the local, Riley sometimes takes up the technique of describing an elsewhere – a foreign, unknown place, a prehistoric grave, a very new or very old music and asking it to declare its hidden messages and singing its song. His several books of prose have worked out some of these concerns in studies of Transylvanian village music, travel notes in Romania, English village carols and improvised music. Since 2012 he has been the poetry editor of *The Fortnightly Review* (online) where the purpose of his reviewing has been to establish a way of describing the appearance and results of poetry without recourse to any of the closed or parochial vocabularies. His poetry is itself the central and generative point of all these possible avenues, and has ventured into intense compaction and expansive narration, hop-skip-jumps and immense rambles, always returning sooner or later to the known percept, the only workable meeting place.

The two volumes of this collection include all the poetry up to 2017 which he wishes to see preserved, and some which he does not. Something like a tenth of its contents has never been published previously.

Peter Riley

Collected Poems

Volume 2

Shearsman Books

First published in the United Kingdom in 2018 by
Shearsman Books
50 Westons Hill Drive
Emersons Green
BRISTOL
BS16 7DF

Shearsman Books Ltd Registered Office
30–31 St. James Place, Mangotsfield, Bristol BS16 9JB
(this address not for correspondence)

www.shearsman.com

ISBN 978-1-84861-611-0

Copyright © Peter Riley, 2018.

The right of Peter Riley to be identified as the author
of this work has been asserted by him in accordance with the
Copyrights, Designs and Patents Act of 1988.
All rights reserved.

NOTE TO THE READER

Untitled poems are headed by three asterisks, those which are parts of groups or sequences by a single asterisk, or bullet. Dates are those of first separate publication, unless this is greatly distanced from time of writing.

COVER
Abandoned mineshafts in the Great Flat Lode (mineral rocks under the Carn Brea, south of Camborne, Cornwall), Western section looking North West — towards South Condurrow, Tolcarne, Grenville, and Basset Mines. Image by courtesy of Dr Keith Russ.

Contents

XIV. Poems, Cambridge (i) 1985-2000

Saint Louis' Island (first version)	13
Place Dauphine	14
Notre-Dame	15
Front Room	16
Ashlar Facings / Pink Rose	17
La Sologne 1991	18
After Mandelstam	19
Castle Howard	20
Alstonefield ('The light fills the ground…')	21
Three Pastoral Poems	22
Gropina / Leopardi / Gropina	24

Small Square Plots	25

Aria with Small Lights	29

Poems to Pictures by Jack B. Yeats
Prelude: Night Shift	42
Music in the Train	43
Oh my Beauty!	44
One Remains	45
Men of Destiny. The Stolen Picture.	46
Music Night at the Old Slip Inn	47
On Through Silent Lands	48
The Little Watercolour at Sligo	50
This Grand Conversation was Under the Rose	51

XV. Excavations

Preface	55
Part I Book I: Distant Points	57
Part I Book II: This Carol They Began	81
Part II: Vacated Thrones	95

Dioscuria 137

Notes 145

XVI. Alstonefield

Preface 151
Part I 155
Part II 158
Part III 164
Part IV 169
Part V 172

Notes 251

XVII. Two Setts and Coda

First Sett 261
Second Sett 279
Coda
    The Towns along the Tisa 292
    Kalotaszeg 293
    The Crowd Yelled Out for More 294
    Pilliszántlaszlo 295
    Frustovento 296
    Schiele 297
    Stuck in Vienna… 298
    Room 40, Frühstückspension Caroline… 299
    A Cold Room in Granada 300
    Terezín 301
    After Terezín 302
    Alstonefield, After Dinner 303
    Across Central Europe 304
    Zum Weißen Roß 305

XVIII. Poems and Prose, Cambridge (ii) 1999-2013

Pieces written at the time of writing Excavations
1. The Songs   309
2. 'Write from henceforth...'   309
3. From an abandoned alley   309
4. 'A step forward...'   310
5. 'The clue to the Neolithic...'   310
6. 'The man in Jack Yeats...'   311

Messenger Street   312

Alstonefield Part VI   317

The Glacial Stairway
    Part 1   327
    Part 2   334

Pyrenean   343
This House...   344
Loutro   346

Bits and Pieces Picked Up in April 2007   347

Airs at Furthest Accord   350

Best at Night Alone   353

Cuban Nights   371
Dreaming in La Habana   372
Sad Fates of the Songsters   373
'Forgive these warriors...'   375
Long since the stars...   376
Vertigo   377
Szászcsávás: the older stratum   378
Four Transylvanian songs   379
Transylvanian Songs   381
The Children of Maramureș   382
Ultimul Drum   383

Weddings of the Gypsy Flower Sellers	384
Bukovina Song	385
Haydn at Csávás	386
To the Memory of Frank Cassidy	388
The Lark in the Clear Air	389
Drowsy Maggie	390
Kings Cross to SOAS	391
The Road + Remix + Carol	396
Shadowy Waters	399
Shining Cliff	401
Kemptown	407
Essex Skies	408
Whistling Sands	410
Lancashire Graveyards	411
Chapters of Age	412
Swavesey Lakes	419

XIX Greek Passages 2006

ExoMani 2002 (10 Preludes)	423
Argolid 2003	
I	426
II	429
III	433
Argolid 2004	
I	438
II	443
III	447
ExoMani 2005 (10 Postludes)	451
Notes	455

XX Due North 2015

I	459
II	469
III	475
IV	481
V	487
VI	494
VII	501
VIII	506
IX	512
X	518
XI	524
XII	535
Notes	543

XXI Poems, Hebden Bridge 2013-2017

Milia	547
'I'm out at night…'	549
5:39 from Lyme Street	550
Food Bank	551
I shall fall…	552
'Stumbling down the moors…'	552
'Round the last corner…'	553

Ferryports
Bardsey	554
Mull in the Rain	557
La Gomera	564

XXII Two Poems Offered, 2017

A Prelude for W.S.G.	567
Henge as Verb	569

Appendix: XV Pieces (dateless)

Alstonefield 1995	573
The Stones	574
Floating Verse	575
What People Have	576
51 Park Lane	577
Alpes Maritimes	578
Third Concert	579
'Peter Hughes drove us...'	580
Asa Beau Oaminii Buni	581
Lathkill, or, Putnik	582
'I used to dream...'	583
'The knowledge...'	584
!Kung Music	585
To a Grandchild	586
Sitting on Ecton Hill...	587

Afterword and Acknowledgements	588
Index of Titles	590

XIV

Poems, Cambridge (i)

(1985-2000)

Saint Louis' Island
First version

Again the bright label suspended in the sky
the new light burning in the old walls. Stone
carves the water: neither an attraction nor
a privilege but a mercantile success, –
a job of work. Water encrusts the stone
with tokens of twinhood, symmetrical facets
streaming in the river wind, a place that
cannot sink to what it has become.

Baudelaire lived here then moved to outer hell.
In memory of Berlioz I carry the heart monstrance
this bright morning through the wet streets and
over a bridge onto the stone crown. Aren't I also
the disqualified lover of vanishing states?
Aren't we all? Beams and signals hover and cross,
the wide eye of the street dweller calling to
the vertical fantasie of state O my lost brother!

Our forehead mansions, our genital kitchens, skin
to skin we read our histories to the world
and fortune is what we dare to ask, not for the
self, that sore, for the life. The vane
skreaks in the wind tossed off the cathedral,
the shops open and tense like bees in amber
and fast in the new day where first and simple
things are right, be grateful for every other.

Place Dauphine

I sit in the quiet place at ten p.m. A few people
playing boules among the trees by the amber lighting,
a dog or two being walked. A triangular square
of 17th Century housing with the river beyond it
still capable of including a sewing shop for the locals.
I eat *un sandwich grecque* with a beaker of red wine I carried down
from my room in Hôtel Henri IV which is OK but
you need to be at the front, I had a view of
drainpipe formations so I came down here
to the public place, in the gentle wind
that follows the river, rustling the leaves…

…guard our declaration, devolved
to a common purpose not any old common purpose but
a common purpose held in the indolent moment such as this.
Like a game, but not one, like a recognised good in a casual
emplacement, an instant of historical success. I love this place.
Baudelaire, come back from outer hell.

Notre-Dame

And then I thought of you.
I saw you in the fields
of your own life it was
truly the finest thing I
ever saw precisely because
it wasn't mine or exactly
yours but a future thing,
an earth detail regained.

Front Room

1.
Cold penetrates the house against
all expense, night cold on my
shoulder, deep red curtains.
Outside: mountains
white across the valley
or a brick street with yellow lamps
depending where this house is.
Where is this house? A cold silence.

2.
Solitude has its own gardens
with their own emptiness,
goldfish in a clear pool
and red flowers spilled across
green banks like scattered embers
bringing patience and delight
to the edges of a morality
where the sun patrols the fences
and redirects to the centre,
opening onto further fields
of self versus self, winning trust.
For the world will mean in the end.
We hope it. And this is you too.

3.
My flickering vision, of a work that sends
the reader constantly back to experience
full of belief in it, anticipating
all its bright corners and painful grit with
regard for the whole in its few notes ringing
across the gap to the green and grey mountains
where the heart settles on itself, for its
harmony. Bread and wine and yellow cheese.

Ashlar Facings / Pink Rose

Pale light on ashlar facings
sent back to the ground
intercepted by a pink rose
and the whole fabric
comes finally close
nothing could be closer.
Carry my number in your pocket
as I carry yours
across divides and instances.

La Sologne 1991

The day goes through its language forward,
I meet it in the evening when it turns at last
to face me beside the lake in the forest
closing its eyes at the simplest point,
two ducks on the water, two herons
floating high in the sky like black twigs,
two pains in one breast,
two grey eyes that set the day at rest.

The days turn through their volume onward,
surer than hand or dream or any doubtful thing
to reach the lake in the forest
and close the story at its fullest hour,
two ducks on the water, two herons
floating high in the sky like black pigs,
one pain in two breasts, the heart turning to face
the night of two grey eyes that saved the day.

After Mandelstam

Pure clear cups
the noble harmony and deep peace
of my household gods set
aside from sidereal pitch.

My household gods, always still,
rapt in scrupulous niches,
as the sun dims and thought extends
I listen to their silences.

What toy destinies
what timid laws
these finely sculpted bodies decree,
cold and fragile.

There are gods needing no worshipping,
you and the god are equal.
Your painstaking hand is permitted
to move them from one place to another.

Note: Mandelstam, the seventh poem of Stone *(1913)*

Castle Howard

We walked by the lake, the day
was officially closed but the bats
had just started trading, hundreds
of them all about us and a heron
flapped along the opposite bank.
Layers of light piling up on the water.
We knew there could not be a dead end,
walking slowly among bats in hollow light
by the great stretching water
and the fancy towers on the skyline.
Which goes to show, that life in this
art of making it plainly survives
what we are. The bats also lightly
missed our heads in sheer ostent.

Alstonefield

The light fills the ground. It comes welling up at evening to the wheat tips, grass sheen, the whole pelage iridescent, slanting and falling to resonant quick streams. And when you look into the distance you see tiers of pale rock breaking cover, tier upon tier like the layers of a crown rising to the horizon where they break like waves into a sky darker than the ground. It sports the badge of earth, the whole cross of moment.

So it is difficult to believe here, the way its quality fills all the possible space, that what happened in the 1992 General Election in Britain was real. That the lie extends to the centre of the pie, and apparently most people will agree to any bloody war on promise of a small increase in income immediately cancelled. But when you know a place really well you have no illusions; its fall is spread on it.

The Inn is cheap and wholesome, and that is the end. There is no third section, no answering stanza. In our own time we go there, take our meal and wine, pay for it and stroll around among the fields in the twilight. The old barn stands in the long grass, the church clutches its ancient carved heart, the land pitches on all sides into steep valleys full of quick silver. The evening is held in the balance, and increasingly full of suspended trust.

Three Pastoral Poems

Corkerbeg 1: The Neighbour Speaks

The goats eat everything, have you seen
the goats today, could you tell me
which field they're in?

They have stripped the lower branches
of the trees outside my house.

The cuckoo on the corner tree my alarm clock,
the beating of the snipe my evening bell.

Alone and melancholy for many weeks
especially in the long winters

Neither winning nor losing, I
attach a cup to the spring.

* * *

Nancy's Bar

"I was a soldier in Belfast for four years"
and suddenly the bar was empty.

We also tire ourselves

and tired of proof, tired
of acknowledgement

move out
even of the short song

and the beautiful quiet talk.
Galleon starfield.

* * *

Corkerbeg 2: Hedge School

Air courses down from the mountain
across the lightly constructed space
left to right, tired but adamant,
to speak adequacy, light from dark things.

Cold in the walls, the wine of age.
The lost masquer settles down for good,
bends forward to feed the small fire.

Waterlogged ground, cross slabs on back field knolls.
Far from advancement or delay
women and young children
hitch-hike without fear.

Gropina

The stars clustered in the valley base. And what do you learn of humanity? *humanitas non solo stet.* And what do you learn of the world?

Leopardi

The world shrinks as the population increases, and the familiar body inflates, and the hiss when the sun goes down into the sea is no longer heard. Whose mind was tensed between star and sea, fierce longing and knowable truth. Whose despair created a typeface. Whose darkness is born into our best dreams, where zero is an aperture of hope.

Gropina

Live in tedium, of course, sheltered by dream. Sheltered from earth figures and their brilliant despair, making the trade routes glitter at night.

Small Square Plots

Seven-line poems with seven syllables to a line, most of them over-written on British poems of the 1930s and 1940s. The authors of the original poems are acknowledged by their initials after the poem.

Now in green and musty fields
the elusive flame day's hidden
meaning floats in the hedge and
flips past my ear like a ghost
saying love is wild and true
to the end, where is the end?
O come dripping to the 'phone.
           CWG
   * *

Summer wipes the leaves a bright
glazier's green, tree standing in
a fuzz of cash, face value as
love contains an orange
on a wooden table: still
there nine years later hanging
cancelled debit on the air.
           DN
   * *

Love that covers death like snow
under a blue sky at noon
pale minute yellow flower
veined through the frozen crust of
eyes days voices promises
of the Atlantic mind a
needle held in constant north.
           JFH
   * *

Love wants to get in at him,
desperately, make him real
and lasting, a promise kept,
open access, a long peace
as the fruit of his process
but the chrysalis opened
and a hairy bear strolled out
                    RB
          * *

Lots of black cold. The thought that
made the world never thought it
would think so small and coldly
at the broad soldiers that bear
the breaking light on the black
flats, the free fens that hide what
we are, father out of night.
                 JGMcL
          * *

In the first idea of rest
was traffic and a distant
war, in the second idea
was a cushion called despair
finally the door opened
onto total loss without
the faintest sound in the air.
                    NM
          * *

Water breaks under the tree
to an ancestral rainbow
between reeds and written reeds
O love is restless there and
calls limb from limb and child from
home to a cold colourless
nothinged edge of air and sky.
                    TS
          * *

Coming back to the big blood
on the screen of days the towns
folding under themselves, what
separates weight and fortune?
The sky clears late behind trees
and lights come on the river,
lanterns fixed against sorrow.
                DC
* *

I love slowly and stumble
through the spaces between words.
A bar opens in the voice
of no one I know, the long
river lights a way edged with
wisdom and my normal weight
prints warnings on the white sand.
                WSG
* *

Day closes in a mad rush
to get the small letters right
comfort to the afflicted
soft words and luggage labels
meeting in the windy street
beautiful eyes fat commerce
what remains of a taxi.
                SC
* *

A rich river with cliff-like
white hotels where steadfastly
I am hollowed against my
inventions in a slow tongue
remembering well, truly,
friendly with fear, run chatting
to a further fallen town.
                AR
* *

Bright architecture brighter
than its function and the world,
love's title-page, archipel-
ago in the sky a Roman nose
in a spread of faceless stars.
Then singing has a good room:
praise of persons, taste of tomb.
                    NM

          * *

No, have not gardened sorrow
but broadened the story home
of a love I held alone
against death's candle fences
skittled seven times to rest
in a garden of mornings
sonant with pillar-box caves.
                    TG
          * *

The grey hotels, the seven
syllables amassed in the
last resort. Thoughts are cradled
in loft rooms of cliff houses
to weigh a beautiful lack,
a sea or carving, against
life provisioned into cloud.

Aria with Small Lights

Late one summer evening in 1997 I walked out onto the hillside at the back of an Italian mountain village, and soon after I'd passed the last house noticed a glow in the air ahead of me among conifers, which proved to be the small village cemetery. The glow was from the lights on the graves, some of them candles but mostly small electric lights of the kind we use for Christmas trees. The cloud base was almost on the ground and the light although slight was dispersed into it as a luminous mist. I walked up to the gate and stopped. In the following poem this action of approach is repeated, by my reckoning, thirty times, in almost every stanza, in many different ways but always as an approach to a space which is not entered.

In an ordinary life I walked one night
on the high ridge top, Vitiana, great valley
of the Serchio north of Lucca. I walked,
nobody about, late evening, stone ginnels
and steps, enormous toads and fireflies, warm
darkness, I walked up behind the village.
There was a glow round a corner. In the hand
of the night haze I wasn't anyone, I had
no history, some kind of foreigner under a wall.

And anyone could become this. There was a light
dispersing into the darkness above a gate in a wall,
a glow hovering in the space I walked towards,
nameless and unknown under lit windows,
on small tracks past the top of the village. Harm
strapped to my back as it was a needed message
I walked towards, a diagnosis. It was a land I
petitioned to enter at the custom shed but had
no language, no history of known good at all,

Because I refused to be reminded and might yet
meet a new mind in a night glow hovering tall
over me in the under branches of a few low trees,
not moving at all but hanging there like police notices
in an occupied city, the blue light you have to turn
under and in the door to bow before the empty page
and ask if you might be considered worthy to stand
to the side of this country, under the wall, with no bad
words spoken against you, the pure eyed calf in its stall,

Standing there while the cemetery glows, and hides its bite.
When I reached the gate in the wall it became further
to what was in front of me than all I had known, the cost
of continuing, because it was a town and nothing else,
a town with all its lights below me alive and burning
through the night, it was the very town of death
busy about its businesses, telephoning across the land,
balancing its currencies against its goods and I had
nothing to offer it. I had nothing to offer it at all.

I was halted before it, I was in a life in the night
not worth telling while echoes of my father
still clung about me. We were living in a hut
or cottage off the village square somewhere. Thence
we walked hence we loved there we drank the stinging
wine. In the early evenings the people who were
really there sang in the square gathered in a band.
There were flesh hooks in their song, there were knives
to cut life out, there were eyes fastened to the wall,

The walls that hang over you with small lights
in small windows near their summits. I'd rather
shrink to a blob of sweat on the road under that
towering domus than claim a thing I never so
much as lived a week in. Or be a ghost entering
people's houses quietly through the closed door,
a thread of ink through lives, out the back and
walk on up to the cemetery, whose lights are knives,
at which day trades recoil, though gentle and small.

The colourless lights, burning in the night
like points of certainty in a page of weather
like the only certain thing left us, that
message from a great distance across the snow
and ice of death to this warm night burning
with one meaning. Which if I could stress forth
on the tables of pasture I'd be able to stand
the silence. I can't stand the silence, the sad
messages reaching no one at all,

The vacuum at the desk across which no fight
and no love can pass, and is set there for
us to make some moment of, and know a lot
less. Leaning over the gate I ceased to know
where love can hide, someone's name burning
like a fag-end on the path, and remain sure
of the pavement under all lives. The walled
garden with the lights of nothing on the ground
was the end of my thin days in liberty hall.

So I stepped no further forward than I might
and there were fireflies coding hope and loss:
switching on and off, hovering in and out
of the bean frames on the rich hillside, and slow
toads moved with infinite patience and no harm
on the village steps under the dim lamps. The dark space
behind the church had a lit shrine in the wall that fed
the roots of separation. Where are you all this grand
pulp of living night so educative and tall?

Big soft harmless toads, I suppose, in slow flight
from untoadness, as I from the shadows of my fathers.
You from difference, as I from like. Reaching this summit
graveyard full of lights piercing the softness what else
could I be but someone peering out of a small window frame
at a human distance unsuspected, like Thomas Gray faced
with the university of the tilled ground, and appalled and
made to sing against everything he had ever owned,
What are these, who suddenly seem so educated and tall?

Who shine at their stations in silence, dressed bright
as royalty. What are these shades behind lethal wire
dressed in stripes and meeting at a point of light, that
cannot speak, so we are safe from, but whose houses
evidently have a party going on and we are not invited.
Like the singing in the square and the lights in the shrine,
like the wedding funeral. We are privileged to stand
to the side and let the procession past, we are not so bad
as to deny the signal of a strict fate during a fancy ball.

And I am truly amazed. I come from a dispersed place
far away and still I know that these points of cold fire
are lives given wholly into where they are, so that
they can never be anywhere else but like a mouse
in the wainscot or a toad on the road eat the same
bread in a different country and trade the same love
strife in a different light. We are holes in this light, and
we are strangers in this country, which takes my hand
and leads me to the graveyard metricising my drawl.

This walled orchard no one can enter without pass
and currency, without name. Yet I walked without fear
into the Campo at Pisa (I had paid) and faced what
silenced thought, leaving nothing but a pause
in the night a faint shuffle on the road avoiding blame
and avoiding love. Piled arcades the shade of a dove
wrapped energy in care and every grain of the land
overflowed with need. And I one of many had hauled
my soul to that construct, glowing pale and ready to fall.

Mother rosebush, share my dark red glass
like a sentence in the silence, a tension where
the buds burn in the night, burn to a point that
points me out as a stranger. Therefore silent, because
somewhere between cash and carry I lost my name
or avoided it, and stood in the field of honour: above
me the timely circles turned in white stone and
wrote me to the new horizon like a train on the hard
lines at night, bright signals before the long haul.

Mother ashes, grand dame, where now is all that fuss?
all that patting and parting, the tremors in the air
as the lamb is led past the mutton shed with its bat
and ball and its brain in a satchel for the next course,
where is all that fear? O it's here, here and same,
here at a scatter of points which is all I shall have
to die with, when I agree to die I shall thrust my hand
in this pocket full of hard won reward and cast
it to the sky. The burial lights wrap absence in a shawl.

But I twisted out of the village grip, the college hand-
shake, on a curled path above the massed houses. There
was a stone wall, behind the wall a glow and a gap
in the wall and in the gap a gate. I felt like a horse
fastened to a cart awaiting instruction, tug of rein
this way or that into some known domain of love
that would deliver us from the unkind land
of untruth, icy and far. I leaned on the barred
gate as a dumb beast in need of honest toil.

What I needed was a mobile phone to hold in my hand
and signal like the fireflies floating in the warm dark air
signalling love, then signalling death. Tick and tock,
fruition and destruction in a slight variant of morse,
buzz, croak, death is the cost of every song we gain.
So chatting on the line as usual and the world like a dove
flutters away from our self cancelling discourses and
leaves me standing alone on the dark ground starred
with former lives, trying not to believe that they call.

But they do, as the fireflies call with their fire and
the slow toads with their patience and my life where
it comes full circle will call and call to you, What
can I bring to your lowly stall from the endless pause
called hope? If I could bring the truth I would be a pain
in your side, an unwelcome immigrant in the office
for questioning. And I stand outside in the dark land
signalled to by the people I knew when I was a proud
witness to human goodwill, wrapped in my pall.

They are no longer with us and their thoughts stand
in remote places blinking off and on in bare
corners of the night to whoever passes and waits,
thoughts that welcome the stranger as matter of course.
Someone is willing to take the dark and narrow lane
and meet the shine of a dark face eyes to eyes
as a mutual trust and if proved wrong let it stand
as a priority. And say so and say it out loud –
the dead can only say the objective whole.

Speak it gently in small lights, candles and Christmas bulbs
strung, rose-mother, in your garden kitchen, where
the night cakes are forced. Held in your skirts they
smoke towards dawn. And here, wishing the cause
of anxiety to be known, but to remain apparently sane,
I cast my futures on a spangled board. It would be nice
to make some connection there, for my number to land
on a fruiting point, a windfall. I turn to face the portal, add
an arm to a shoulder and we sing together the songs of shortfall.

Facing the music, the gleam in the fiddler's eye, as we must,
me and my ghostly other we fill our lungs with air
arm on shoulder each to each and openly declare
our immense disappointment, and deep sense of loss.
The details are unimportant. The tune is again
in the minor, to a slow rocking four. And not a trace
of gloom shadows our faces, boldly we face the band
in the triumph of our time on earth to have and hold
the music that sits across pain, curved with the earth and as loyal.

It's me and my double-ganger in duet, a bit of rust
in the pipes but never mind, the people are out there,
tiaras and tie-pins twinkling in the mist, in the smoke that
rises from the stage lights we sing of beauty and old wars.
The sky is solidly behind us, day's tincture on the wane
as night pulls from ridge to ridge its pierced surface,
its black furnace, over us all. Together we sink, and
sing the stars to ground in our decline. Pulling the earth hood
over our faces, we burn to nothing behind the wall.

Almost nothing. Some pieces or tokens of mutual trust
gleam on the earth, and read as a transcript of care
across organised cruelty. And these are things that
we have always had, for which we owe nothing because
we are already there where success is in vain, where
patience nests in the fruiting trees and a fine lace
of stars hangs round the neck and illumines the face
of the sleeping worker. I creep in beside him and
together we sound the night's distances in the blood-
beat brother to brother, Simon and Paul.

It would be good to get it exactly right for once
before we part for ever and wander away where
the rivers touch the sea full of shadows waiting
to return. Not to get it wrong, the passionate force
that speaks us while we're here and speaks us fair
if we deserve it, shining in the night like old bone,
the corner against harm. It would be a fine grace
to issue wholesome energy forth but here this grand
sequence of goodwill collapses, I don't know what good
all this wishing does, I don't know where to crawl

And hide, from the accusing fires. "You might
in some court or school, get away with asking. Here
you have to answer." But it would be a good thing
surely, to view the earth-flares with gladness or the
sky fires with resignation, or simply to stand there
in the mist the flames of distance on all sides and gain
from somewhere a willingness while the sun's
in hiding, to let this darkness be. It's yours, in your hand
squirming with shining lives like small prawns cooked
in white wine. Love these delicate creatures and eat them all.

It's yours, the voices say, the voices in the night vat,
the candles on the birthday cake, warming the black air
under the small trees on the top of the hill, singing
far behind the wall, Somewhere a voice is calling.
What is mine? – Anything you care to name,
as long as you don't move; while peace holds this fair
prospect is yours. And up here nothing moves, from base
to zenith all is still. Isn't this then the very land
you wanted to enter? Doesn't this motionless moment hold
a four-way tension across the world? So they call

From far away, from deep under the tricks of light.
And I'm still here at the gate, seeing from afar
the small flames of history like a traveller pausing
at the top of the pass to view the burning houses
of the home valley. That was my uncle's, that was where
we first met, that was the school, and the whole frame
is split for ever. I have gained this empty place
full of darkness and energy points. From my hand
it falls like sand but I remember yesterday's gold
light on the white arch, distinctly, each in all.

Old light, Italian, passing into the stone as I sat
there paused in a personal shade where
slow toads walk and funeral candles burn, causing
an absence in the day, a blink in the light which is
full of history and tracks all deaths and sorrows. There
in the burning light on the sculpted portal the lost names
file in at the door on a hopeless quest for peace
and belonging, refused point blank at every office and
no reason, for there is none. We shrug. We have sold
the light to the tourists and wait with candles in the black hall.

A book, about war and death, is open at a black page with white
punctuation. But all I can read is the story of a lost partner,
an old man in Dorset seeking the art of forgetting
in slow sung syllables before dawn. How does this
help the southern victims of corporate greed? The air
holding the light says it does, says that blame
disperses like a silver cloud in the night and ceases
all its clamour. Then the song is slowly sung, the band
wrapping it in distance saying we shall all when we are old
turn our losses on a silver palate under a dry wall.

And how does that help the victims of massive corporate
indifference? Oh it does, says the tidal rhythm, care
is balanced on a sense of what you are and the thing
you will finally be. What are you going to be? – this
old fellow walking slowly up to the graveyard where
his memories are errant fireflies and a single name
fills both staves? Or some tight bag of successes
counting its gains in the broken backs and foiled
lives of a continent, happy as a pike in a waterfall.

Life's own loss and failure truly owned will be a pride
to inhabit in some corner of the earth, a sorrow where
the new earth pivots. And some creature will sing
it forth – not the bearer, not the old man on the hill, this
pleasure falls to the reader, who lurks behind, whose care
for distance inhabits the loss, whose truth came
and stood by the widower at the grave. Caresses
of 1965 are set in a nosegay and placed on the ground.
Turns and heads for home without a sound.

Poems to Pictures by Jack B. Yeats
with a refrain from Handel

Prelude: Night Shift

Where there are lights there are people,
In a hospital ward at night, shifting
And groaning, talking quietly not to
Wake others, switching on and off a
Dim light over the door – from outside
A flicker in the window as the pedestrian
Passes under the tall building in the middle
Of the night, walking steadily home
To light a candle and carry it up to bed.

Where there's a light the mind is in question.
There are thousands, across the city,
Cross-shifting lights of which any at
Any time serves to tell, to guide
Someone to somewhere, the nearest
Toilet or out into the soaring arcs.
The pedestrian lies in the bleak loft,
His light by a cup of water on a bed-
side chair, reaching for a page about eyes.

The night sky opens and shuts cloud-curtains
In the theatre of everything we aren't. They stream
To the horizon as the shepherd in the play
Calls his cares back and the flashing machine
Spirals to a final top. There the greatest distance
Is absolute contact. And the watch lights
Gather quietly for the last time round one
Who dies before dawn to prove
That time sets all things right.

Music in the Train

No escape from a small country. An old man
Stands up in the train and plays his violin.
Ghosts pour out of it. Everyone nods, this
Is a music to die to, knowing that you are
Bound to and the train rattles on.

We pay a dream tithe to the ancestral hat
And head into the city looking for work.
I never asked to be out of this I was never in.
I never longed for another. Green hills out
Of the train window, touched by cloud,
Draw the very breath from my throat until
The only dying left is into this line.

Which is I suppose too a way, a rather
Circuitous way round the hill but a way
For all that of supposing, and launching
Your soul into the guess, that the work you do
When you arrive is good work, and time once
Properly located sets all things right.

Oh My Beauty!

At some point of a life
An arm goes over a shoulder.
Then we know what we are.
A helpless wish, a wishful help,
The best of what we are.
The city rears to a heraldry
And the stars fall to the side.

The sky reaches over
A mind or shoulder
To yellow meadows and brown
Hills where strife is over and the city
Falls to a market. The stars
Lie in the grass like twists of bestness
Spelling Time Sets All Things Right.

One Remains

I would like to die lying on a hillside
In the West of Ireland one summer evening
Crossing my legs and resting my right cheek
On my right palm with my latest companion
Standing beside me already wondering
How at that age to find a new friend. I
Like to think there are people I don't
Yet know who'll be willing to ease my way
Through that day's work. I shall gulp
The sunset I shall turn the slope on edge
And one stands there, he or she, asking me
If time sets all things right.

(i) Men of Destiny

Walking into the nation bearing
The sun in their lineaments, blood
And salt on the ground, everything
As it actually is.

Pure light stinking to heaven
Bursts through the rib-cage,
Heart-fire returns to the land
Wrapped in flesh, rises to cloud and
Floats away over the hills,
Anthem to an unknown future.

Then proudly forth, star on the ground,
Frail vehicle chained to the
Compass wound saying Men it is Men
not Time sets all things right.

(ii) The Stolen Picture

Men, if only they would. The woman
Casts a small pink rose

Across the blue morning, we speak
At last of the world

And it is too late it is fallen and lost.
Time brings lost things back.

Music Night at the Old Slip Inn

Nothing less than exactitude: exactly
A 40 degree lowering of the eyelids
In respect of a national hope and the degree
Of emancipation that might result, exactly
A high B-flat at the keystone of *The Last Rose*
Lingering into a curtailed glissando
So delicate as to be unannotatable.

Sings his song, as he often has, a worker in the day.
They listen, and the moment stands still in its
Becoming, where national is never enough, and
The spirit of the commune tunes the incus
To a fairer reason. Becoming what? becoming history.

Yes, this also is history, this pub-singing, that constructs
A momentary refuge from hope, as from despair, a fragile place
(the exact sustaining of the final cadence) a place
Of now, the very banner of the struggle. For here time sets
All things right. And the future, with luck, might set
A few things at any rate a good bit better than they were before.

On Through Silent Lands

To make of the heart a question mark
And forward artefact, a woven thing
Held close and shedding purpose
On the ranges, slowly articulating
Resistance beyond what a life
Can speak to, the swellings of
Oppression that crown human heads
With fear and disappointment. So the
Stressed consonants, the shreds of colour
Fleshing through the dark land:
The heart   The wish   The demand –
A good life in an unjust society,
                A difficult thing.
What sign does the heart make
When the shadowed limbs falter?

                On through
Silent lands, crossing creeks on
Wooden footbridges, long tracks
Winding over the mountains and
Down great wooded valleys. Mud
On my coat, sky on my hands I go,
Announced by lark on high as
Hedgehog and hare watch from their
Grassy stations. So the world has a chance.

                Through it
A traveller passes pressing a hat
To his chest as if the heart
Needed protection from the rainy
Convexities of the universe,
And from the wholeness that
Burns a mind to stone. And from
The heart's own exclusivity.

And thus continues for weeks over
Silent lands to the goal of speech
Many troubles beyond, to the world's
Rebirth in kindness, knowing
Also that time (a known thing at
Day's decline) sets (easily as river
To sea) all things (whatever's
Wrong with them) right.

The Little Watercolour at Sligo

The point of pain
At which the voice either
Cracks or cruises. The little fat man

Makes it, whoever he is, drunk but
Not too drunk in village night he
Stops to sing, his head rises, his arms fall,

His mouth like a typographical O.
And it works: he cruises out across time
He brings history back home in a small purse.

Nameless and small, he
Sails a stranger's psyche, saying
Cast your (care) crown. This

Is success, this is being, this
Is where love fastens us to the earth
And time sees to the rest.

This Grand Conversation Was Under the Rose

The person in his/her moment supreme. Of the
Successions of which history is the sum.
So the grand conversation can start. Art
And poetry and all their costly trappings
Immediately vanish for ever – there's plenty
Of time, no one's making a recording, sit down
Here and be the failure your heart's ease knows.
Don't be modern, don't be threatened,
Be just, be welcome and be generous and the earth
Is yours for the duration. The stage is set
Because the heart is in need, adverbs and
Prepositions everywhere begging to be used.
Like the surface of the earth rolling into itself

We know and have always known what this
Gift is for, placed on our lips. It is for
Time's reconciliation. It is for eloquent farewells
And that grand conversation under the rose.

Notes

The poems' titles are those of the pictures referred to, with the exception of:

Night Shift: *no reference.*

Oh my Beauty!: *actually called* My Beautiful! My Beautiful!

One Remains: *more commonly known as* Death for Only One

The Stolen Picture: Bachelor's Walk: In Memory *(stolen 1971, recovered 2007 and now in the National Gallery of Ireland. In memory of Irish Volunteers shot at this street in Dublin in 1914. A woman casts a pink rose over the site.)*

The Little Watercolour at Sligo: *title unknown, described from memory.*

The refrain from Handel, "Time sets all things right", is from the oratorio The Triumph of Time and Truth.

XV

Excavations

(1995/2004)

Preface

These are: meditations / constructions on 19th century excavation reports of the contents of prehistoric burial mounds in northern England, mostly of the period now thought of as an uninterrupted development from Neolithic to Early Bronze Age centred *circa* 2000 BC, with emphasis on the apparent funerary disposition and orientation of the body and its parts, and other internal features, in relation to each other and to the whereabouts of the tumulus. The archaeological evidence is sometimes given within the text, sometimes not. The primary sources for parts One and Two, Mortimer and Greenwell, who both worked in the Yorkshire Wolds, are as given in the headings and notes. A "wold" is a plateau-like area of high ground in a curved chain of chalk hills, uncultivated (wold = wild) until the early 19th Century. The appendix, 'Dioscuria', arises from the excavation of a tumulus in the Peak District of Derbyshire, by Thomas Bateman.

The reports are taken as they were found. A modern archaeologist might attach greater weight to the effects of soil-shift, redisposition or destruction of burials by subsequent buriers or by other forms of intervention, such as burrowing rodents, etc., and would also want to consider the results of loss of flesh by exposure of the corpse for a long period prior to burial. But no amount of cautionary rationalism can invalidate some of the amazing things found by the old excavators under those grassy hilltop mounds.

I feel these pieces can be read in various ways, according to the reader's inclinations or experience of modern poetry, from pure text to monologue. My own preference is to read the piece whenever possible as a kind of *khoros* sung and danced over the exhumed remains, as at that point near the end of many of the Greek tragedies when a screen is drawn back revealing a tableau of death (empty figures and masks, the actors from which are now survivors in the foreground). If so, it is a Chorus often striving between lamentation and celebration, whose members speak together in different tongues from different places and times, offers of harmony bought in fragments and the relics of a common humanity authenticated by a common fate.

Technicalities:

Italics about 90% represent quotation from the archaeological sources, usually fragmented and not necessarily exact, but there is a 10% anarchic principle within which they can also be anything else. This proportion is greater with **bold**, which basically represents quotation (or feigned quotation) from old texts, the majority 16th or 17th centuries lyrics in English.

Each piece is numbered with my own number to the left, and the number the excavator gave to the tumulus on the right (for some reason Mortimer usually represented the single century as "C" while otherwise using Arabic numerals – perhaps this had some connection with his profession of corn chandler). A number such as XXI/8 (or 273K) represents the burial or deposit numbered 8 (or K) in the tumulus numbered XXI (or 273) (Greenwell's and Mortimer's systems respectively).

Abbreviations:

OGS = original ground surface (i.e. the ground surface upon which the tumulus was built and into which the subterranean elements were dug, not necessarily lower than the present ground surface).

An indication such as NW-SE indicates the orientation of an object: lying north-west to south-east. If the object is a human body the position of the head is given first. NE/SE indicates a body lying with head to north-east, facing south-east (therefore on its left side), though this relationship is normally spelled out. Cremated remains can also be oriented when the deposit of ashes was formed into a longitudinal shape rather than a circle or a scatter.

Distant Points

Excavations
Part One, Book One

From the Researches of J.R. Mortimer
in the Yorkshire Wolds

1.   1

the body in its final commerce: love and despair for a completed memory or spoken heart /enclosed in a small inner dome of grey/drab-coloured [river-bed] *clay, brought from some distance* and folded in, **So my journey ended** moulded in the substance of arrival **I depart** *and a fire over the dome and a final tumulus of local topsoil* benign memorial where the heart is brought to witness the exchange: death for life, absence for pain, double-sealed, signed and delivered – under all that press released to articulate its long silence, long descended • tensed wing | spread fan | drumming over the hill.

2.   C39

folded in river clay, the boat on the hilltop /lying East-West facing upwards *the right hand on the right shoulder, the left arm across the body* gradients of sleep, to die, to dream, to mean— *beyond his feet to the East a row of three small circular pits or stake-holes* dawn trap as the compass arc closes southwards and the heart is secured by azimuth, all terrors past: **She only drave me to dispaire** /dead child, cancelled future in a satellite cloak hovering to SE. Yet the loss, folded into history, sails adroit in the clay ship over commerce and habit, bound for (to) this frozen screen where [cursive] we don't live, but do (love) say, and cannot fail.

3.   233

who) *crouched at a right angle, head to East facing North, right arm doubled back, hand on face, left arm bent at a right-angle, arm across body* – armature of memory and affection, relinquishment of wish – squared in his own frame **perish in despair | die for the fair** and other (wares, treasures, trash) So closely the arctic weather becomes his word, and his lost fortune rings the horizon, armored in latitude **that most rare brest** against the warm, denying thought.

4.   6
South: destroyed children. We turn our backs; only the North is kind. The forged cold.

5.   18
Upward chevron on the shoulder-pack, the stars between dogs' heads (Orion's eyes set to vengeance) **suspended heart** attaining meaning | meaning the shepherds' call across the valley, the hunter's triad in the forest **where kindnesse dwelles** /hanging **in middle air** his **auctoritie** feeding back the overplus (of pain too) as service. His right over a temporary clearing. His prior pacted death into the curve of light at pain's edge, where the City spreads.

6.   21
Distance joins us by the third person *each holding a part of the same child.* Looking so hard eye into eye across the motorway and the chord dissolves – So it was in the long hills, with the flashing tailback: endless demands, rival claims **that the heart may break**, overjoyèd at the world's convocal edge.

7.   43
the food that finally blocks the face, as a town blocks light • pains of succession *tightly crouched. But beneath this was another body, head to South facing West, six black flint discs behind his head ... five more of these scattered through the body of the mound, and* one on the western horizon in its own house: There, **be there my trust** | fixed there |**never part** | I blocked my face with knowledge facing the plangent sunrise and a sky shard calling me to fidelity turned my life round to a short song at a great distance further. Distinct ringing of the earth as the black stars gather to the nail-head.

8. 72
Turn our heads the same way, many years apart | *separately, and on different horizons but the two bodies in almost exactly the same position* [heads to WSW facing SSE] a chord that burns through a life across the grey ganglionic nuclea to reach a platform behind the eye (arctic clouds massed in indigo, faked in gold) *dorsal vertebra pushed tightly into the calvarium* glowing red, and behind us the moon of broken things and infant souls. A new created world springs up.

9. 276: Dog Hill
Our limbs become hunters and tear us apart from the centre outwards, one step from home. The bird knight stands to the side, resting | *one complete foot on the original ground surface, a little North-West of the centre.* Metatarsal, thin as leaf, on the child's pelvis. A new created world springs up.

10. 273: Duggleby Howe
Red in a white matrix the fire stars, lives rendered to a point and sealed in the blue clay dome, to hover over the theatre of memory *a finely ground and polished plate of almost transparent flint in front of the face* **My feerfull dreme** | falling angels, hands in front of faces swirling into darkness | to where no earth or sky or any mortal claim has any place **nevyr forgete can I** love's harm.

11. 70
The central hole in the small sky, with white markers, focused on the heart *head and thighs violently thrust to the side* (left, North-East) or focused on the head but missed it – *twisted, and a small hole in the rock to the right of the head, containing* (food, rubbish, the usual suspects). Facing the future disjunction but refused to see and so to act *Both hands in front of face* **who seek their gaine in others wo** *Here Psyche descends* et se répand sur toute la terre.

12.   116
Lying front to back across a red streak, *a pipe of ferruginous earth* (that your heat stay by me and not spiral in the smoking glass) Ageing to South-East with the coral and deepening, hands *as if reaching for the cup* that only the child obtains **So living die** and crest the circular sky in declaration, and leave not well alone.

13.   88
The entertainer *(shafted arrowhead under thigh bone)* bursts open and casts his bodily parts into the family office! They hold themselves together, focused on a burning hub that persists from generation to generation: **All these were men.** I come to warm my hands, and deliver a letter. The sun extends an arm athwart the corner of the rectangle (where timely care lapses) singing **Humble dum humble dum / Remember oh thou man / Thy time on earth is spent** in a succession of psychosomatic illnesses leading irrevocably to/ **Tweedle tweedle twino.**

14.   52
Sewing, salting, sailing the self out on the world / blades ringing through the eyes | *A one-note bone flute, or whistle* A pygmy idiogram that wraps the mind in succession and brings the body home in pieces *a skull, with the other bones of the body jumbled together and piled up against it. The under-jaw was fully twelve inches from the head and on the opposite side of the deposit* : the whole body in the mouth. Turning, burning a point a memory into | trampled ground, into | distant provinces.

15.   54
a deposit of various tarsal and metatarsal bones, skull fragments, jaw fragments of six individuals, crammed into a skull calvarium and set crown up on top of the grave Speak together then, for greater gravity [**ther is no life like ours**] and (when the pie was opened) plunge spiralling into the earth, from this eminence – bird knight, cartilage flapping in the wind.

16.   94
Our empty spaces either side the bed. The tune is engraved on a black flint double-knife behind your shoulder and the map of earth where the leaves meet, the frail moth flutters at the moon. So those fair lids close, on darkness burning cold and memory is printed in negative, an enclosure in the night sky the parcel depot of our changes. There the few words spoken, half to oneself, come finally to rest in a surety of tenure that lays distance on the cracked glaze of a sounding board and **Heaven her bright stars through earths dim globe shall move** O swallow swallow

17.   208
And the heart floats above in a small boat over a crack in the earth *of sand and clayey matter, which formed an eminence, being more resistant than the surrounding subsoil to denudation*. Solid absence, on which *a few cremated bones in a dish-shaped hollow lined with wood* "like a small boat" rides the pains of succession | denudation set in motion by calcification during Bronze-Age land use, the present ground surface *some three feet lower than that protected by the tumulus* and the body below, bundled into a crevice facing south, artefacts leaping from the skin. Quietly drifting across the estuary. Such noise in the air, such conclusion.

18.   211
A bowl, a northern sky ring flickering at the rim, a dish of nascent matter behind the comfort-seeking face, the agreeable body, a stewpan of/ *a circular hollow ten inches deep was cut into the edge of the grave behind the man's head, full of dark earth mingled with animal teeth and bones, ox horn-cores and ribs, three flint splinters, a broken bowl and a palm of red deer antler with four tines* globe of hunger and waste, god-food /by the black blades a theory moving through earth's equivocation to the cup, *placed in front of the face, just out of reach of both raised hands* so the text passes forward through his cancelled idiolect, held in the halo of its own cause, geography of need, pitted earth. The past speaks me in bitter fragments towards the impossible and the sign is close to the

head : *a broken shard of a much larger vessel* **In this system the living person is the only complete and irreplaceable thing** (frail and dusty moth settled safely on my arm) Belief spins through the northern gate from ice to desert across any possible city in a tangle of red and black, creating immeasurable harm | where flowers fade **Be not afrayde** | and caught back in the very tide of its own hunger to an East-West diurnal in a caul of opening throats, where each vowel becomes a field of thrift.

19.   55
A knife grows in the heart | extent crashes at point and bound | the question closes. Bodies in a generational sequence sunk into the centre, that space "cut too small from the inside" – cot, factory, and war. The heart closes on the knife, plurals rise and disperse at surface as the globe turns but are drawn again to the same closed question, that cornered thing so proudly policed, that time sucking badge | and with nothing to answer, no longer know, **whether the roses be your lips** and cast a smoking heart to the wall, flower of the.

20.   58
the/ *one deposit of burnt bones in a shallow scoop at the centre of the empty ring*—the entire person, directionless and unrelated entity *with no artefacts or accompaniment of any kind and nothing else in the entire tumulus* But so well remembered your forgetting, so well forgotten your name, as you would wish it | or the single rose, or the drop fallen from that rose, or the shadow that burns to a point, or a final hour in the eye, that stares **Merrilie upon the plaines**

21.   12
Take your head to your thigh and lose your teeth (looking for a baby's voice) or stretch the heart between two faces and find time sharp enough

to cut through silicon | and in that cut a rosy blue air appeared | in that cut a sky resigned.

22.   201
Walking alone *head to North facing West* (position of unusual rectitude) in an inner garden strewn with completed lives, one of which shadows him in ash: one day, knife in heart. Desire focuses behind the body to a pre-linguistic parcel, never seen, always there, heavy with curses, hot to the touch, impelling that restless and unhappy shade. Believing fervently in rights.

23.   99
Limbs and organs act independently: the head moves to the waist and sights Venus. And would drown in it. Flakes off a flint block become tools and weapons, completed by fracture | **this darke night. Vnder my window** the body disappears, leaving the head floating in the air, looking out of the darkened house by a northern skylight and seeing a possible explanation for the survival of harm in the form of an anthropomorphic boundary-stone on the horizon. Half lit, half ink. Quietly ticking into the dawn so **Let my change to ruine be** and sequent harbour

24.   101
the edge of the Zodiac (below Venus) that part of the sky where no heavenly bodies rise or set… | paired lives, symmetrical, both gazing North with empty eyes *front to back, heads to East* disgendered. *An increasing richness of ornamentation and originality of design* augments to South, to warfare, and along this line, she/ written into this line, she/ *head to South facing East but face turned upwards* | joins and separates (diphthong) wrapped in sexual hesitation, She/ «youth of my delight» **falls perfectly.**

25.   C69
a buried politics where now thin grass hangs on rendsina: empty centre *cut through rich brown loam two feet into the chalk, and left vacant* | tongueless voice, (distant) points of loss at the crossroads. A well sunk through the moral surface into inarticulate yearning, dreams and figures, an ice-wedge cast under the sun's maximal journey, heading for further death. Fructure has run down into the valleys and gone to be a sailor on the wide waste seas. The mirror under my feet shows bands of angels tumbling to nonentity: they expire before touching the ground in a fizz of bilberry dust, podsolized before our eyes. Thus polity unfaces truth and torts succession from the zenith to resentment. Though the accompanying singing, half sad, held knowledge back from the edge of despair *on a circular chalk pavement* moon of the bereaved, to whom all this is rind. For I talk to you constantly, though you are no longer here.

26.   62
head pillowed on rock, gazing upwards, and all else is ink, scattered. Including his own body, and his cup *made from five separate segments of clay joined together by overlapping* somebody's lower jaw on his neck – spoken into nonentity and a scripted remnant, a few shards of the person gathered on a line of latitude, a transit camp number *North of centre the other side of possibility* | and survives, a few fragments of someone else's speech because true-spoken **Making all the shadowes flie**

27.   31
My right hand taps me on my left shoulder. Will death never be serious? To sing, and dance, and to raise the arms in the air. And let them fall, meaning **rest awhile** familiar faces, spare a dime **you cruell cares**

28.   C43
massed shadows behind the head, where if the neck were touched it would be sensual | head to E facing N *both hands before face* and a stew, or dough, a mix was made, *of burnt matter: charcoal, with earth, lumps of chalk, human bone fragments and probably flesh, in a dish-shaped hole behind the head:* god food, unformed child that shouts through the bone. And then brought forward: *this matter* this biological heat *identical with that of a "core" or boat-shaped mass of black stuff hovering over the body* **that was you, and not you** but I/ took it, as if it were, and would be spoken, a silence beyond all speech. «So shall your heart be easèd» the dark **terra** whispered through me, and I believed that, sad infamy.

29.   275
Heart soul or mind, whatever one life is or becomes as a written /resulting/ thing, *a compact ball of human ashes in a circular rock-cut pit* | whatever the life performed, to be represented thus, in the figure of its hurt, neuter, something that laid avenues open and passed its message through a tripod: *also in the pit two large flint stones to NW and SE* becomes a clock. Saying sleep, listen, act, soon, hush. Saying nothing. Silent motionless clock hovering over the sleeping community (covered in the season with clover, daisies, coltsfoot, «to silver turned» | and set so still: every hope countered every despair raised | and an immense weight pulling to the working East, civic renewal too late: *ten adult skeletons on a rectangular pavement of flat liassic stone from at least two miles to the East, impinging on the eastern side of the pit* O the vain hopes of early risers. This industry is counterweighted by a single child, SW of centre, head to SE looking NE, close enough in to join the carolling [everyone is to blame] [and love a cell in the darkness, a house on the cliff, before and after, unremembered] bleaching to the arctic, whatever a life is, meets its (patron) pattern. "Les Illuminations" for high voice.

30.   16
A short song, bringing the movement quickly home. The contracted skeleton of a young child. No grave: *lying on the ground* one jet link two feet away to South, placed on the ground *facing North* | straight line, cast time, full sign *over a fault in the chalk* a calcium night light in the hollowed town, never far from home.

31.   41
By which some future. The bone-light in the clock-tower: not-I, not-you, not-ever-anything but the aesthetic self. Because formed because protected because reaching a close (aesthetic: "…a power, a concentration, a figure, a voice"). A blue dome, fenced, impinging on that tight dark space, a blue clay lid to the endless calling **you and I and Amytas** where all perfections keep away.

32.   C83
Bridge of flesh the child believes in plural pronouns, talks of "us". The others are *back to back and head to foot, in separate hollows* at right-angles to the world | the child holds the local together across the long memorised solos of history and all the soil of fall/ *about two years old, set horizontally across the edges of the two graves so as to join them at their northern ends* and facing South to the source, sings itself, a turning, separated, empty thing of polished limit. That tears roll off.

33.   28: Life Hill
carefully dismembered (They are chucked into holocaust graves as complete as they reached the end at; if you don't care who they are or how they die you certainly don't care how they lie) for a purpose, a scenario or buried score where the limbs gestate in the vocal cavities where the past becomes the future in chains of blood (Antigone) | where a fallen god/ *a shallow*

grave holding a carefully dismembered human body, mostly skull and leg bones... widely separated: one skull fragment from the South top of the infill matched pieces from the bottom North **Los smitten with astonishment: Frightend at the hurtling bones** *two feet exactly in position at the south end of the grave,* a cremation unit exactly above them |where a fallen God stands on the earth asking "What is this?" **The Eternals said: What is this? Death. Urizen is a clod of clay.** on which the dancing continues, world-loss survey, naming separate states **With numerous fete weell part and mete** or touch casually in the night, seeking warmth with honour.

34.   C63
And for a sign, *four large flint flakes in a row along her back* /a sign to whom/ *a yellow pebble the size and shape of a hen's egg set at the end of the row, at the base of her skull* – route marks, ironies, sentences of affinity and yearning, the couple apart/together *back to back and head to foot, the woman to the north* /set as a sign for no-one to see and everyone to know/ *and two assemblages of human bones side by side a few inches above the couple: that above the feet of the woman mainly large bones; above the man's head, which was turned away, a much smaller heap: front and back of a skull (separated), half an ulna and a piece of tibia.* A few delicate voice-like notations, mnemonic for what performance, what singing? "clear as a road sign without a road" | of lines forking through lives and circular arbours, sanctuaries of the god | of the renewal of love through growth into worldness, progression up the spine year by year to the sun's marker – making a sign of hope to all | Antigone, Elektra, year after year.

35.   294
and seek and seek to the final denial, a door open on the world | **be neighbours in the grave, to lie Urne by Urne, and touch but in their names** (as Paris touched Helen, in name, as Achilles, in death) spelt with a flint blade by the wrist, food vessel, ochre pebble, harsh crown | five flint splinters set in an arc around the top and back of the skull and touching in name make sentences across the hill, on chalk marl, bisecting

habit and season | ecstasis in Leuke, the White Island ("Passing sailors could hear Achilles and Helen at night, singing the story of their lives in the verses of Homer.") squaring the circle **the mortal right-lined Circle must conclude and shut up all.** Indeed the complete halt, the message opened for ever... Life is a pure flame | and makes but winter arches.

36.   C61
The final man, flat on his back in a rectangular pit, black knife at his shoulder *knees raised* staring upwards *surrounded by six circular dish-shaped excavations of various sizes from two to five feet across, scooped into the white subsoil and filled only with a very black peaty soil* and the final man's final words, floating like rooks in the pale and future sky **Come, come, while I have a heart**

37.   C62
They spiral into the pit grammarless, shelf-browsing as they fall, noting the marmalade, hurriedly accepting concessions in printed cursive, accepting the most costly gifts and proudly. Shades in Avernus, porridge in the pot, third Jaguar on the state | What the country means is the term of centrifugal love in knowable distances, sea shores and mountain ridges, hope wrought across transport in the occulted rhythm where the land evades the nation. Any stranger knows it immediately by local small-scale patterning, concentric circles and rows of triangles on the lintel, a transcending grammar of world/body negotiations, the syntax of exactly here, was where/ *two secondary or intrusive interments made with some apparent knowledge of the disposition of the primary* theatre. So they turn their backs on the confused and cheerful clientele and process patiently to *South-East, heads to South-West* red balloons on high, warmth and risk on crossed axes. And let them weep, **for all the teares my eyes have ever wept** those self defeated winners.

38.   C51
Two bodies buried one under the other, very close together. Both male, the lower about 15, brachycephalic, top of body to S facing E... *The head (minus lower jaw) neck and right scapula had been severed, and placed near the pelvis, thus under the shoulders of the upper interment, almost touching the food vessel behind his head.* The older man, dolichocephalic, head to NE facing NW... The departing elder, the star farmer who tuned the whole horizon to the pitch of a pre-City across the long stones, securing the calendar on ecliptic hinges. The miniaturist lies broken in his shadow, a diagonal section, a small song or Irish joke out of philosophy's mazes, his future secure. But surely the idea was to pass on a **work**. And some third term, probably female, barely remembered, reaches out from westward *one ulna, one humerus, one radius and one or two other fragments of a small dismembered body* to reclaim the flesh after sunset, as the stones fall. A **small pattern, a brooch or perfect guidance to the perplexed | and insists, nailid I was for the** blooded rights.

39.   40
Speech cancelled into music *the lower jaw removed and placed, intact, on the chest, teeth down. A small pottery vessel was inserted in its place, touching the palate; its contents included the bones of a small animal.* **And Lockd me up with a golden Key** Head to South facing upwards, legs flexed and turned to West *young and slender* left hand thrust into groin, right arm across chest *two yellow quartz pebbles, rounded with use, just beyond the fingers of the right hand, beside the left ear* | sun pitch, clay star, black blade fracture – speechless with horror. Bite my heart, three-personed sky, and I'll earn a living, out in the streets and bars of earth. And spend into the whole astrology, at speech's vigilant reprieve.

40.   82
Heart floating in flood-loam under the sleeper a completed memory settled across dawn where gravities and negatives scatter behind leaving an arc of generosity open south to a baby's raised metrics.

41.   80
Sun rising stone setting. Paired limbs on the eastern rim *sandstone and carboniferous limestone* | crescent soul burning the earth into focus | the dream of certainty *facing South head to East* stretched on the generative line by the wheat-fields, not ours, and the cars that block the streets not ours and none of the recked numbers ours; leaving "us" (heart of one) with a burning stone from bank to zenith. As similarly not mine, any you I track in the grain of day.

42.   81
The bone pin that fastens her hair. The flint scraper in front of her mouth, *almost in it* her voice, her *head to the North of West, torso curved back and head raised so as to face the same direction* her voice a blade *her right hand touching her thigh, her left hand at her diaphragm doubled under at the wrist* her pain *her left foot amputated at the instep, and two worked flints placed where the missing bones would have been: a double-edged knife, very sharp, and a splinter* her dance, her carefully struck fate. Set with her back to the diagonal fire-trench and all that heaped suffering unspeakable but not unsingable, as she does, perfectly, *her perfect skull* her profession. This painted future of the planetary mind I believe entirely, as she/ **says she morned for me** her courtesy.

43.   81
Prostrate she stands and dead she dances and her singing is a blade cutting flesh from bone at the cone of love, where time stays a while. The sea blazes in her almost.

44.   C40
Buried one below the other: topmost a child and an old woman, laid out in line East-West, the woman's head to E, the child's to W, feet in contact.

Every step I take is on the soles of your feet. Then an adult laid E-W with a child just above, skulls almost in contact. *Every word I speak.* And at base a large man on his back with head to S, but head and knees turned to E/ every loss I know is a child's voice in the empyrean singing «in hearts let some seed fall» inscribed **False world, fare well** as it will.

45.   C36
Crudel' amor that remembers nothing after so long but five toes, a left calf, and the right side of someone else's head. | Darkness from my mind then take | to the white crevices, and **sweet flowers Ile strow** where promises departed, where ice spread on the stately board.

46.   112
tangent of hope through half remembered speech and the deaths of three children. Sweet echo in the southern cosine, **sit downe under this shadowed tree.** And I will promise (never to forsake you). So too: *arms thrust forward but hands doubled back.*

47.   212A or 278
folded in globes of song, distant points, bruised arm, three gentle sighs fading to green pasture **before my watry eies** and the hawk above high hanging while the stage lights dim, the sun setting behind the wooded hill.

> *Note.* Mortimer points out that in tumuli 221 to 229 and 245 (Huggate Wold) the Great Bear, known to him as Charles' Wain, seems to be set out on the ground with remarkable accuracy, only one tumulus (no. 245) being somewhat misplaced.

48.   224
those clere fiers on the ridge top, they who «needs must part» and their being **vannish into smoake** | into a column *what can only be described as a column, in the middle of the burnt area bisecting both the tumulus and the primary burial, two feet in diameter, extending from the original ground surface almost to the top of the mound, and consisting of burnt human bones mixed with chalk and soil* and the changed vegetation over it, an eye in the grass | by night fire by day smoke | Lower limbs in the furnace, who found nothing here but careless love and cast his/her star between consummation and consumption. Ripening in flame towards the lost consonants. And deserves this singular brightness as her/his rest. The rest floats towards the sea on the wind.

49.   Lost number
The body falls from the eastern sky into history and breaks apart, lost on earth, teeth biting toes. And doesn't stop falling, falls through. In hell a pile of limbs waiting to be fed. Here the furnace set, that points the passage through tense the only place it ever meant, and makes a descant of the eyes, turning on the boundary of speech **that cannot love to die** and sets the colour of justice behind the new factory.

50.   222
The scraping-blade before the eyes at sunset. The wedge above the crown to south. The black disc behind the head. Never shut of them, **star brighter eyes** that tear the skin to **worldes heavines**. Hopes that drill the skull, and compass the head in coastal darkness, faint glitter on the point.

51.   226
though there are many double burials, how rare it is for the couple to be set face to face set through each other *both heads to East* in final disagreement,

forward fear against pastoral stability **Who ever will say No** /hope suspended as Fructidor ends again.

52. 227 + 245
A disposal of strange and hated stillness which mocks movement | **false world** the fall of consonants as speech closes, *scattered heaps* to rest, sunk in white walls. A span closed on itself, dispensed, *burnt earth and wood ashes* where horizons meet there is no life. There really is no life at all.

53. 229
As if held in pale hands, circled or entrenched and the hands open enough to let out a small bird. By which the dying enter the ring and patiently cloak themselves in forgetting and lie down in the apertures prepared, conferring their cardinal points to the history of the race, lit by a small flaming heart on the ceiling. In peace one might say, morphemes fluttering out to the vast resonant Ō, and the shapely snow.

54. 218
such slight remains in such a toilsome structure, the heavens and magma ringing the bits of dirt which is all that's left of us. Or maybe they were so drunk from the wake they lost all but four flakes, but, being what they had, was centred and sealed and raised for remembrance as is proper as thanks for leaving so completely, for that love to continue. Held in the ellipsis, falling like rain to the spring.

55. 249
Hollows in the earth, **the secrets of our hearts** declaimed from ridge to ridge as white tumuli, writing the edge of belonging on a winter arch.

56. 264

Head in a flint-cloud – *interred cross-legged in a sitting posture, and protected by a small wooden enclosure, some traces of which remained* – head in command, fragmented lives and shopping floating above: *a female head, an ox skull,* a cup of child bones **that were his eyes** | all that success fallen due at last, a revenge of the fields and the innocent working population, stones of the province heaped over his throne and massed to the centre *the bigger flints in a cone within the flint heap, over the burial itself* the emanation presses on his brow straight down from God the very dust, slowly falling into his space. The sleep that charms his cares wipes his account.

57. *Hunter's noon.* 2

An artilization of sight, honed across terrain. Following hither and thither the appetite of the adored creature to the finesse of a bronze blade, all the groves loud with mutual cry. Cenotaph on the northern ridge end, *two red deer tines and the lower jaw of a dog* ears that sweep away the morning dew. The skills of the money market are just as delicate and purposive but, lacking any grounding valedictory, close on the self gracelessly, the money dematerialised, a funereal trace in mercury against the name. And the name is forgotten, like a soldier. When the exchange becomes an asset the hunt becomes a teatime sneer and Falkland grunt, killing freely down the avenues of lime.

58. 254

Reddish dust on chalk rubble | handfuls, scattered in **gentle showers** *wood ash, burnt soil, cremated bones* almost smoke descending, as dust enters the house. And on this bed *an oval merely scooped through the soil* genitive domestic plural | pressed front to back *facing South* tented, lie.

Tragedy, industrial silence, a vertical gash, burns through the night (while they sleep) reared to Northwards where under Betelgeuse he reigns, earth Captain in Boreal riches | dust-free, ecstasy of pure cold, sings his pain

tout a par moy, affin qu'on ne me voit : and his lost arm points «Behold this harmonious pair» casts his book and sings anyone's pain but his own. Then ends again, and falling signs, his heart to soil, and failing sings. The song falls to enter, Like hollow murm'ring wind, or silver Rain.

59.   C93
To burn, or bury, or both, a life **pursu'd with doubt, enjoy'd with feare** that «died before its day» | to cancel all the detail, and the self becomes a thing, point or capsule *small heap at centre* head nowhere facing nothing, speech fermenting in the chrysalid, where (and) **sorrow shall cease.**

60.   C96, C99, C92, C93, C94, C97, 236
What else? **sable night** closed profitable eye **All things in sweete repose Their labors close** and all that fear, hope, and all that mourning fail. And are spread | Prince Henery, had he lived

61.   237
separately, but all on the same axis *two adults and two children* NE-SW As if there were an answer pending, the first-person plural created by music, set at recognition. Diagonal, as "we" offer the crown in an image of sacrifice, a sharp crown. Then the third child, *a baby at an adult's feet* **I heard a maiden** is set across, NW-SE **singing** of how fragile the arteries and consequent reticence, of how fertile the cuticle. Then the wide wilderness of what **still shall be** where strange fruit hang, gather the flesh, up into one ravelling cry.

62.   238

The mind recoils, empty room at the back grey dust on slow shelving, templet to atrophy and the glad glance long forgotten. No one left, no one there, shuffling around in a dressing gown, envy of the world. The spirit spins past, whirling its own and two or more lives in loving money. Then ceases, no money left, no motion in the lungs and the dark space above the eye is tuned again, stretched taut across a void or grey rose. The tins and pots in their various places on the shelves and in the cupboards. And tensed out of this omission is a fruit or mind that lightly touched sounds sweet airs back to the world, of articulated silence, and the irony of love.

(as at the end of *The Honorary Consul* what a triumph that was: of course fear, of course failure, of course not-us but precisely you, the ravening cry that holds the earth, angels take up.)

63.   241

To become a foreign object in the god's eye, death injected into day, into the fields of life the very houses | *this tumulus evidently raised over a pit-dwelling...* To become an alien object in a memory of affect ...*a cylindrical or drum-shaped mass of black matter and burnt wood, containing an inverted urn with the calcined bones of a youth,* in the middle of the room. This erases lunch, closes the account, the machine eats the card. The dry leaves that rustle in the night, the rivers that slide away. Because life is elsewhere | black hole that cancels the heart and holds the earth. And what is the name of the god and why is the room empty, and how is life deferred? Because, **I needs must love.** While I live. Albion, white pit.

64.   265

at the West end the apparently dismembered bones of two youths, one skull base up, the other base down, both jaw bones separated and placed one foot away from each skull... corage whirled in to a melodic crown on the central absence, the limbs, riddled with separation, spin onto an untouchable point, as if there were an answer to this scream | *fragments of one vase placed in two heaps one foot apart, with, when reassembled, one fragment missing*... The accuracy of these artists terrifies me. Singing anthems through the hole in continuance and. What then is love but mourning? What desire but a self burning? A rush to death, where those bitter spaces fold. And who bears the weight when the sweet dawn curtains call the valley back to its traces? For there is between night and day a small crack, a chance to change everything.

65.   209: Kemp Howe
O the actors poised in passion's starless silence. The sweet synthetic tone of a carol against the perpendicular stonework. A parallel shining through schools, black and white.

66.   280
head to East, upper torso lying on its back but crouched at a right-angle and knees turned sharply to left, and the head also turned to face South... remembering all the tricks of warmth, twisting aside, avoiding the sky */both hands raised to the head, the left touching the neck, the right arm doubled back with the hand behind the head* but clear, clearly coloured clearly set, a whole row of sorrows parting the air, **rote of stedfastnes** in the hands' guardian delay. Spun then in passion's careless reach who thought a life was a sum, with double sorrow **dowbyl sorow complayn I must** of the failure, to clear before dawn and bring the disadvantaged to their gathering or the self to its principal. As it did in the wrested moment, earth **Like heavn still in it selfe delighted.**

67.   281: Hedon Howe
And to make rooms of stone, set at the wind's four quarters, a voice in each and a carol at the centre. **Woffully araid** indeed, broken apart or sunk without trace a lifetime's labour entrusted to a falling temperature and shrinking faith as the great cry is restored again *We have a right* /Let them, fallen warriors, we shall build our cells with links of air.

68. 284

But look, a tumulus in a valley-bottom is altogether too esoteric a thing for me to begin/ and *nests of frog and toad bones the size of an orange to a melon, at many points in the mound* what on earth were these people up to? A complete disregard for centrality or orientation, reversed strata, family buried drunk. A plastic bag rustling in an aspen.

69. "X"

Who now a sheer nothing, is held still in a tension, a triangulation across the land. Buried speech speaks. Of Northern separation: spectacle to let, lives lost into routine negation while the comedian bites his own hand to please the owner. **These are my children** their slow running blood. To South-East they watch and manipulate, assume the currency: hand-down life that knows no necessity, resting on its literature. The heroes, mindless killing machines. So flee westwards held taut on the string for we have but a short time and full of trouble, enjoy the mock-up of native plenty, errant child. But tilt finally back to the boredom, the allegory of supply, child on an errand. To settle for very little, "anywhere", trusting in suspended potential (everything, that is, still speakable). Or those who, like Ilyich, suddenly pass at death into adulthood | *two large flint stones in the middle of the grave, to NE and SW, a foot apart, cremation of an adult between them.* A wing-reach, a purchase in the wilderness, a formal courtesy in the desert | fireweed, spreading over bomb sites.

70. "Z"

And this so clearly nothing (nothing left and nothing else) bury it well and heap a mound over it, to prevent it escaping. But a *smaller mound*, for it is really nothing. So they rest side by side /grey and grey. Hope strikes and holds, at the fancy edge to any known limit, the waste that stays | Small clouds scatter sky clears above sheds and light fills empty bottles.

This Carol They Began That Hour

Excavations
Part One Book Two

From the Researches of J.R. Mortimer
in the Yorkshire Wolds

71. C39
grave the shape of a knife blade, and the economy floated on, and the generosity it saps, falls into three degrees of pain, left right and centre. The fourth is an opening *the cremation of a child* hovering above and southwards like a guiding star, inverse gravity where the razor-sharp gnomon says it is time to go. And gladly part, taking the narrow pavement in the thin rain and leaving us with nothing: All for nothing (left); Nothing for anybody (right); Nothing for certain (centre). These pains heal where undivided need wraps the standing light in diaphane, miles along.

72. 6
and so a garden where these pleasant corpses/ **lyly-whighte rose methought I sawe** the children in the sled pulling and pulling against the ice, whose light it is, heaped up as it crosses the earth and day dawns | **This day this gentill day dawes** back, rises back, crests. Withdraw and hope to meet again in a nothinged garden that death sets apart from the arbitrary work-force. I must home gone.

73. 106
Packed in stones, packed in law as they fit, impermeable history of/ boat-shaped mass of/ *non-local clay stretched lengthways over the body* the eyes begin to see. The penis is useless, the legs are stuck in a dance-cramp, the arms refer the heart back to itself. But the eyes (long departed) *see*, to SE by moonlight (losses and hopes, fermented or cemented) see what? See under affect to the headland, where the heart is longer than hunger, dark against the shifting flick'ring blades.

> Note: the heart is longer than hunger.
> *We travelled four days without food, and when on the fourth day we caught a hare, having discussed all day the best way to cook it we finally gave it to a passing trio of Arabs to eat, as an act of formal courtesy in the desert.*
> Wilfred Thesiger, in précis.

74.   44
All night by the rose I lay. But there was no rose. *a circular flint disc, five flint splinters, and a lump of burnt wood formed the entire contents* I had lived. And do, a desert in the garden while the night singers convolve.

75.   72
As even the nothing we become may be compacted or thinned, or moulded to a globe or stretched out *like a cigar, South-West to North-East|* this eye I now speak as, closed, and all the dear crystals stilled | phosphoric residue, doesn't remember can't forget: **My lyff was lent To an entent** and stretch my mental arms on the migration routes [ther stod she] kindly aversing the pole.

76.   3
a mass of brecciated material and wood ash | the slight, hovering movements of the human jaw during speech | earth scourings. **From them shall I never vary**, from them never rise – but always be/ The waiting child. The town archive. The blood flow. Sailing away.

77.   291
(Greenwell 1866) *an inner mound of clay with chalk and flints, and a central innermost conical mound of chalk rubble ... on the top of this, lying on charcoal* [male, head to W facing S] ... *four stake-holes behind the head, possibly representing some kind of canopy* Listen, the economy of transhumance: white sound under the star awning, summers alone in beehive huts or bark tents pitched for the night in the high valleys | eyes (closed) scan the heart graph for return, eyes (gone) span the terrestrial film at zero option • Mortimer 1895 (by the way) confirms there was no central grave under the chalk mound. Me, I was never more at home than hovering above on a daily problem of transfer, head in a windbreak between snow and sand. The fire dust was sweet stuff to lie on that night.

78.   273K
the base deposit of the most complex abundant and prestigious structure in the entire field *with a vessel at its feet, of Windmill Hill "A" ware* | if it is feasible, about this, to feel passionately, or awkward not to, O Pioneers! entering the land, ranging for clearings, marking the wych elm | a despair in constant parting: from the known, from the closing sea at my back, from the ocherous grammatolatry of beasts in transit, witness to fruit. *head to East, facing* the sky. That instead, we might bend, and carefully plant, and staying wait, and these were my sovereign desires, to stay and hold the year to its yellow promise. That counts the errors from fear to delight.

79.   273L
But some will not lie, some will not wait, some will not linger at the counter poisoned into joy (the sweet bite of dark liquids, the slow solace of settling froth). Enclose their hopeless dreams in houses of night that they face ever the one right angled sanction, **and sweetly weepe** [in crystal showers] a buried kin.

80.   71
A roebuck horn. The rest of the syntax is omitted. (But you were there weren't you, and know how simple it was, leaning on what we have, and if that is all we have, that bears us still/till, everything I thought I leaned on suddenly had me for dinner. I became powder in an urn *inverted in a rock-cut pit* (too small) one roebuck horn in my heart. You were cast by the plough.

81.   65, 66
Sing to me, that half of you that's left. The upper half, containing the air chambers and the arms and hands to hold the fiddle and bow and the fingers to stop the flute. And I'll lie *crouched, on back, knees turned over*

to right, head to West-South-West listening to the singing **Sleepe fleshly birth** /of right and wrong stilled, of heart relay, of hope's gimlet in the neck turning to that music **of the spheres** or very sound of death, the crack | not quite horizontal, as if pulled down slightly, my upper half faces the sky and listens. The rest was burnt.

Sing to me, what's left of me, half a person, the upper half, that breathes and hearkens and learns to lie still. *hands to face* no pelvis, no legs, no choice | of left and right sundered, of gravity consigned to healing *remains of a child to South-South-East* the head not quite vertical, as if drawn forward, over, to listen, to something that might answer the pierced star soprano and restore to good all the time I've spent in the notation of that snap.

82.   67
to that music, or trying not to | male, not old, on back, *very tightly crouched, both hands to the sides of the head* in a circle of stones – an industry, a deafening silence *worked flints under the finger bones of each hand* blades to the ears (the very heart of music, before anyone knows how it may settle) eye sockets listening upwards | that singing, those twin stars corpusant on the mast head and the approaching accord **high treble** that pull the lost limbs to resolution. Bound tightly, as on this earth we walk and/ final top pitch of the equation where extent snaps. So tuned to love, nothing answered, the body signs itself to total coil. And ends, knowing at last how to live.

83.
So fallen warrior, the rain forms a pool in your midriff, showing the colours of the sky. A music seeking a people, serene and clear light *luce serene e chiare* along the horizon in layers of thin cloud, held under your heart in the immediate format, a fidelity. *Dolce parole e care* soft and caring words soaking through you, forgotten to, what happens to, as the rain continues to, fall, soft and caring words remembered… A cladding on the earth, as the child picks a way.

84.   97
For look, your eyes have gone, to less than ash, and where is the sweet month now? Is it not perpetual holiday? All sentience becomes a blade *a black flint knife* at the core of a bag of grey flakes *possibly of a young adult and a child* mingled together [infant/father's joys/fears] *under an inverted urn, placed on a thin bed of clay spread on the ground surface* at the centre of the ring. So struck and finished, finely ground to a sharp edge as the sides close, beyond which nothing, except : close SSW of the urn, *a hole in the rock, three feet in diameter and two and a half feet deep, narrowing to a point,* full of *the sides reddened by heat* full of *burnt wood, greasy mould, a few human burnt bones, one nut or plumstone* all brought to a point, that pierces not but opens. A fruiting point. So **never shall affection die** Is that not for us perpetual holiday? For us children a future?

85.   94
If the space beside us is sharp, if it cuts, if it has a tree, or a foot, marked on it, something that narrows and spreads, if it descends. What then is the direction of our patience? "Persephone led me gently to her mother."

86.   208
And at the precise moment, in the perfected sign of harvest *head to West facing South* why is there a saw-blade in front of the face, why does the vessel have legs as if it might change its mind? Do we long for a warmer answer? Turned at the finish of a life to where the life "came from" where the blade or the clay "came from" where the sun augments its angle of declination and the answer is here, city of, this is where. Why does here then have a blade dividing it? But also a calculus *close to the pelvis* a stone to work by, a human stone. Where **sighing shall cease** and that also is here, if you work it out.

87.   90
A drone a continuous murmuring in the air. Some sink through, and end a grey-brown question-mark over the fell, a packet of dust in the ground. Some solidly stand it out, roar in the face of death, and somebody has to find out how to dispose of this relict mass. But both require fuel, continual reassurance, *and some sort of canopy* | when you go I'll continue to write you long letters, that they may be some sort of canopy. Describing the river valley.

88.   57 – 55 – 58.
Meaning spills, over the edge. The vortex has stabilisers, contingent but discontinuous *two small mounds exactly to East and West of 55* housing nothing much: a minimal human unit (E) / one jet button (W) / the star-warrior has friends and relatives, whose superseded sanctions form a belt of further purpose and even comfort across wheat fields and factory estates in the path of the sun's decline where wounds are dried. The clenched night has a sort of day as a sort of canopy a sort of gravity or moment hinged on void points. Fa-la as they say at the end of some songs, like a speeding ambulance.

89.   26
Now cease my wandering eies/voice to a faint sibilant, a light ash showing in section. The person becomes a substance cut into its own ground, heart stuff **One soule, one love** *showing as a line of lighter substance in the clayey matrix* whose belief sinks into its own history| *an inner chalk mound forming a new ground surface through which/* the eyes **Distracted spirits** survey the traces, the few or singular lives that have formed a permanent equation | *burial of the skull and arm bones only of a young person on the edge of the central grave, and three stake-holes…* three life-spans or fixed stars three steadfast hearts forming **One steadfast love, Because our harts stand fixt, although our eies do move.** And the residue drifts on through generations, drawn (in silence) from this lesson, of intellectual desire in the theatre of closure, where the long S winds.

90.   27
annulled, gains an entire form, an aesthetic, as a blade fractured doubles its worth as an ore wrenched and scorched exudes its cutting cash | and lies *head to North facing East, tightly flexed* in double hope: and again a boat-shaped mass of confection ("greasy earth, variegated in colour, with small cavities and some patches of conglomerate cemented by bitumen-like substance") hovers over, its *narrow keel-shaped bottom touching the body* /sentences of terrestrial mass, and future, sailed on me until I could believe nothing. Nor wanted, but my dark earthen pillow and no removes. Hearted circumference, as the blade presses my front, was what I had in mind.

91.   115
Crushed under a mound of impedimenta. Knives and devices and things to throw at unpopular comedians. What I wanted was to cut through all that to a quite clear diagram, not with but by you, and the fruit coded into the wine, the softly repeating compacted day. What else is there to want?

92 *(Lament)*   118
Voices lost in the fading edge, national verbs *houses that leave but little trace* finance companies that suddenly vanish from the screen | The generations heaped on top of each other, each holding a piece of black night in a clenched fist or a clenched something else (heart, deed of contract, bundle of ash). As if planar return settled the active line, as if stratification answered desire. It isn't so: the wound stays open, carefully traced in the angle of the skeletal arm to the forehead, ligament at its highest tone. Orientation of hope revised *head West facing North* into hatred, fresh air. And they fall to the scruple of a service industry, head bowed, erogenous zones offered for a momentary title. And one by one are added to the founder's pile, and I insist the augmenting number the increasingly weighted polyphony twining on twining **wrapped all in wo** is the very crown of it, the sunk and scored name (by desire, the light) shining. Along the horizon into a future that these failures never for a moment harm.

93.   104
So descending, sight given into the ground, for future reference. So the whole land, and its index, in tears gains the waiting soul. So in tiers they take their places, **say simply what you know and the earth is yours**, heads to south over a simplicity so plangent as to be a garden of facts in logical space *two beakers placed on the floor, to north and south, an ox rib beside the northern. This was the entire base deposit of the tumulus; the two inhumations were tiered above it, separated from it by a layer of wood* and facing east. Ambition and its content donated (simply) to necessity/ and reach to where (dark severance) all is lost, lost glasses lost stick – "he sank his head in his hands" (Shostakovich, or) donated to succession. Colour then becomes distant light.

94.   C49
We're talking about the sum of privacies, and the moral generosity of a people. Where the self takes on the structures of supply, and the tools and weapons that create a debt to the body, **Thus under sylens I do endure** as suddenly the "heart" or emotive soul, suddenly hurts therefore exists and from such distance **The sterre of Venus… Sharper than thorn** or the immediate moment than which what could be further? But people make things and pass them on. Body echoing body, inverse to body, stretching away, your eyes upside down in front of mine, stare at each other and don't we see then such a world of hurt petitioned?

95.   C52, primary
Paired at the destructive centre, precession of the open vowels to south and ranged on that line for a marriage completed: the song, the purity of Orpheus' original intent : **Ma solamente per la donna mia** I ventured thus far only for love. These are the kings and queens at the centre of the hill, taking voluntarily on the self all the gravities that hang in the air. The sum is unrepeatable, cannot be given or bargained for. The overtones clash at the slightest shift to secession. Post to press the echoes resound, o tears and shadows of my native ground.

96.   C52, upper and satellite
And still we complain. "Fuck!" we yell as the biscuit crashes to the floor/ *blades, and the blocks from which blades were struck* But you see, in succession is a structure of work. It rains. Cars pass. People walk dogs in the night. The dogs delay and then run. I too head for a closed space. If I was honest I turned, ever so cautiously, the trust I copied about its own pivot, set round with dark and fertile tokens as a phrasal shoulder heaves out of the earth in response to a circular cry.

97.   75
Deeply funnelled into the roof of metaphysics the ground | **far from eve and morning** empty or full, the light that breaks and closes. Deep in the facts that support birds and cloud, brushing the slopes to westward for the common aim: a perfect hand. Then sets out for the highest shopping, love and law/ **Whyls lyf endure Loyall and playne** and gains a final site | deeply embedded in that wild future, that planetary spasm where the chances of the tribe multiply, the pains of lessness fall /into the ground, and lies on the right side *facing north*, far from company or solitude. **What shall I equal to thee,**

98.   75
that I may comfort thee? Where she also lies suspended, *half-way down* near or far, it really doesn't matter now. But in the same alignment, *on her left side, and with her feet thrust into a circular heap of cremated bones* | where and when, moving through the human successions that brought us (bring us) to this final separation to (this distinction) and the rain reaches the silent fields in the middle of the night. A gentle hiss begins. Death voices it alternately.

99.
Leaving me wrapped in nothing, shouting *hab'ich nicht* did I not, live / love / finish: yes-no questions to which there is a vast silence and a great length of territory, great chalk hills sweeping down into marshy valleys | where any true bond is consummated, every error joined in the lift of bird and cloud. Fallen warrior, despondent lover, bee envoy. Singing in the rain.

100.   C71
I must therfor with silence build The labyrinth of my delite *in a straight line from the centre northwards* "looking for the source of the chill in my bones" in the slow succession of menuets.

101.   40
The slow succession of minutiae. A little flame inside the silex. Listening to the yellow crystals. Pitching time. The hollowness in which music extends, the hunger, to be paid for. The slow draining of sexual regard. Momentary safety in the focus of landscape details as colour grade. Hexagonal morsure on the spinal canal. Everyone suddenly burst out singing.

102.   81
Slow smouldering inside the silo. Red caterpillars wrapping themselves in themselves, days of eating finished. The hilltop tumuli, encasing heat, mark the cross of lives, central vacua aligned, birth graves of gods at points of stress. And the deposition of a dancing girl fixes the holocaust, by turning from it with a gleaming knife in the mouth and the severed foot sharpened to a sky point. A slow succession of lost children bars the north gate like a trench of fire, a failed education, a mass grave in the roots of palm trees. I dreamt it was discrete, access to the heart, but it was a tilted crossroad on a hilltop where five generations lay still and waited. The stardust turned out to be most precise and elegantly pranced the night away.

103.

Leaving a simple state *a cremation placed in a trough in the floor of an oval pit five and a half feet long and aligned East-West* striped by the dawning light in the narrow entrance *the deposit of ashes, also aligned East-West, was two and a half feet long, nearly the length of a tightly crouched inhumation* | unlimbed, unsexed, stuck in the crack between days, but something performed, or learnt, leaves a sign, – of what, sign which way? I don't know, it led to a bone on the shore in blazing noon. And here, (you/she/it) who doesn't necessarily exist at all, beside me, beckoning or tilting to affirm, again and again, the head bowed over me, the long hair falling to the sides of my face. Willing to give the self entire into succession as a unit, through a particular, for a glimpse of renewal. And lightly graze the cheek in gratitude. The bone glows on the edge of a life.

And look, the money runs shining into the ground.

Vacated Thrones

Excavations
Part Two

From the researches of Canon William Greenwell
in the Yorkshire Wolds

104-116. *Preludes* II

/a
both hands on top of his head loss beaming from the horizon to the centre, where no one lives, no heart moves. A dark Sudanese photograph: a hand descends holding a vitamin pack but it is too late. North/South • white • black • God • nil. The dial spins. A decision is made. A cricket hacks the weightless air.

/b
A colony of untouchables at the limits of navigation, drunk as lords. Reader and writer [we] lie on an East-West axis in the council chamber wrapped in earth colours, echoing words in symbiotic transport. Lyric is our nomad wedding, sibilant in ecstasis. It thieves its vocabulary from memory but disregards the submersion of pain in time (both hands on top of head) until it is too late: the starry compact is signed, a distancing of everything we live by, a still margin to the daily tempest right outside the currency. The ancestors shift below us, the exchange bell swings slightly without sounding, the dial spins and the question is one of advantage, to gain by inertia. Then all the harm. As if *virtù* were singular. As if corrupt statecraft weren't the natural result of two centuries of artistic bohemianism. Look at it there on the bared clay floor: the human shape at a right-angle.

/c
So what it faces is what its length laments, and from the limbs' contention the eye looks out to North singing **adew mi hartys lust**. So the spirit is strangely appeased at loss. So, conquest.

/d
So the wounded, and the starved, the music in the night at the crossroads, valuables buried under the floor. */a large wound in the right side of the frontal bone, but some three months prior to death and not causal* Both hands on top of his head/ then they unravelled his story and danced in the space his will created and set out a map or life on the floor "such that time and place are understandable, and can be wrought." Arts of peace.

/e
Deeply concealed. The sun caught in the arms of the little pylon that hums over the fell. Under the ground the fallen warrior faces into a wall, the halt he always meant as he advanced, falling sideways. Then the arriving world is set behind him *a cairn of oolitic rubble ten feet in diameter and three feet high with an outer layer of yellow clayey soil which partly overlies the body from behind it* and the extent of his understanding from North to East is marked on the dial *two holes just beyond his head and feet, on the edge of the cairn, two feet deep and full of sand and broken pieces of stone.* Deeply concealed, as is the national custom.

/f
This structure gathers all the heat of an active life against fortune, scorches the ground with it, signs its fracture and gently half-seals it under yellow clay, edge-set as eventuality gains depth from singular cries. Marking the invention of the triad on the long zither precisely where "nature" defeats itself. Then an eye-line emerges from the limbs' disarray, from the edge of the dome, and darts North-East, delocalised affect at the focus *both hands on top of his head* only to crash into a low stone wall, redirecting the possible world to about 15 degrees' aberration from reliance, and narrowing. Hope is finally wedged against society as an unknown to which all this furtherance directs, full of weariness. A dusty light pouring into a gap.

/g
This clay bone soil stone, these statements, nothing is gained till the articulation is set and fractured across succeeding languages (weariness is a succeeding language). Memory of warmth, completed heart under a porous dome, moments of success, a brown hare by a five-barred gate paddling its paws at the sun. Building a life, that is delivered to the dancer's feet wrapped in brown paper, and rests now *under a white porous dome, sealed under a further, dark dome* all under the grassy blanket **under the leaves so green** and the plough shifting to iron innocently softens the curve of the swell [**a little pretty bonny lass was walking**] while the villages hung between these tumuli sink each generation deeper into metallic soliloquy and a final succeeding emptiness, and silence. But with an interrogation-point hooked onto the chest, as to what exactly empowers these arcs of movement, what attraction or resistance to what finality. There might be a silent flash of blanket lightning reducing all these visions to pre-industrial trust, or pre-death spasms. But always the unanswered question or the unquestioned anger pulls a line across worlds.

/h
Those whose power is not immediate set the agenda of thus buried peace. *two secondary inhumations, both of old women* Who sink faltering into latitude aslant a brook, who remember a lot of old songs, who see without saying, without connection, whose children leave home, whose pets die, whose wars roll up like cloud. Secondary persons, the earth is alive with everything you desire.

/i
Everything. *a cluster of small objects in front of her waist, probably once held in a cloth bag –*
>	3 bronze awls
>	1 boar's-tusk point
>	1 beaver-tooth blade
>	1 flat circular jet bead
>	1 pierced snail-shell
>	1 dentalium
>	1 piece of rubbed belemnite
>	1 fish vertebra
>	3 cowry shells

19th Century archaeologist and cleric: no comment. *both hands to mouth (pieces of night)* | 20th century unemployed writer: no comment. To enter eternity carrying a small bag of pivotal details without market value, prey to every professor of shamanism in the Northern void. But in the jammed contrast of whorls and points, local and remote, something answers militarist leaders in their own terms.

/j
As an old woman's knitting gear does, any quiet hour on the road out of the town, by low walls, the soldiers passing by.

(k)
Explanation: In this (preludial) tumulus the central burial (the wounded man) is the northernmost of three burials. He lies legs flexed on his left side facing NE (both hands on top of his head) partly under the NE edge of a small cairn of "oolitic rubble" with an outer layer of yellow clayey soil. The centre of the whole circular tumulus occurs on his pelvis. There are two holes or small pits, full of sand and broken stone, close to his head

and feet, at about 12 o'clock and half-past-two on the circumference of the inner dome. He faces into a low wall of flat stones on edge, about the length of his body were it extended, and running WNW-NNE at a tangent to his axis. This wall could form the base of a flattened isosceles triangle with the 2:30 hole as its apex. To SE two or three feet beyond his feet is the skeleton of an old woman with her back to him, sandwiched between two layers of flat stones over and under her. This is the one with the cache of small objects on the front of her body. She is set head to SW facing SE. Just to South of her is another low wall of about the same length running exactly E-W and just beyond it is another old woman, described as "very old", set exactly E-W, head to W facing S, her body laid "on a rough pavement of small stones". There is a pottery vessel of the type called 'cinerary urn' in front of her knees on its side, its base pointing towards her body, its bell continuing the line to SE. Finally there is another hole, larger and deeper, to the West of her feet, and thus directly South of the man and his cairn, full of rubble and with large flat stones over its top. This hole is also exactly in line with the SW-pointing head of the first old woman and could form an acute isosceles triangle with the northern wall as its base, which is to say that a line joining this hole and the one at the wounded man's heel would if continued bisect the northern wall. These tenuous dispositions are viewed as abstract and not mysterious.

/l

No comment, we dispose the daily wrong as best we can. Somewhere is an abstract painting or a long story that coheres all its inner tensions against each other, flexing the absolute against necessity in such terms that the excavator flinches, recognising his/her home lease in a blanket flash, a yellow cloud, the harm of venture set against the harm of settlement and wrought into a linear harmony standing on three feet, singing words to save the world. And all the fondness meant by "a pavement of small stones."

/m

But the abstract screams right out of the picture as any warring, hunting eye at the moment of true capture faces the cold refusal to NE and speaks for once and for all, "This is not what I wanted." I want to live.

117. *The African photograph.*   II
He lies under coarse weave on hard earth both hands on top of his head saying in a language of angles, I want to live. But have come gradually to know that wanting is a distant signal, a far light or soul-point in the polite plains. So I learn to do without a life as I learned to do without a meal, and the big boss can have it all now. I pay outright, I settle the running total. And smile slightly at the descending hand with the vitamin pack as if I needed assurance at this stage. This is total heat-loss, Mr Jim. I don't welcome it, but I hope for something to be saved, at least, this bit at the top that I shield with my elbow-bone, and remember my part, **loke down upon this londl** here above the eyes up to the crown, that bit there, remembers love and can't be misread. It was a bright tone, and should survive.

118. *The purposes of this writing*   II
that the 1990s held a poetic opportunity, subsequently lost to politics *the moon in the branches of the little pine* of, reaching *and keeping* the full and singular presence absent from any set discourse: the person on earth and its reflection on water, at night from the edge of the slowly moving boat with the small stove behind me, that intimate and regal station, anyone's, entirely its own oeconomia and likely to continue, tracing the earth, drawing, life after life after life.

119.   III
The train passing in the night, slightly shaking the structure, indicates plainly that I cannot want to live. The stains on the porcelain similarly, the spaces between the stair treads mounting to the loft, and the row of three inner chalk mounds *in a line East-West, the only burial being on the flat top of the central mound* head W facing S and smiling at the very idea of living. Perhaps a traveller, a modern politician, floating out for a term, pocket of hidden agenda *two water-worn pebbles* and protected head. From thought perhaps. Or the winds that bring difference, the impress of populations on the earth. But where he finally looks, when

wholeness finally covers him in its great arc and nothing can prevent it, where wholeness finally breaks him, and he lies in the pressed earth… two black holes *to South, the further much larger* seeming to confirm, that what he ultimately desired was to live, and didn't know where to look. Or listen, to the passing freight, the sainfoin shaking in the wind, spots of blood on the smooth agreeable slopes.

120.   IV
Mullet, star, and millstone, on a ground | picture of an infant, nameless in a prospect of chalk, her knees in a pile of juniper berries *head to NW facing SW* tilt of perseverance on a stone bed | O link girl, why droop you here? the very song outweighs you, stretched across history **make marble melt with weeping**

and secured from above: the twin stars of commercial travellers and ships' captains *two ox-teeth side by side in the earth above the grave* **those brite eies** set in the black (gleaming, blue-shot) underarch that diffuses through the atmosphere, hollowing the trusting heart | out of that then, out of the herald's submission out of the word Please

and out of the silence that succeeds the word Please | a loud and triumphal cut into white rock housing "a child of two or three" cast as a five-pointed star. Lament on a ground, and nobody knows what, if anything, was lost. Or why they wept at the strange device.

121.   VI
Burnt soil. Burnt umber. Angels, smell of burning at their approach, the air heavy with earth particles after rain | scattering ashes and feathers through history, and leaving an earthen certainty in the nostrils: that there can be no removal, and no (bolting the door for the night) lesser expanse. Soul streak through lump of clay, facing the Zodiacal horizon alone as the angels brush their teeth and go to bed. In the dark that is never quite black, the red seeds shuffle.

122.
Angels, these strange ironies we construct whose wings never seem quite to fit, never quite contingent to the shoulder-blades. They ascend and descend with scribbled notes between theoretical factions. They pass high above the winter avenues where the victims of our anxiety rock their souls to rest, o good dog be kind to the trade.

It is possible to promote security at the expense of every living gain. To build walls round money and walk children on a lead from cell to cell.

And they rest, wings spread out on the grass. When they rest the earth is known, and the whole of intellection passes, as it is, into music, and regains the present tense. There the Angels make constant love/strife, the children dance on the edge of viability and the rich sharp berries are set on a town table for the recognition of working people.

123. *Trojan Women (double essay)*   VII (= (a)) and VIII (= (b))

Which is suddenly shattered, by theoretical complacency. The Ironies, those careful observers, flutter their wings and flee in horror. A soldier stands at an old woman's door, pointing a gun at her. "What race do you belong to?"

I conceived the idea that in this art of funerary ceremonial the opportunity of a death was taken as the occasion of a total theatre, of which the final disposition left in the earth was the dénouement, of which the excavator finds a fragile and usually over-written map. So it was a language peculiar to its occasion, grounded in finality but responding to a history. Looking in that light at these two tumuli, neighbours to each other on high ground near Sherburn, I saw them as essays on war. In them the human image is abstracted, fragmented, disordered and replaced, domestic referents are intrusive and inverted, distance is disoriented and brought back to an enclosive limit. The person is separated, figured, and amalgamated. And all these statements are stressed in an echoic but varied duplication between the two mounds so that they cannot be interiorised.

In both tumuli the central "grave", in both cases precisely in the centre, was found to be "empty" of the human body, and filled instead with (a) "a mass of broken domestic pottery with a few pieces of human skull near the centre" (b) "chalk and animal bones, with a few bits of human skull and ribs, and domestic sherds". (Domestic (cheap) pottery not normally deposited with the dead, who always got the best). Both of them had directly to West (result side) of the central pit a disorderly mass of broken human bones, (a) "of at least eight persons, with a few animal bones intermixed, on OGS" (b) "of at least five persons, on a layer of clay placed on OGS". Both contained a triangulation: (a) three holes close to the central pit, to N, SW and SE, one and a half feet deep, filled with chalk and symmetrically set. (b) two holes, at some distance to NE and SE of the central pit, filled with chalk and (NE) animal bones, forming a triangle in relation to either the central pit (obtuse) or the deposit of broken bones to W of it (symmetrical). Both mounds contained further human deposits in eccentric locations: (a) a young woman between the centre and the bone-heap "two large flint blocks, roof-like", over her head + 16 flint flakes and a knife; also a child far away to NW close to the outer edge of the tumulus where no one is ever normally buried. (b) South of and close to the NE hole, an area of charcoal with pieces of human skull and ribs mixed with potsherds, but more importantly, "Throughout a great part of the area of the barrow detached human teeth were met with, strewn upon the original natural surface of the ground."

Including the continual and wearying war lived with day by day... Not the sudden threat but the continuing refusal, the constant struggle for equity, and purpose, against advantage. And the time lost stoking the furnaces of the smoke industry. Language wrenched from its earth and floating independently into nonentity, the secret agendas behind public acts.

The continuing refusal in fact to operate a country at all, a nation, state, or anything like one in large or small, any mechanism of trust and reliance, any hint of common good...

Such pains sends the body into hiding: a foot in the woods over to the East, some ribs in the farmhouse wall, parts of a skull three miles away down the motorway, so that no venturing soldier, no appointed agent of power will ever be able to locate the killable centre or the accusable statement. Human racks in the sky, passing from war to war.

But the listener listens, it is a duty. The message is passed on, vulnerability confirming the human core: it has to be risked, the heart reconstituted in the mind. What anyway would anyone read anything for, but to confront another mind doing what a mind can do: thinking, but also falling, in: debt love error vain and time. Doing things that only a person can do. And the mind hearted becomes a pathway though a landscape of sown teeth, readable tombs, of fallen warriors and lovers betrayed. One word at a time, peace starts to gain its own vocabulary.

Be it, risk it, stand there in the doorway and make the sentence that completes the life. I do not run in any of your races, young man.

124. (*Rothko: works on paper 1944-1969*) X

Ganesa dances, bearing the head, the head that wobbles and sways and impedes the thought (of the day) and the sense (of the world) the gross lost head. Dances parameters of science and night, stumbling through the routines, stamping on the spot, trusting in humanity. The chalk swirls on the dance floor and spreads to the edge like a message on a blackboard, in a schoolroom, in Rwanda. A message too late.

There in the page held out from the page, and the distance that clads proximity, for it is time to go home, if home is still there. Quietly under the hospital walls to the top of the town. To see the layered musics twining into the far fields, and the icing on the multitudes.

125.   XVIII
Beyond memory, through the quiet night the soft flaking of detail in the breeze, past forgetting and returning, to a final pronoun, featureless grapheme, full stop. And what a noise is there then what heaping of costly materials on and over and in the margins *massive heaps of flint blocks* over something after all, a tiny nest to the South of the big empty grave and the point that sings across the wilds. Claim and loss, it all goes written into the future so slightly, as a pause for breath, as necessary, as the filings of my vocabulary are magnetised to your brow and attain/s grammar. Palaces, lived in.

126.   XXI/8
"...a man and woman facing each other, at the level of the original ground surface, on a filled-in hollow two and a half feet deep", their ages about 20 and 17, the man "partly over" the woman: "his legs placed over hers" (set in a ring of modulation the boat steering by St Mark's bell) "Her hands were up to his face, as though his head had been held between them" *Es tanzen Mond und Sterne / Den flücht'gen Geisterreih'n* (the moon and stars are doing the bird) "The left hand of the man was under his own hip, his right hand on the hips of the woman..." *Wer wird von Erdensorgen / Befangen immer sein!* Who indeed wouldn't gladly, take a kick from time to time at this "beautiful earth"/*schönen erden*... Greenwell refers to Warne, *Celtic Tumuli of Dorset* (1866) page 62: "Two skeletons side by side... The head of each leaned towards the other so that their foreheads touched. The man's right arm was across his breast, the right arm of the woman by her side, over which his left arm was crossed to hold the left hand of the woman, whose left arm was bent in that direction across her body." And mentions two couples, "the one's head on the other's breast", and cf. Bateman, *Ten Years' Diggings* page 68, and XXVII below. And how rare these conjunctions are. And doesn't suspect irony, and neither do I.

127.

[Irony?] Better not to know | who inhabits the dark space, alone in the garden at night smoking a cigarette, brushing aside the white flowers, speaking under the breath *mein Leben an den schönen Strom gebunden* my life tied to the fair course. Better be asleep elsewhere, mouthing, turning the dream. Then stroll the genitive earth gentle shepherds, hand and hip in company, while s/he whispers in the bathroom. Divinity, the soil in my teeth. A person unrecorded. The nightingale's filament pulsing to the moon.

128.

irony] passes to a distance, diverting pleasure to succession, turning from the betraying mirror to follow the dark lines of fervour and disappointment **that from those eies beame** /through affect, and stretch across the land, where any number greater than two reverts to solus on the way home. For such is our frailty, spying the roadside pits, history of, child mortality, acts of despair extenuated from that simple embrace or marital greeting. A wedding present from Olympia, meaning trouble. Passes casually into distance by the outer curve of the escarpment **long ways from my home** and how the whole tribe howls and cuts itself at its unbearable daily loss, mineral dust breaking through the pores and prophesying defeat. Of course defeated, any theatre. **All men are bad and in their badness raigne.** But a fine starlit night above the ramp, where we pass in line, beyond comment or pain.

129.   XXVI

My Dearest friend the surface is untouched, the surface is clean and intimate and bears the heraldry of love as on a circular shield.

OGS unbroken : no pits, graves, holes. All burials placed <u>on</u> it.

Entire and clear, salmon mounting the stream under the tissue of war. Blown in the wind, the dust sweeps forwards and back on the piazza through the long night, moon like a dandelion, red wing beating on diamonds and rice, hard cough in the vast gap: the earth plate steady on its shifting bass.

the body of a young child [head to S facing W] with the cremated ashes of an adult arranged in an arc "close to the child's back and partly surrounding it" /the body of a young woman [ENE/SSE] her face in contact with the child's head, L hand on breast, R hand extended forward from the hip and holding the head of another, younger child. The lower jaw of a young person behind her back.

Whole tensed membrane, completely opaque, verbally replete and resonant as reason. Must it then fade and thin? Along the motorway at night with/without you beside me burnt father arched at my back, my) child hovering at (my) brow (her) limbs turning into the future. The road rides a causeway on the last miles to the city, yellow glows at occasions in the fields, outlying factories guarded by light and convening before us to the slight horizontal strip that means (hope/despair/immersion in focus) that means, and passes at once into impossibility. As delight scatters in scalar glist, **their helms in the sun** massed flexible laminae, really, the reason. I don't know how, but | the pressure bent to the surface of event and held, in the hand thrust forward from the hip | strikes the timely orison until a certainty is recognised | And mounts in clear streams under sweeping ash and clouds of carpet dust towards the breeding ground, the round terminal seething with lunch packs and understanding.

130.   XXVI bis
Central burial to WNW facing NNE, crouched as usual, knife under shoulder, large flint blocks over & beneath. 10ft. to NW, a head on its left side, a food-vessel in front of it. 19ft. to SSE, a cremation circle with a miniature cup to W of it. 1ft. E of these the head of a young person laid on its R side facing North, a barbed arrowhead in front of the face, its point touching the teeth.

So to the matter, to the focus, to the clouding cone where separation (and the cat sleeps in a curl all day) narrows the sky to a circular hollow (one day the cat will stop sleeping) fiercely guarded enclave where trust throws back an azure coating on the inside of the biosphere, folds it closed stains it red and hits it for a boundary. When the cat stopped sleeping she was frozen in a wild arch for the leap into number.

Rain on its grave in the garden, Doppler-effect running through the night as good ideas, and helping hands, trespass upon intimacy, fade and thin, break apart. Sliding fall of less than a tone, pale face (there is still a face) staring desperately through harm, ear to drum-head, sentences ground to a blade. Under the weight of the factory wall, at the sun's marginal stay, the whole green ground and blue lining of earth-sight sealed into a tradable form. A red ball stitched round the equator. An ancestral promise/premise.

And doubtless the same silence descends on crucial moments of decision as the shadows lengthen and only a head survives the blankets, turned to face, as I across several centuries, no solution, particles of love-strife between my teeth. Wondering when the promises will ever be fulfilled. So silent in the silence, no-one touching the stilled dial, that maintains a city between compacted desires and the whole circus steps down to its single centre end and purpose **my ioes interred In simpell wordes** completed exactly at vanishing point. And there it goes, for six, knocks over the sponsor's hoarding and is lost in the crowd, where someone quietly pockets it for a valuable souvenir.

131.   XXVII
1 1/2 ft. above the centre of the tumulus, a cremation capsule containing the remains of a man and a woman mixed together... war economy or ultimate embrace? Perhaps this should not be taken seriously. *Perhaps this was merely the redeposition of two primary cremations subsequently disturbed...* Perhaps the things we find lying on the earth were put there by someone. The implied third party. **Turne all my thoughts to eies** and I see him (her) bending to the ground | relinquishing a purchase | Gurney improvising through the cottage night, Scelsi in a palazzo wrenching a tone to its core. And there at the core they are consumed to a point, but still there, as if of each other the substance.

132. XXXI
Heap the hypers over us we ejaculated them and fell extinguished!

133. XXXIV
In silence articulate, the high song unsounded **As to the dead the dead did thes vnfold** • so pass by *qui transisset per via* [all-you] and forget. A silenced clause of the continuing equation, we cancelled numbers lie compacted under green shade and slide major triads across the industrial garden. Under the capstone a cup held between us: so difficult for the living to understand, that we do in fact have it both ways, light and weight, mutually enacted. Well, perfection is but human and love at the glowing limit.

8ft. E of centre and 6 inches above OGS, an old woman [S/>E] (the old woman went on her way long ago, leaving her salts on the table) *and a row of three skeletons facing her in a very closely compacted group, almost touching, all flexed to the same degree and the three skulls in a straight line E-W: a child of about 12, a person of about two (hands to face) and an infant of about 4. The knees of the old woman and the young person touch, and the infant between them is in the lap of either but facing the old woman, with arms raised and hands up to her face.* Three generation tracing her sight back from hope to home, holding it up to her mouth, a cup open forever towards peace.

Wee should beginn by such a partinge light to mend our fears at the article (and our thoughts at the verb) for there is only a moment's space between falling bodies when the calyx opens direct to whatever's in the sky and nobody knows, nobody knows what moves across those dark continents, where power lies. Nor ever will, but the rows of soldiers' heads in line for tomorrow, basket of silver fish brought to the market. O kind hearted woman, accept these transcripts of scattered lights as the suicidal routes fan and tighten across the plains, this dentelle.

For **I have learnt a lesson.** Where distance turns on the rim, neither self nor other is world. A cold resonance between lost travellers, seeking relief from love. *At the centre a man on a chalk pavement with turf laid over him.*

134. XXXIX
Either/Or, the ground slants, and divides. The dictionary speaks of diremption while a soft glittering moan runs from the pavement into the national computer. Quietly, by the starred button meaning long waiting without thought of result. For people are not what we see of them, even when we see them most. ¶So a line is drawn, a straight line *a rough chalk wall from one side of the mount to the other, 50 feet long, WNW to ESE, passing some ten feet SSW of the central grave* A line separating sight from knowledge and asking no more, **love I or love I not** *the upper part of the body covered with turf, the lower part of the body covered with chalk rubble* green under white or white under green over or under Rothko's floating horizon, the earth at its fulcrum comforts desire (but doesn't halt yearning) – the dictionary speaks of cadence. ¶Latin terms, sockets turned to SW and lost promises across the lawn; an elegant figure, as it were by Boccherini or Wittgenstein. But to centre the entire institute, by reaching a true concern across the dividing flux, full and rough as it comes: then what is lost is retained, *a bronze dagger held in the right hand, with a flint blade laid on top of it.* ¶A high voice across the fan vault and straight down to the young question on the slab, **I did but see her** and so carefully poised, asymptotic curve where the day ends and finds its object, firmly and slowly **passing by** relented gravity, moon behind hill. Circular token where lives recuperate their absence. ¶So these signatures augment their worth as they traverse the entire economy hill to hill across the vale, industry and speed, a life that passes by. Messenger creature, loaded with celestine, save the earth from nugacity. Wondering what it means we hope to yet, surely.

135.
Doesn't halt yearning, no question of that, and bear it to the grave, to be represented there /lying at my side or a passing affectionate clasp, arm over shoulder | generation makes machines of us. And soldiers, pumping. But doesn't halt the sentence written through you across the night scaffolding, a simple request for support, to stay my fall as the celestine deepens and opens into space. Where the blue is airy, hands are tied in marriage rings. Where it sinks towards black the wild hunt is up. We turning shield our eyes, represented in a curled posture, as if sleeping, as if pressed into a ball. Which wants to be born, and open, showing its

azure lining to the bees. So as requested, generational light shoots to the closed aether. Go then, trace the course to its thing. And collect the old lady's pension for her while you're out.

136. XLVII

Yearning for a pitch that wasn't/can't be, seeking a tenseless junction. Finding nothing | **Writes in the dust** *an oval ditch, wider E-W than N-S, into solid chalk* a white ellipse on the otherwise yielding text. Promises are rarely actual. Striving to maintain social justice when law is the king's new clothes | **If ye love me** [keep my commandements] so where the |centre| at the/ where the/ true, whole, entity >>body, or statement, would be *is a patch of earth very hard, as if puddled, to a foot's height* is **where we danced that night.** And in that metope the promise born, and I (I) shall give you «another comforter» **e'en the sprit of Truth** (and yearning cease). The moon in the branches of the small pine, for instance, or the dripping tap in the stone house. Unbroken ring, repeated: spirit of, lower case, home. Accept the offer at point of departure. Have it where it says the moment's extraordinary reach. Says death shall not die, and every jarring love is worded.

137. *The Sibyl*

(XLVIII) ending at a grammar of filled absences, S/E of home. *chalk rubble, burnt earth, charcoal.* Replacing present offers, which do what surf does on the hand. Replacing present promises, which divide into the years. (XLIX) and this relay has no beginning, these elegant figurations bridge forced gaps in the story, coiling flex (distant messages) to a substantial coin: *three skulls in a hollow, in trefoil formation.* This emblem of the immense resource that loves deploy on occasion as the informed eye spreads the light across night-crimes, diplomacy, Zeus in the crannies of newsspeak… | this, there-are-three-of-us, keeping time to the heartspan, speaking in riddles, gives the lie direct. Evernew tongue never entirely new, mantles the dimming sky in a green cloak of undistinguished cut/ **Shee is distracted, bring her home** what hope there is for hope abandoned, that it is broken and stays, refortuned by solitary lectors.

138. LVII

A big tumulus, 56ft. in diameter, 6ft. high (always that smooth and elegant discus) *and crowded – 16 burials, and not one of them complete and in proper order, all "disturbed", all with something missing or displaced: a few minor bones or a head lacking, a femur, two tibia reversed... the 15th a pair of hip bones and the 16th a woman's head on a man's thigh bones. And all of these lie in one quarter of the ring, in the NW segment, and define it: one at the centre, one W of centre, one N of centre, four and a bit on a rectangular pavement of chalk flags lying to NW of centre and aligned NW-SE. all the rest between that and the centre.* These traces, deliberately set,

or little more than a dry smear on the unbroken surface of the earth. Fallen walls, boarded shops, swept dance floor, white arrows painted on trees

NE segment empty. SW segment: one clay vessel close to the edge, symmetrical. The SE segment has one refilled hole through OGS ten feet from centre exactly symmetrical, a yard wide but not very deep, forming a line through centre exactly to the chalk pavement, a NW-SE axis across the entire circle

human residues, post-fear, post-loss, post-null. Core of laughter. But the fear remains, handed over. Like a wire taut across a drumhead

individually set E-W but collectively SE-NW and what that means: survival of public options: romance, war. The "gloom of death where all ranks revert to private." That desperate stone raft facing the wildest hopes and pulled irrevocably across the fulcrum to the sucking hole, the same end for all. *all burials on OGS or slightly higher* so that the hole to SE is the only point at which the circular plane is broken and seems literally to counterbalance all the damage set across from it *a headless body, hands in front of where the face would have been.*

To seek an answer, and to sigh and sing and to work the night out. Musicians working together, black and white, gypsy and peasant, intellectually united. The gift passed on, to the outsider as to the child | sits on the old man's lap, two hands on the one bow, and the anxiety of it. Of the separation inhering in focus. A circular cut in the ground, refilled, model of daily purchase that tightens mourning to a soft fundamental (when I close my eye into the real and denial burns on the horizon) across a central colourless void. And stop waving a red flag because they have all passed into the line.

So the war continues, run through the entire phonetics, "the dark mass of copses on the hill" (Sassoon, 1918, in a château garden, waiting to live) and beauty hung on the line, costed in the street, O faithless world **that tare, that rent, that peirsed thy sadd hart** burns on, from station to station down the coast, distant languages succeeding each other, losing nothing, giving to all.

139. LXII
Purpose or produce of, love and labour, human residue that cannot be erased. And remains in the films of death, taken on, a question deflected from mouth to script and back that persists through generations of certainty, imaginal buds in the reaches of the mind, carved shifts in the music while phagocytes patrol the streets at night... | a hollow in the surface of wish, a fragment to the East of innocence, a vast history unnoticed in the flick of shadow when a recognition stills the hand **as by an angel grasped.** The surname of my desire, the swan arched on the river, the cecity of the book.

An enormous shaft, 9ft wide, cut from the top right through the inner mound to 9ft under OGS destroying, obviously, any original deposits. On the floor of this shaft two stone cists in line NW-SE one holding a body, the other a compact cremation capsule | setting a new law, of equivalence by contrary, protestant police, substance and idea on the scales of justice. *and the shaft was filled in a sequence of eight layers: bedrock | chalk | earth | pavement of sandstone flags | chalk to north and earth to south | burnt earth and charcoal | chalk | topsoil.* Burials and fragments in the upper layers... *but the entire intrusion occurs in the same pottery stratum as what remains of the original* (beaker) *construct* And represents the recession of memory as a series of eight discs, each one burnt on its upper surface. These states, these years heavy with resentment, fired into certainty from beneath.

I remember crossing the road, holding my mother's hand. I remember a thin flow of blood reaching the gutter, turning and falling into a grid, and the butchers coming out to scatter sawdust on it. Everyone standing around defeated. Cutting down through everything since, one by one. Death's hand steadying the earth, take it without fear.

140. *(a small pot by Elspeth Owen)*
All the early colours sprouting from a household grey.

141.   LXVI
These people are not suffering. They are not bored, they are not asleep, they have no pride. They abstain, and the immense energy of their histories, separated from them, rests *in situ* though in *Sheffield Public Museum and Art Gallery* more difficult. Make them welcome, say to them: enter our reach, tell us all, tell us if/ **Let neither us deluded be good Lord with dreame or fantasie** if we, are many and one. These people are at vanishing point.

Neither fast nor slow, Mr. B., is the tune that visits me. "…and I falter and see very little, but perhaps entirely, and hope not to dream any of it | as in that anthem of Mundy, I think it was, *Let neither us* in a pavan movement, who did very little, that I know of, but perhaps entirely | who worked it as a trade, like digging graves, painting walls, as was needed, that certain possibilities may be preserved…" If you write a single word, the dead rise up before you demanding a city, and democracy.

The chalk folds trending North and South, the length of England : the demand between pleasaunce and corage. To set a purpose across this horizontally as the ridge curves round to the sea is comfort indeed, shielding our eyes from the bright banners. The language for staying and the right to a life that means, sets a line straight across the meniscus of sleep, so much sharper than the rhythms of nomadic obedience, "follow your instincts" up and down the same hill for forty years. This line, that separates hope from fear, we strive to reach its far ends, but live fervently across it, where light and substance collide, diagonal of wind-swept rain in the street or the sweet tilt of the banker's cap. **They clothed me in the clothes of Death** and I | lie flexed for ever in the path of light. It stalks the slopes, it grounds the metropolis at start and stop, it infiltrates the processor at every angle. It is dreamed into hope in the flesh against love which harbours there. Then set me down (this is my stop) where the light is brought down, the evening prim and rosy.

142. LXVIII
Two interconnected (pits, lives) *both in the same posture, both on their left sides facing SW* | But the simple statement is immediately (confact! episcape!) is a [ritornello] is a/ box of [– vibrating heather –] Concord, and peace, if they are to mean anything, posit a governor, an overseer, a far sighted *an older man* facing the opposite way [SE, head to NE, and N of them] and *with a bronze dagger.* So. **He went up to his chambre** the hope too in the despair, the **aire**, the hope passed on with the fear and **wept, saying** | Would I had... (died, loved, spoken, etc., **for thee**), but clearly do not have. And the whole nation on the move as the air passes swiftly over the field rows and long banks the parting couples at night's fair-ground – repeats that I do not have, but am, in my faltering trichotomy, scattered across the valley pastures | migrating plant forms, stubborn against the future, annually articulate | for you.

The heather and thrift, stubborn against the sea wind, building theses across the brown slopes.

143. LXIX
So raise the head, *as if looking upwards* **I would give you the earth if I had** but have very little, less than my self *extended* askew from the horizontal (I) fall sideways through the gates for (I, you) never quite believed, until diremption was on the wall at last and o, flagrant/ raise then of all things the long lost eyes *hands to the side of the head* lifting it up, for on the edge of final relief is a wish to witness, and be set Here in that meeting of sight with understanding, and leave a clear record, a firm knot on the cord passing through us. Stunned thus, set thus (delighted, amazed,

aghast) that some long-term physics might accord with the quick guesses of the self-dot, endless in its grasp, that I would be ashamed to offer. • Otherness is a beautiful creature and difficult to see but by straining, the neck, the dictionary, the plume tossing on high, as the river winds between hills and the messenger continues slowly, up the mountain trail on a donkey's back by stupa and trig point to (somebody wants you to get over the mountain because they are waiting, for your words, why, to resolve a current despair | weather coming look Up.

144. LXXIV
Simple and undivided, all cover broken all dream displaced *a cremation capsule ten inches in diameter, in a hollow, a "very slight depression" at the centre* severed from all blanketing connectives | present active, unclaimed *and cremated on the spot, the hollow having first been made there* | person as unit: unconcealed stupidity focused to infinity. Thus safe in the fold of song, no reductionist could get you now you (who could not be further reduced) and the language becomes strictly applicable.

Then apply it, at night, across the salt, arid expanses, are points of light: stars, ships, villages, squills. And the hopes passed on with the fears: that the world is good, that the music claims this goodness out of the hope and the fear by eliminating the delay: extent rests on the cross of times at an articulate point, like hung ground. Then the world might be good: for we had a foot in the door once: Stantes erant pedes nostris in artriis tuis Ierusalem and was set aside, flew away, the love-child wrenched from home, polishing the cross-talk. Then **He went up to an high chamber over the gate** ascendit coenaculum portae the porters' lookout over the trade routes and wept or **shouted, with a loud voice** | would I had | but hadn't • social failure (war) so much more than the failure by which we come to die, the failure of nature *and wept, saying*

In pace in idipsum dormiam. And stake a life on it, horizontally traversing the sun's energy cone, you to you. May your peace be a constituted solid, holding its enmity to heart. Then a civilisation: the elements are here, and the junctures, lacking only the will, or burning desire. I'll wait for you at the gate in the evening, when (the only right worth claiming) the mists rise up from the mountain streams.

145. Coleridge on Aeschylus LXIII
Most gentle and sweet mother, thy hand, I am alone/ a pronoun, a bearer, suddenly alone, 3000BP and *saying itself,* as *"Idea,* which knows itself, and the existence of which may be inferred, but cannot appear or become a *phenomenen"* or has already died, into existence, saying: I never bargained for this. And no tribal philosophy, no hole in time, has ever dulled the shriek that follows.

Against which heaps are aligned. Though the day still dawns, gently, as the seasons turn, in the garden green below the bank and the fresh flowers where loss is cupped in a rising cadence. Hope and adversity in the shadow of frost, that rules this ever succeeding day. There I finally **am merciable.** And between the heaps that are aligned I enter my kingdom, be it a glance or a fall. Leaving to the disposers the echo of adieu, a kind of tempered howl **my love my faire one** | Smear of a passing god in first light, heavy on the leaf.

This carol they began that houre singing and complayning and many complained about the complaining but it was a gift, "by which we are to understand reason theoretical and practical… unapproachable by the animal basis – that is, by the pre-existing *substans* with its products… but yet endowed with the power of potentiating, ennobling, and proscribing to, the substance…" ***lex legisuada****,* the dance compacting earth to an equality. Then how to live, and die, between the heaped substances: arts, of observance **Afore thi hart hang this litell table** these numbers of the clouding set.

& the return is guaranteed, the carol sung in the night by the border guard, the throat waged into long song, drunk or sober, learning or guessing in the process how anyone gains at last the right to say. While the song curves in the air and settles under the lip. These contrafacts are sweet lessons on how to live.

O love alas what shal I do We have listed the blood far too cheap. As the song grew they heaped and delved, and put increment against absence *around the complex of burials and structures, an oval ditch aligned NW-SE. In and over it a layer of* "puddled earth" or 'hardpan": surface soil hardened by pressure, as of ***dancing feet*** "that a spade would break only with difficulty" **thowe I do fere to trace that dawnce** encircling zero as the music regains the throne of measure, making copies, months and engines. The name is finally alloyed into space, the guarantor. The dancers break the ring and she turns her wrist out across the green **the voices of children** to the old woman's door.

Never any help really, but the penny to be turned, the hat to be passed, the slightest shove against history | "Nature, or *Zeus*… can only come to a knowledge of herself, in man! And even in man, only as man is super-natural, above nature, noetic. But this knowledge man refuses to communicate."

So the knowing that knew itself was chained to the rock and forgotten, as years blossomed into days.

146. LXVII/1,2

The landscape comporting an action, reaching and ending, to East (seaward). The wolds curve round in a great arc from south to east and this final ridge-end cluster lies within sight (6 miles) of the sea at the Bay of Bridlington, where that cold morning (Greenwell:) "…hundreds of ships were lying at anchor, sheltering from the strong north-east wind." Smoke of Hull in the far distance which 1880 maybe meant something in the hand and a looking up and onward | a shelter, and a yearning triangulated by the spire of Beverley Minster in the middle distance… Or that cold morning when

It appears that this huge mound of chalk fetched from elsewhere and quarried from below ground at immense labour, a hundred feet in diameter and still nine feet high [always that gentle discus] *was raised over the grave of one child approximately a year old.*

These cold mornings recur across millennia. And the child lying with its head to north, facing east, at the east end of an oval grave lined with wood… the frail craft departing *and no objects or artefacts of any kind, but the bones of a young woman evidently re-interred from elsewhere, incomplete and fragmented* | the incomplete and fragmented utterance of this child's future | who happened to die when this tumulus was needed. Or not |

Sentry on the ridge-top, facing dawn. And another cold morning spread its grey distances into the thanking heart.

Honoured in loss, **in absence mourn** /powerless before the vertical demand, the self thrust into the earth, where need and knowledge burn – and funnelled into a hole where /person at vanishing point where/ a god appears, heavily disguised as the specific hopes of a child not yet able to speak.

147. LXVII
– guaranteed hole in the forehead vast plain stretched before, of industry, or waste, sheltering nothing. The god appears at a juncture, where the possible person vanishes, leaving a space/ "...flocks of bustard and flights of dotterel and the thickets of water-loving alder" among which a thin line of thin kine, and berries, which is where we still live, and vanish into (the dry wine of, microtechnic pastoral.

And these streaks of phosphorus on the ground indicating paths, of exit, the dead infant giving birth to the Ancient of Days, because the world can never be the same again, because a baby who did very little, next to nothing (but entirely) occasioned a naming, and a new structure, and after long perusal, a hope. Apollo's cup-bearer (clusters of knowing sinking to the heart) (an orbital route-map, a fire of delay, a dynamo) redeems all lost promises.

In my youth, at school, we were much engaged with questions of eternity | *all other burials, and there were about twenty, were at the top of the chalk mound, mostly in earth-filled* (dark) *hollows in the* (white) *surface, several with chalk flags beside, above, and over, parts of the body and head. But there were no burials in the NW segment, and the SE segment contained only children, seven of them, of which five were in a straight line to SE.* It seemed there was something out-there, a location, open to recognition.

Thoughts of gratified desire flew diagonally across the sky leaving the singular result untouched, lying on the ground, facing the light. As if there were an historical hope, and formal question, in the surface glitter of a small prize donated to a baby. And lust formed a sign to southeast illuminating the god's vast scattered demesne, charging into dawn pursued by (a bite in the heel) generation. Meaning I fork on the outskirts of love like everyone, and go tired to bed to await the exhibited pain.

Beneath which the original transaction still holds, under all that prizing and placing under all that echo, the child-exit lies intact, at the plug-end of a "slight hollow" in the Original Ground Surface *heavily burnt and with many animal bones strewn on it, also 79 flint saws, 17 scrapers, 3 arrowheads, 2 points...* this infant lies in industry (& waste, in what s/he can't use) in a hollow in society its boundless despair at the silence of boundless love/ to have died, at one, out of, and into, that band of abandonment . . . . . within which a (clearing in harm at which) an agreement (every noun in the world enters and stands round the edge of the theatre, merely witness to the soul's departure, ,to no-one knows where, goal of desire, promise met, the fruited verb// To be in position at the gates, facing the very arrival that creates the world, like a cup to be grasped. As if the lost eyes saw

saw a crown in lowness, and a triumph in despair.

148. LXXIII
Wingèd thing, balanced and hesitating thing-like thing, fixed in the ground as hung in the air, young-old and /burgeoning centre, dips to the earth so the whole structure takes off and cuts straight across > NE to SW the hawk over the hill and the red-haired singer holding in the air her singular belief "We have created man under stress" to await the releasing movement of a languageless consummation. Which comes and passes over like a migrant Boeing. The house settles back to its nightly murmur like an electric tug on the Danube you're in the other room writing to lost friends.

149. *Thesis.*
Where the person vanishes the god appears. There at the fulcrum of the marked space the node that empowers the tone. Bearing love like a train of falling dust and petals vanishes into a point in seeing where the power over distance resides, that commands every duty. Again and again, appears, "There, in front of you, can't you see him?" (it) genderless emanation of, an entire life at point | creates an imago at the edge of day when the light is on the turn | appears then, half visible half a contour of the closing foliage at the field's dark side. *(Eurydice, Elaine of the cold white hand!)* Appears, and never stops appearing, in the grain of the worktop, remembered honesty in speech, wherever the person's act is final and lamp… appears as the person departs into, because s/he must, the world. Come back we shout but it is too late, we get a certificate. Would give every god there ever was for another touch of that warm hand.
Thesis abandoned.

150. *Ekelöf's Dream*
Dead hand in my hand responding, turning, dead taste in my mouth like stale rice. Histories of fear: How the king was dismembered. And when only an arm and head were left was asked, "Are you still sentient?" Yes: the big blue eyes staring out hard and clear to the horizon muttering **She and onlie she** | what shall I do without *Che farò senza* and where do it? – on what map, on what paper smeared with dismal farms. The answering silence

2. The answering enemy, the Warrior who tried to kill my voice but missed and struck a hole just above my eyes, black ticket to the cancelled future, small with insipidity and unresponse, caught in the dream unable to [wake, die, love] at the mercy of time's silence again. But also, "a kind of turning" [*ett slags tillvändhet*] these, who craved for life, and lie, like left-overs on a plate, rubbish in the street. Plimsoll altars, full of static, all the messages wrenched to a capsule, until the unfolding. Until the soul is called out of it (because someone needs it) – father, mother, wife, turn again.

151.   LXXIII
Then burn on, **You black brite starres that shine while daylight lasteth** as these spaces once filled by people, like spaces in the thoughts of other people, expanded and contracted and hovered and struck and finally settled to their cornering fates. And are arrayed here as points through the surface of the earth | whose colour, at the cauterised edge, is dragged by gravity away from cerulean fire towards the clay of the valley and sideways into love at a tailing point or new struck edge… /leaves, fallen, at night, on the car bonnets like petals, like advertisements for the future. And day passes into night, true night without word, without telephone call. In this silence a colour grade pulls the eye down from strife.

Crimson turning rusty. And a vertical crack opens in the ridge-end, a hollow track **my last and most true friend** | Enter then the Queen of Night the great prima donna herself. Oh then Oh then everything stops: the London traffic the scent of gain on the world-score screen, stops, and listens: a someone asking in a pit: where are you? And speaking a name into the hollow where desire prepares a final bed. Over which the rain on the roof cuts distance vertically through the self, until sleep is despised as a cheap return. Then an answering silence in which language is cynically weighed, and maybe on the fulcrum of love's pole **is raised a body spirituall** that the eye, touching, closes, and knows. Like the sculpture under tumulus 73.

Three inverted urns in a line (ENE-WSW) *the middle just missing the centre of the ring to E* in exact symmetry: the outer two both 3ft. from the centre and raised 2 1/2 ft. above OGS, the middle urn *sunk in a circular hollow* and *surrounded by* the cremation of a "young person" /sunk and raised again like the action of wings, wailing of the wave's fundamentals the very instruments of understanding and forgetting, beating this way and that, stupidity and wisdom. Takes flight from the edge in the quick brush of earth currents and answers despair at a curve, a guidance towards the reaches of the long valleys. And moves through the air, owl creature, on the pinions of care, whoever s/he was, laboursome but surely, sailing on, to the world's first answer on a cresting front, loving all that is left behind *adios, pueblo de Ayacucho.*

151A.
And look back down: Clay caked to the bone, where the answering fact keeps its council, and always will. Until there is not even bone left and in that post-final annihilation and nowhere else I declare my trust (what you trust is the first thing you think of) Inside that horological despair a fine line shines at a meeting, as in obsidian.

152.   LXXI
Dark disc hovering over the centre, cloud edge over the ring-road/ *compacted of burnt matter, with a plentiful scatter of imperfectly calcined human bones* /in the municipal library they switch on the desk-lights at mid-day and pursue a relentless commerce in the deepening gloam | salts of mercury and cobalt into the dermis which stay impacted, passed on through generations of histiocytes until the entire chemistry closes down. ["The money has to come from somewhere" *but the money is here*] Then blue brightens back to the ore and we edge creatures exchange limbs in the indolence of the gulf stream: *not a piece of flint in the whole structure.* Kind, but longing for a working-place where //What we have is not a poverty problem but a wealth problem: there is not a shortage but an excess. And no one prospers until all prosper in their various currencies. No one evades this condition, no one opts out of the unwritten agreement. Secret gain is an ugly veil before fear, and the resulting cruelty increasingly blatant. **Yestr'een there was four Marys** and once the name stood hard but clear on the heart's floor.

153.   LXXXII
To forfeit the edge rather than lose the middle | A young man walks on a long road, a green and gravelly road between stone walls in Ireland or Scotland or Eastern Europe, over hills and through valleys, meeting no-one on the road, striding on and the impatience of that healthy stride: to love, to get there, meaning death also is on the road /has wrecked the hope of cities and brought beauty to a leg for sale [*at the actual centre, nothing at all; but two graves equidistant to North and South, respectively*

an E-W cremation and a tilted infant like a wain under the bed...] very love has harmed, because it must, our truth and knowledge. The lust and healthiness of that stride, whether it be to a joyous wedding or a refugee camp in Croatia | and to regain the certainty rather than lose everything to a central void. Walks on, over the moors and mountains, between the graves of kings, the factorised fields, all that grey ash sweeping the ground and the burnt posts on the horizon, victims of nationalism decorating the route... Keep clear and there is a hope it is a true meeting, a thing read back from its results, a road you may never need to walk again. Keep clear as the day folds the sun crusts my heart is inditing.

154. LXXXIII
And we shall found a *res publica*, a thing of the heart, a forward thing. From (not at) the centre a spreading lustre is cast back, that opens the edge darkness to language. Dim things become visible, a table, telephone, silent, barely distinguishable forms in the black paint behind the portrait /become sayable, as attenuated desire teaches silence | **Sodenly afraide Half wakyng half slepyng** naming the artefacts that succeed us. *There was nothing at the centre, but exactly due East three urns in line* (dim things) emerging from the obscurity **And gretly dismayed A wooman sat weepyng** | the line of demarcation turns on anxiety to attain distance: the child grows older and further from, and learns to walk in fear... | a strange, dark thing made known and inhabitable: cursors (across the earth) from the soul of, the beautiful reason for (being) that maintains the planet's course at a slight differential from a point or middle where/ the song rises *while the seas, do ebb and flow* – where light arrives and is cast off, light dispensed, across shadowed ground. And back to the centre, cracked with worth.

155. *(Installations by Gary Hill)* LXXXIV
"I have arrived at a place mute of light" | In the darkness the violet rods tune in. Pages on the floor slowly becoming visible, open books and documents **these were once** (hopes, fond farewells, life works) illegible,

moving surfaces slowly stirring, dim forms of lip fingered, skin horizons stirring back and forth, cold burning | fleshly ghosts pale grey wandering in the seething paper ruled with horizontal lines, silent forms meeting and separating in small cells scattered on the ground, dim quires turning—slowly, repeatedly, touched lip, cast eye, turned back. Some seven or eight (of them), each *less than an entire body, and burnt on the spot.* the white wine of homing suspensions, when any elsewhere cancels itself to complete fall. And the echo, the ghosts in the corridor, the lives that were and shall be, totalling themselves in the margin. May we keep a charm or right of way, a unit, a piece of cheese, a pen in the hand, a yellow seal **The small rayne** a voice recalled, awaited, a message understood, these things that mean, these things agreed. After so long in darkness, the star sputters in the breast pocket and love is not fair. But love is not the end.

156.   LXXXV
It is so perfectly fair, to thrust death into the jaws of this transparency. *A natural rise of chalk at the centre of the tumulus held the cremation deposits of two children, one very young, both cremated on the spot* or to mistrust any statement that breaks the membrane. Here we live as we have by the mark of succeeding names and the stories told the children, that come from over the horizon *among the deposit two urns, one on its side with its mouth facing west, the other standing on the first* simple tritonic motifs repeated at length gradually phasing into a branching complexity and returning to a different point. The stories, of animals talking in the dark and the ultimate reward of sacrifice, are told and listened to with complete concentration. Distant thunder on the dry plains raises a few heads. The children sing dead in tune.

157.   LXXXVI
With favoure on hir face ferr passyng my reason /calcined bone, clad in, robe of honour (slight but clear trace, pale streak drawn through clay the cloud behind the ridge, the crown of wild celery, solidified light... A precipitate settles on the rim of night: lines, of the *ossatur,* this curve

and that angle /to SW facing SE *hands in front of face* as if inhumed but in fact cremated on the spot, the entire skeletal structure in position as placed, a tracery of ash | these, (hands no longer claiming, but indicating, the touch/ cross/ clasp of, offered desire **were once** (powers of the land/ | Close then, close bracket, close life, close episode, and yet it means on: this curve, and that angle, in the light, as a precipitate in the glass a falling and fallen substance a thing that settles (finally) to a pictograph, to an intricate sentence, the arrow through the crescent (a Pictish grapheme) **were once** meanings | And the world like a chaconne returns again and again and virtue flashes on the legible borders of the social, the jewel in the night showing again and again what we are like, a moon facet drawn through clotted darkness. There **I heard a wyfe sing** this form is what I am, take it.

158.   LXXXIX/i
It was perfectly clear that two bodies, of a youth and a man, had been placed on OGS back to back and then cut through the middle, and the lower half of the youth and the top half of the man removed, leaving two halves in approximately the space one body would occupy, but askew: the torse facing N the thighs facing S, the upper half of the youth on the lower half of the man…

willing neither to go nor to stay. And what settled this pact and drew this conflict out to its summit was not world but/ not voice, and not memory, but/ was this, this laying down this keeping (the child from harm) this justice. Which said, as you have been so you shall be, the pair of you.

159.   LXXXIX/ii
Pale ash in dark bowls. The dawn light standing on the hill's flank, the strata laden with earthen cells and scallop casts, a dome of comedy over a life *of extreme misfortune*. Then the light runs down the slope and away to war, in far countree.

People take it as white cloth, hue of death and obedience and wear it, standing around the closing centre. The diameter is the current scope of love, and occasion of contemporary despair, opening like a flower from there to light the band under the chin, so we are very suddenly changed.

A young girl casts her ring into the pit her future in the eyes of the man this dance is named after, who lived through immense misfortune such that time no longer had any power over him, and he migrated to the pale margin of the continent (pained majesty at the margin of content) among slow tombs and careful records to his nightly rest while the waves weave. As thin a strength as a phrasal verb, that stakes a house where the wild ash courses. And the final shape of his life laid over him in the form of an earthen mound, *its entire surface burnt* and five bodies set into its hollows, calcined, palled script on prepared ground.

This turning of light ahead, this curving down to land, this palling… is (is it?) where.

160.   XCI
100ft. diameter, still 5 1/2ft. high under plough, and containing one pot, 11ft. ESE of present centre and 1ft. above OGS. And the urn is "quite plain".

                                                                                                                              C
45ft. diameter, earthen mound 2 1/2ft. high, containing one pot, 4 inches high and 4 inches wide, 8 1/2ft. NE by N of centre, in a slight depression in OGS. Also one piece of burnt bone (human?) 7ft. SW of centre. And the urn is "of a rather rude description".

Paucity which stands at the very crown of day, a kindness tracked against power and right, the simplicity of it, sole property of the flick'ring shade the focus that passes in a blink of the earth back to the eye.

And all sorts of riffraff getting their own tumuli these days, another roadside shrine in whitewashed cement at a bend in a back route, illuminated by a wax nightlight 1 euro 50 for six.

We nod to it. Trouble in mind. Sitting in the grass mending a coat in the liquor of dawn.

161.   XCII
The base inhumation of a child in a hollow in OGS, the cremation of a woman above it, the inhumation of a man above that. There was nothing else, only this central three-tier structure.

"Oh lift your little pinkie, And touch the winter sky."

162. *Nurse's Song*   CI

"Oh lift your little pinkie, And touch the winter sky.
Love is over the mountain, Where the beautiful go to die."

Where the light returns to the eye like a tear running back in, the *foramen ovale* re-opens and the singing echoes back through hollows in the earth to the pain centre now stilled, funnelled to a point of nil gravity, an immense weight lifted /*massive exostosis on the shaft of the left tibia, agglutinating the lower third of the fibula*/ **The sorrowes, which themsealvs for vs have wrought** ...*another large deposit on the inner side of the foramen nutritivum*, **Ar burnt to Cinders by new kyndled fiers** with smaller growths inbetween and **The ashes ar dispeirst into the ayre** names hovering over the graves (in the night it snows I trust you are warm) | a dedication.

Sorrow was my revendge, and wo my hate in less light than the dead cast, a switched-off TV at night, frost in the tree's shadow **Who lookes not back to hear our after cryes** but lies buried in the ring of sky, the town street in a lemony glow of consequence. Whose silence speaks, because there was a guardian, a carer, a dedicatee. Who rocks the cradle, who monitors the breathing, who /maintains an observance: a complete stranger, who nurses this written-off thing to its closure through the night hours as the pipes sing through the vast building. Until finally, **Wher hee is not, hee laughts att thos that murne | Whence hee is gonn, hee scornes the minde that dyes** and always so, always to the upper side of belonging an unknown leads love to the bent hills, where ice coats the blade and the mind grazes narrative, which lives on. Brillig 'twas, and yours for a star turn.

163.   CII
Lives on through shadowy quarters, sorrow my revenge, sadness my hatred, my **frendly fo and ruler of my vow** the hunger passing through the skull reaches a knife. A knife *south of south-west.* A warm knife.

In that orchard there is an hall, **hangid with purpill and pall** in that grave there was an arrow a star-cast writ pointing to the fine-bedecked powers that stand behind/before the mind and redeem the world in excess. Of truth. That falcon

hath born my mak away while I write what they say and my life veers to a pointed nil west of Tuesday. Nothing could be clearer.

164.   CV
If it is clear a paradise begotten, if it is a pit in the earth a breath traversing the vocal chords the few and gentle moans of accession. Numbered like the tiers of a small theatre (five).

Retailing a story, as we walk on the soles of the dead or the response of the entire fault [Tapiès, *The Step,* 1966] and make a forward thing on its resistance, a vow on its echo (as the wood tucks into the hill's end) and scoff at nations, that starve the market. While the distant soft sea in the wind lays crystals in the grass **whither I go that understand I not, neither what shall become of me yonder** | *removal of the mound revealed a circular excavation 36 feet in diameter decreasing by five tiers or steps down to a floor 14 feet across and 4 1/2 feet below OGS. Here the single burial was laid, well off-centre to North: a middle-aged man, crouched, head to SSW facing East. Behind him a ditch two feet deep ran round the edge of the grave for half its circuit* /**this mystery have I desired to know, but none can impart right** (as to why the throat should burn and the tongue fill the mouth | as to why, we would agree entirely, and yet fall to silence under the earth tone and the resonance of the dragging sea, because no fate is deserved. No handy deities close this rent.

No compacts qualify the urgent sense, of radiant lack.

SO poor thing lie there less than you are *hands to face, fingers doubled in* (a flicker in the eye where the lost shoppers pass by) no longer remembering, a walled spring. So poor thing lie there so much more than you ever dreamt. Cream of event. You dreamed of a warm spring, spreading across the land, a socialism.

165.   CVII
The person entire, and left with "nothing". Owning nothing, part of nothing, wearing none of the tribal filth. Whose account is elsewhere, and clear as day. Whose speech defeats linguistics, and the sky acres bloom.

166.
and dreamt (but didn't dream, for it was already there) that the sky was cast in a powdery grey on the slope and carried as a precipitate in surface water to the small river, European as it curved by the domed wood. A dark crusted ink stands in pools in the pits and hollows of the paper, seeping out in fine threads to a fuzz of tailing closes under green wash, almost Japanese. A row of small brown leaves. The clefts in the edge where water runs off the plateau. Recognitions and agreements, musicians addressing their instruments, enemies of fear residing in the manifest of speech or worth absolutely nothing.

167.   CIX
A child of about eight cremated on the spot and the ashes gathered to a heap twelve inches in diameter a button that colours the entire daylight, a shout in the field and a whisper at the elbow *on OGS at the centre, surrounded by lumps of charcoal.* An urn was placed on the burnt bones and among them was a "pin" made from the wing-bones of a bird, also a piece of flint, calcined, evidently part of some small implement to maintain and support uncertainty and bear it on its track across the nations, over the lapse of Either/Or, to its founding horizon **wherein true sorrow dwells** and faithful heart.

168.   CXI
in a small vocabulary, where North is fear and South is ease, and East-West run the days so **lulla my onelie joie** bowed under a diagonal, as the rain falls, and the sweep weeps in the streets he cannot clean.

169. *Waiting for 112.*
A small vocabulary, where North is risk and South is comfort, and East-West runs the trade, brightening the copper wire. Then lay my profit in the ground, as a finished thing, a welcome agreed between contraries. And leave it there, departing at a particular tangent from the dialectic, turning aside from, the whole person a line extending from a point (for we drift off the earth and everything we make is left behind us, the greatest retention an account aligned to a sector of the whole, a line turning this way and that in search of its end | **for Musick's the cordiall of a troubl'd mind** anywhere at all. Meanwhile the sugar creeps into the berry, it's a disaster of a kind, the bass that holds the sequences, a weather front, a war, creeping down the earth.

These things are set at the edge of the balance sheet, to which no metaphor belongs; the earthline swells and closes, holding the horizon coiled like an infant in the womb, everything we were and could have been, the future never reached, is fixed at the diversion sign where war pours into the ground. Remember me.

And set my failure in the soil, that/ ebbs and flows against a **constant marke** which is | what my love remembers. Remember to wake me when the North sends a promise a promise down.

170.   CXII
The flesh decides, the rest is disjunction. Pale moon on the rise. A white disc beyond which failure, +/- horror. Like these tumuli, or the furnaces and barracks on the roads out of the town.

Surfaces, through which amours shoot collide and scatter. The black disc in the white envelope records movements of flesh to and from itself, flights of spirit as the result implicates a new mind, which finds reparation on the furrowed edge of the consonant, reluctance in the wooded echo. Then this becomes that and O the flowers, the cypresses, the high flying voices, the scarring of the sky!

Disposes (of) us *on an axis* ("we" = sentient humanity, also "two elderly women", one above the other head to foot, axis NNE–SSW and a lost narrative concerning a "young person" *haphazardly scattered in the infill between the two women, but the leg bones set carefully in their natural positions.* There's no answer to this. The sign is forward only, **more I learn less I know** (of wisdom, of what the stories are *for* I | can't help | falling in (love) | with you (or) the bygone snow.

(and the clues are in the disposition, very clear. A climatic maximum engenders a question, as the fields re-fruit the fence of love falls. Plenty demands more, money burns holes, the fat kids want their Brazilian beef. Memory of a cold and focused fewness pulls at the compass rose. Only the singer calls the answer, the spinning circus full of burnt result, spiralling in the air and dispersed towards the future coast.

So take your dialectic away | **O let we gwan!** The leaf, released, spins in the air and comes eventually to ground, entirely one and many. The choirs for which Fayrfax and Sheppard wrote, those expert children, rehearse in the earth.

With what tenderness and reach (therefore) clearly. Birds, and meteors in the cauterised sky, wine in the cup, love in the very letter.

171. CXV

The word that sings out of the ground, and the sound of mourning between the shoots of (a term shifting over millennia from "grass" to "wheat": *emmer* and the wind passing and shaking the leaves) *No home but the struggle* but no struggle worth half a thought that doesn't want to spread home across the earth, wherever the light wind creeps and the broken leaf settles, to sit there in justice. A whole and singular thing, a self. That stays itself and stays sited as the world offers faster and faster transport to nowhere in particular. And the fast transport shakes the earth until the self and the roof and the steps of the Institute slide into nonentity in a smoke, a cleansing smoke a smoke for getting rid of people. That drifts across the town most natural seeming of a Sunday afternoon, raising a smile in the ethical couple, that their dependence is full of continuing labour and the planet well mined. The smoke comes from behind a wall where some self fell an inconvenience to the great hurry.

So, (male) *headless* to NE "facing" SE *arms crossed in front of his diaphragm, part of someone else's skull on his knees* and what he has left to see with sees the answer, the homing pigeon settling on the loft roof, the luminary over the horizon, **Out of th'orient crystall skys** it sails, it bounds down to earth and he knows it, his self so completed by fracture that the plain clearness is no longer a threat. In fact sacrificed, **That I may neer disdayn.** Well I reckon so, how about you? *A sherd covered in fingernail impressions.*

172.   CXVI

If the self is at a frontier if the self is a frontier creature, there is no relinquishing, and no restoration, *Navigare necesse es, vivere non* | and Isaac's burden falls easily as a leaf... The cry at the threshold of nonentity, **torne down my face A littel while** and for this respite, for this ethics, creates an enemy (at a frontier) the heart tuned up to assembly. A public thing, a learning, not a meditation, a circular field. A crown made of layers.

circular, 23 feet in diameter, and the whole surface covered with blocks of unweathered flint under which the buried body faces the land of origin or the uncharted future and always faces both ways by the accounts of a whole life here marked on clay | free at last, over the threshold of nonentity, to regress forwards and relax upwards *the grave aligned NW-SE* a "large man", no skull no arm-bones *all the bones of pelvis and vertebrae mixed up and out of place* /*and clearly has never been disturbed* | the dry friction of wings, that bend the spine to the earth when **my mornyng ys past.**

Lost connection, where you are now or how a promise reaches me. Speaking an entire land (arrived and departed) as a trade, to which navigation is necessary and setting it on the rim of hope like a weathered stone… silence and stillness of an unnoticed passage— | marks, a letter, scratched on the clay (never let yourself be led to feel ashamed of slow reasoning by step, or slow movement by thought) until it becomes possible to think of a country "dear to the heart" for its bleak edges, its ambivalent signs, its overbearing common sense **thyke as sterres be in the skye** (galleon field) a country of response thick with (peace) O Pearl!

173.   CXVII
Unrepeatable. Circular, *the whole surface covered with blocks of flint* echoing back or echoing forward *a woman facing S in a rough cyst of flint blocks and chalk sunk below OGS* | Comfort, small pale wheels floating in the industrial matrix, **Io venni in loco d'ogni luci muto** as promises have back-formed years into marks on stone, repeating each other, *facing SW, right hand under her head, left hand extended forwards* and we, slowly uncovering, layer upon layer, not understanding, revealing, mark upon mark, mark cancelling mark, footprints in the sand, rewriting memory to a set of affirmatives and departures /exact or not, but curved, floreate, lifting frail emblems from the earth in a stillness, with hints of marine débris.

174.   CXXI: Money Hill
Antigone, calling us back to the ethical when we thought we were wild-self ranging the intermediate heights by state permission; and placing murder on our lips. Then denying philosophy, so that there is no "we", only a singularity of just exchange by a code that "we" cannot know, only "I", Antigone, my privilege. Opening the sides of the Pennine Way where harm is unbounded, stretching over the denuded pastures, the buried schoolchildren, the stifled hymn. Antigone, in what we thought was mutual tracing a linear wound. So the pit is made, but the/ ground is/ /cancelled. Antigone.

And the circle cancelled *an oval mound, its long axis tilted slightly N/S of E/W* over the grave of a girl of about 17, facing SSW and a massively stressed SE-erly pull below her: a child, an old woman, a cremation, all to SE. all remembering what she refuses to remember (Antigone) and steps over, to a singular property within sight of the frontier. *Round her throat a necklace of 126 jet beads.*

That strange habit of counting in sixes and twelves, always plus a unit to the hand measures. And putting flowers on dead bodies. Princess of the north, the resistance.

175. CXXIII

Then fall, and with an art of falling, to a state of shelter. To a history, tension of forms across the possible, written into a closed fire that arches over succession, fall exactly into that. And lie there, in more space than you need, your history forming an empty cavity offset behind your back like a rucksack as you religiously face SE and sneeze for luck. Fall no other way but back to the lapse, where nothing is surer, the core and sudden end of love. Through a thin stratum of dried blood, tomorrow turns over.

Dioscuria

1.

In your stone boat you sail the green hills home, joining year to year. The twin stars cross with your eyes, sailing the side horizons of the trade route, dragging a hope/ a crescent in the tides of reluctance **when life shone warm in thine eye** and the needs of the people.

frost on the tilled earth beneath which the human remnant *the bones softened by the acidic soil to the consistency of soft cheese* white pudding on a stone plate, that wills the fixed boat out across the screen of duty | Sailing from Byzantium with a crew of small furry creatures. Eggshell craft with matchstick mast…

In your stone chamber, *the body upright in a sitting or crouched position* a few objects to hand | a green screen that damages the optic nerve, an unheated loft room on Stephen's Green through the winter, the singer of *Der Winterabend* waiting through 78 bars of floatage for a visitation… And persists, stares harder and harder into the glowing resistance, fixed to the post/ *large limestone slabs piled over the grave, with a second burial on top of them* guiding twin *bronze knife, stone axe* | Christmas angel in a loft conversion looking out over the winter gardens at night, watching for cell decay at the cross of star-sights **Timor et tremor venerunt super me Et contexerunt me tenebrae** for the darkness is my road-map. And the message sleeps in the continuance, waiting to be counter-pointed out, written on a bark scroll: the chronicles of a people, the record of a lasting coupling, the stabilisation of the globe.

So sorted, letter delivered orders received objective sighted across miles of waste, the mapped swamps. To navigate askew the trade current, diagonal to the pull, the needs of the people…

And it does, this is the amazing thing, it moves off, arpeggios in the left hand
– "everything is a pathway"/ the bank, and all the sweet pathetic remnants of now, recede into the mist.

2.

Drifting over the black marshes/ A few signs of life, the whole earth, everything on it, all its weather to the last goodnight.

Fading scene (we were asleep and dreamed the whole thing) gathering solstice (we wake into what the dream posited)

And the dear pain gathers on the edge of day and orchestrates its answer before anyone moves in the streets of the town. They sleep on, nestled in dreams of trust and failure. But the whole flock of strife has been up for hours. In the sheer polarity of simple numbers, pure hatred is pure hunger and the elven drivers lap back the hours until the final agreement is reached at which, yes, agree to go. Either/or. To school with a gun, to quiet corners of the countryside with a prayer-mat. To make of the self a burden or a lack. And yet someone else worked for many years entirely without gain and made a different image, signature of a finite mode bound in earthly form, formed in beauty…

I was there at the time and I saw it with my own eyes. I saw it in Florence and again in Arezzo, to the north side of the cathedral axis *her long hair about her shoulders* making a triumph of despair, and a final home of earth.

Hee haw, I said aloud, and the future was uncoded.

3.
An affected heart, at which world and future are paused. And in that pause a long, winding music with miles and miles of rolling hills and valleys **where Jove abounds** where lime and potash leached from upland granite break into yellow and red promises. Meaningless unless shared.

But rose, what bitter dust lies in your roots tonight, what trans-continental messages restore your future to irrevocable action, while back home the deadly prophets stare. A freeing movement across coloured counties, and translated terms. Meaningless until shared.

O brightly burdensome rose, retuning the cuticle to an immense concept of societal hunger.

4.

Living in a white rock landscape the star zones must become more casual, the questions of children more open and the identity of the earth located in a horizontal theorem, reaching across forests and rising scrub finally to re-know the other as a death ticket which maps the entire song.

The entire song on the ground, day after day, striking the surface gently/ fiercely, holding it, voicing the verb and focusing breath across it, so/ a friction, a knowledge, a dance measure, an open space between arcades where the body quite openly reclaims itself and the separations written into history dart to the side and turn back in blossom, marble putrescent with symmetry. Marble florescent with flesh-lapse. Resting its premise on redeemable goods (as if fear could be just brushed aside) most feared, most loved.

Exactly what [under your stones, under your leaf and egg tags] is what we have here, almost more than enough. It would be gentle to assume it so, the white rock far concealed under words and orderly setts, known by its results which table their own time. But here (me) it breaks into loss: where were you when I called? The gentle tribes that roamed the land and set up burial posts on green knolls.

Made a future. Save it, store it, back it up for it is longer in the throat than any agreement, hold it without fear if you can, the white reel cutting the daily confab. Jesus, I adore those daily confabulations from bed-light to crown but dark in its brackets the language flinched itself again and pointed with unbelievable grace to the constant factor, the third term, the hole in the ground.

This cavity is the end. Line it with sincerity. When right-wing capitalism gains the entire world, when nobody anywhere believes a word, the time is ripe.

5.
There is no rose of such power there is no rondeau of such grasp there is no ring so virtual /and the number of my days encircling round, **for in that rose is hevn and erth contayned** as A MATHEMATICAL LANDSCAPE across the night across the very thought of death across death's champion domain like an Essoldo striplight in a quiet provincial town in the middle of the night **in lytyl space** contained | and have it all, the Hutu stories, the Jewish music of Transylvania…

How do we have it all, after it is gone?

lip against lip, the hurt of pronunciation

no longer seeing anything, but this little space, loaded with nitrate recuperants, and knife-thrower's music.

6.
All mein Wirken, all mein Leben All my work and life given to (you, to you) My time, bending over grave-pits (faithful to) signs left in the débris of wars and normal living.

How the tones lean on the green fells. Like Buxtehude, like a man vanished completely into a resonance. Really, no bits of person whatsoever but a space in which a world-meaning resounds, the soaring towers of zero. And isn't that the final home to which all of anyone's work and life is voluntarily donated, the greatest knowable thing. It bores and twines across the whole of now.

Lest there be too much death.

PRINCIPAL SOURCES

Part One: J.R. Mortimer, *Forty Years' Researches in British and Saxon Burial Mounds in East Yorkshire*. 1905.
Part Two: William Greenwell, *British Barrows*, 1877, and articles in *Archæologia* LII and LX.
Dioscuria: Thomas Bateman, *Ten Years' Diggings in Celtic and Saxon Gravehills*... 1861

The many fragmented quotations incorporated into the text are mostly from 16th and 17th Century sung poetry but include other things, from mediæval songs to Housman.

NOTES *(The numbers are those of the texts, not the pages)*

19.
"cut too small from the inside": a phrase from a poem by Ian Patterson.

33.
The two longer quotations in bold are from William Blake, *The Book of Urizen*, 1794.

35.
The quotation in brackets is from Peter Levi, notes to his translation of Pausanias (1979, volume 2 page 71), summarising Philostratus.

38.
brachycephalic: broad-skulled; dolichocephalic: long-skulled. These two types are or were held to represent two populations of prehistoric England, the former newer and possibly intrusive, bringers of metal working and singular burial, the latter the population of the preceding phase, stone and wood-working pastoralists who lived and buried communally. New populations are supposed to have pushed older ones northwards and westwards.

69.
Ilyich: Leo Tolstoy, *The Death of Ivan Ilyich* (1886).

78.
Windmill Hill "A" ware. A ceramic form belonging to the earliest Neolithic people of southern England. The occurrence of the vessel here is highly anomalous unless it had been purposefully preserved.

86.
"came from": anthropologists have found instances where in the disposition of burials the dead are set to face the land which the people are said to have come from, be this fact or fiction, and shall return to, dead or alive. There are cases of heated arguments on this subject during funerals. Earlier 20th Century British archaeologists always attributed evidence of innovation to successive waves of people coming from "the Continent" (south and east).

100.
"looking for the source...": from Jack Spicer, *Book of Magazine Verse*, 1966

124.
Rothko: The works on paper were presented in a book by Bonnie Clearwater, New York 1984. They are mostly late works, smaller and generally brighter, sharper, more optimistic, than the gloomy big canvases.

The Indian deity Ganesa is "a god of home and hearth". Like the Rothko paintings, his figure is dominated by horizons: elephant/head zone, person/body zone, tortoise (world) zone, as if his "wisdom and prudence" associate with the encompassing of levels.

126, 127.
The German is from Schubert songs, mainly *Gondelfahrer*, D808.

135.
If you love me... /...e'en the sprit of Truth. From an anthem by Thomas Tallis. Sprit = sprite = spirit, also a pole supporting the sail of a boat.

138.
Two quotations from Siegfried Sassoon, *The War Diaries, 1915-1918* (1983), May 4th and May 15th 1918.

142, 144.
David's lament for Jonathan, in the English Bible and the Latin Vulgate. All the Latin is taken from C16-C17 English anthems, and familiar to many people.

145.
Coleridge, 'On the Prometheus of Aeschylus' (1825). *Miscellanies Aesthetic and Literary*, 1892.

150.
Ekelöf: see the poem 'En Dröm' / 'A Dream'. *Song of Something Else* (Selected Poems), Princeton University Press 1982.

153.
Croatia: was where, at the time, one's thoughts immediately turned when "refugee camps" were mentioned. Since then they have spread everywhere

155.
Gary Hill: American artist working in video and installation media, encountered at an exhibition in the Stedelijk Museum, Amsterdam, 1993.

161, 162.
'Nurse's Song' by W.H. Auden (not in any of his collected volumes), rather touchingly set by Benjamin Britten as the refrain of *A Shepherd's Carol* (1944). "pinkie" means finger in some lost language.

Dioscuria.
This sequence is what remains of an intention to continue *Excavations* into the work done in Derbyshire and Staffordshire in the 19th Century by Thomas Bateman, Samuel Carrington and others, and possibly beyond that. It arises mainly from Bateman's uncovering of one tumulus, at Parcelly Hey, Derbyshire.

XVI

Alstonefield

(1995/2003)

Preface

Excerpts from two letters to Tony Baker

(1)   6th August 1991
Dear Tony,
[...] speaking of which, on the way back from Liverpool last time we stopped for the night at Alstonefield, and as I was strolling among the fields south of the village in the evening I suddenly had the distinct sensation that it mattered, this place, that its very existence mattered. I surprised myself, because obviously there's nothing there that any version of cultural modernity needs for half a second. Limestone hills, sheep pasturage, meandering river dales – what does any contemporary claim want with any of it? Yet there it was, all round me, manifestly necessary. As you know, I lived nearby for four years so I should have known, but everyday sights do diminish so, don't you think, and sink to marginal residues of our upkeep, if we don't have a theology to polish them with.

And I began to think of the place as an arena, a theatre of outrageously manipulated light in which the soul puts on a show for the people, where the self's instant of being is depicted as the lost masquer bearing a lantern among towering land-forms, in search of his company. I could see that it would be necessary to enter this scene again and again in search of the plot, threading questions and trials into the labyrinth, the complex displays of rock and vegetation, sheep-pens and graveyards, set up by the masters of the challenge, the pluralities that devised this spectacle and left it there like an open book. And a writing was needed, an interlinear commentary, to work the self through the fairground of its purpose and throw a shadow image back to all the rest of the known.

It had to be like that, it had to be a performance, because there was no trace of those pure and simple instruments with which we wage our self-wars, like "nature" or "society", and the human mental heart seemed to be cast before the eyes as an unhoused proposal, a thing of many possible directions, carrying everywhere on its back a balancing or compensating device which always begs to differ, always seeks the exception. For nothing up there is quite itself, everything bears the shadow of its contrary, including nature and society. An upland pastoral community run by machines; a week-end break zone for the wild soul which betrays refused planning permission at every turn; sublimity locked into sordidness on the high pastures, elegance and care struggling with cynical exploitation in the valleys... It finally seemed, set there in the centre of England, the very literature of what people are, the star-wars shooting round anyone's living-room in Bradford. Am I rambling? I hope so.

The manic "Estimate" Brown, you will recall, stopped at Dove-dale on his way to Keswick and hated the place – shrivelled valleys, miniature grandeur, he said, the horror without the sublimity or the immensity; meaning it was separated from 'society' without offering that surrender of the wild self into its full theatrical suicession as of the Lakes or the moors above Haworth. It wasn't simple and it wasn't enough – it was half way there, it was untidy, and awkward. Well I don't know, I adore all that surface water further north, the constancy of the music, but I've lived through enough manifestos and I've begun to believe in peace, messy and running-failed as it is, the blank horror these states face at the prospect of having to live without an enemy. And anyway, that segmented limestone dome ringed in darkness (ringed in squalor, actually, and waste) cuts natural light into the most "untoward thoughts" without any help from theoretical Marxism.

And since we no longer have to give personal names to the entities that debate within the arts of perception, the narrative is less predicated – I like that. To stay with landscape objects and chunks of thought, like living in one of Ben Nicholson's paintings, and our entire traffic is set a questionnaire, concerning worth and tenure, which I thought could be played as a continuity impelled by hidden reserves, like the Irish bag-pipes, without any, or much, sparring against the kleptocracy being needed, and certainly not to have to ape the kind of de-relating *coupure* you get in *The News* visuals.

[...] the slender fit of grey stone buildings and dry-stone walls into a very diverse ground of curved grey-green slopes – at every turn spreading outwards, white steaks at the edges of the view always curving upwards to a provisional horizon [...] particularly as it was twilight, and the moon was large in a clear sky so all the near fields were silvered into a texture like the gloss of human skin. And the pub is a good place for a cheap meal for the wandering, and suitably impoverished, definitely proletarian, pastoral or pasteurised, writing person, at the end of a day.

We must take a walk there some time.

[…]

(2)   10th February 1993
[…]
I keep going back. It's still there, every time. I stay in a B&B in the village and moon around the landscape, sometimes alone, sometimes I bring someone with me. I don't write, I don't carry notebooks; I walk in the valleys, I stand in the fields, until I get home. I'm making sure it's still there – "it" being not exactly Alstonefield but the challenge and serenity it conveys, and for that there's no alternative but to be there, there's no channel of information in the world I could trust. If someone comes with me I listen carefully to the same scene working through a different life, however fragmentarily, in the hope of sharpening and extending my own sense of where we are.. So there are also matters raised not mine, and not settled by anything I know, which have to be entrusted to the language as to the hills clothed in weather. And can be, for this tactic also discloses the limits of personal poetry. An enormous fight starts between "the" and "a" which tenses the entire discourse: traditional stagecraft versus objectivist texte. As yet inconclusive, unfinished, and I'm increasingly unsure which side I'm on, whether the world can be captured in a small ring, or should be left to its usual dissipation in detail.

The house I usually stay in has a very 1930s feel, especially about the windows, with cast-iron radiators beneath them, bay windows with small panels that let in a lot of daylight, and look out onto pasture marked out by dry limestone walls, modest heights mostly implicit in the distant folds of grey-green which can prove quite formidable when you actually visit them. The whole landscape is fixed under a geometry of stone walls, parallelograms and asymptotic curves charting all the wave-like thrusts. I seem to breathe a pre-war atmosphere known from poetry, fiction, film, or the generations remembering – a theatre of pauses, dream hotels and branch-line halts, a roller-coaster of green roads, calm metrics ruled over depression and despair, a working industrial city beyond the hills forming its new image of man, with Nash visions of eternity sitting quietly on the grass, and a literary tramp at rest in every barn and haystack… It was the period that bore me, which everyone always remembered with affection:

"The war put an end to all that" whatever it was, it's difficult to say. It lived in the country hotel as in the Marxist meeting above the tap-room. Something was held in the hand which meant something. Stability and change as coextensive, a central healing balance between the cruelties of monetarist disdain and those of underdog resentment. So a hope. The war put an end to it. But it sits for me unrecognised in those dull fields like a Chinese poem, a spirit flight distilled to leaf patience. A deific glow that scuttles out of sight when you turn to face it, but integral to the entire geology. Because it is a sedimentary landscape, however distorted in the details of the disrupted surface: the horizontal successions of settling fundamentals underpin everything you see, layer upon layer.

By the time I get there it's usually getting dark. I install myself, go to the inn for dinner, and then wander over to the churchyard. Which is a rather obvious prosodic gesture, but everyone needs help getting started.

Well, we didn't get that walk in yet.

Love to all, P.

I

Again the figured curtain draws across the sky.
Daylight shrinks, clinging to the stone walls
and rows of graveyard tablets, the moon rising
over the tumbling peneplain donates some equity
to the charter and the day's accountant
stands among tombs, where courtesy dwells.
Thus a special and slight enclosure is set,
slight as the dark spaces I fill tonight and
silent and motionless as lives become, swelling
with truth, scattered with glowing plaques.

Darkness opens the sky to space. Fallen
light sets up its booth in the stone-yard
where the theatre of eyes flickers and dies.
The moon sails the eastern sky, rides
the upland fields in sole possession,
the scattered runs of grey wall the walled
yard and the speaking stones, that say there is
something made in a life not to be lost
however small it is not to be crossed,
not to be cast in eyeless wax.

But is kept folded in this unvalued space,
space free of us, where the moon slices time.
Void of us, where we didn't take any
advantage but sailed away, leaving
old bones kicked around the churchyard
and carried off by dogs and wrote out
the only true thing we are, a record
of love. Every impossible meeting
happens here in darkness and silence
and the slightness of the piecing mind.

A beautiful thing, the moon on stone, and
central. In a momentary breeze the trees
sway slightly and clap over the churchyard,
patches of hawthorn and yew claiming some
marginal light part towards the edge
leaving the moon's direct file on old names.
A farewell to the world that opens the world
and sets standards of dealing. How
could you secretise the language on this
final stage or place a reserve on hope

When the world is watching you? Mirror flashes
on the horizon, distances steeped in petrol,
lives snapped to zero across thronging waste and
planning ethnic cleansing in Mansfield. Death
pressed through the dream into constant
separation as the waking world coats itself
in speed, factorial of despair, that
defeats the bearer absolutely wall to wall:
the action without cause, the daylight caves.
We turn our backs, only the night is kind.

Of course we turn our backs, what is there
to speak through the coils of resentment
but denial, heart loss across the mirror
that coats the bank, what is claimed but self?
I retire to a distance, I have the right
in the late evening and on through the dark hours
keeping to the edge of the necessary plot:
trade, marriage, maintenance, the sacred cast
of continuance always at risk, fixed with loss,
moon marks on stone, trenching the calendar.

I thought I heard in the still night air
a mother suckling her babe and singing
softly in the darkness: Poor little mite,
the cruel captains of earth will wrest
thy virtue to their standing in spite,
and all of thy trust in good will
have to find its own way to the centre
without me, who am not there. Poor
accidental thing, she said, poor rabbit,
what ardour you bear to an unknown point.

Her milk was blue in the sky, it was
time to go. The moon like a knife in water
slid silently down the firmament and sank
into the trees and hedges, shaking themselves
in the dawn wind. The question frames
the response in emergent green: my life
may be kept in some spare cupboard as
needed from time to time or not but the light
spread again through the grass stalks
and the flesh trembled in its window.

I must be blind, to see such brightness
in such delicate light, to see the world
in its hope as a leaf turns in the
movement of cool air, a memory trace
sufficient to keep a name in stone,
the letters full of moss. I would serve
for ever the few ecstasies that form
such a purpose, the child's space at
the table, anger stretching into the future,
obedience glowing at every joint.

II

"The sky will not help you, the soil and trees
will not help you, to die in peace." So don't,
carry your account and rankle with the fox
in the valley, ever on the loose under
the chains of despair, ever alert to
the movements of the gentle victim
we know well, the soft breathing
in the wooden box, the leaps of inspace,
we know the lamb. Whose anger paces
out in the stone day and crests the end.

And know at evening when a path
to the heart opens for the cold and
dark airs of the earth full of locked spirits
and disputed graves. The light bows and
turns its back on the receding uplands
coated in false frost, the hill crests take
the surge of territory to its break and
mark it as on paper, ink under blue wash.
Making clear what I thought I knew, that
truth is at the rim and rings like cash.

At the rim of land is a return of knowledge,
spilling from the lip. Several pages of worked
time graft my trust to this fair lecture as
the staves ring out. Secured in the reprieve,
balm and fescue stretch to the succeeding line.
What it means is that I might have done nothing
but help a different sight into the world and
wouldn't that be something, wouldn't the graves
smoke in the small hours to bear such a legend?
"He spoke to us and it was safe to continue."

A sight not mine I mean. The fields are dark
and the sheep with their long ears are alert
in the night, where we purchased the wine,
of separation and sipped it at the rim where
the bubbles winked. You were with me
though you may now forget, how safe it was
to take affection under the wing entirely
and trust it the whole length of the dark road.
The bulk of love obstructs all my fantasy.
Calm the lamb sleeps its future.

How can anyone believe solo the very idea
mocks itself. Day closes from the start on this
limestone chess-board and today the autumn sun
smote the western sides of the tall grass stalks
and lowered gradually until the cream of being
shone back and then it was total, all colours
clenched in grey-white over the hill's back, it was
the rose of time in the earth pocket. Fear it
continuously, is how I came to know the spectral
city in the end, all the way back to the B and B.

Now I sleep in Alstonefield. Gods and goddesses
walk in the dark fields and stand in a ring in the
churchyard waiting for light. Of which I have it all
over my pillow alone except the permanent.
Gradually in the wine of sleep a completed memory
compassed by care makes a globe of love. Very
little I can do with it, alone. But it is like
a repair depôt that continues through governments
and wars at the end of a small back road where
carefree labourers stroll around dark and competent.

As any night. Looking out of my window at
dawn the voice of desire is raucous but filial
because of the narrow gap containing the
river invisible from here. There the war is
final and formal, where gods and goddesses
enter their own. The fields coated in water
do everything to light the mind can bear
except block it like a town. I think my
dressing gown is a thin and crucial history
of lads and lasses up to good before my time.

In the days of pink-toes I lived down the road.
I picked boletus in the woods, effed around the
local employment situation and drank a daily
bout of distance marked in infant years.
It was my wine to rest by the stone wall at
summer's end far from Cambridge, where
cthonic severance dictates endless toil.
When a meticulous light brought a sequence
of detail to sever the intimate, I thought
to trust the gloss on the stem of travail.

Now the narrow breakfast while the world
stands outside garmented in fall, the plunge
and stay of the valley sides, limestone edges
scrubbed to a gloss and shedding soil.
Garlands hang on the outer wall and the voice
is clenched, saying there is never
enough passed on, the body substantiates
only its own and when the sun returns
the day is closed for the night. Here my life
turns to the earth, and peers into the pit.

Hanging on Thor's lip, the whirlpool cave
hung over the valley while the miner's hammer
sounds traces of enriched water to an under-
ground palace shining with promises. Take
what's available and depart: a gentlemanly
mode in the bed of state. I don't blame you
for running love for profit, O lubric self,
but I know the victim well. I know the sore
throat, the scratched palm, the sleeping bag
in the shop doorway. I hear the passing bell.

It rings, and the throat opens into song
as a matrix clutching the future across
fallen cloud, seeking a long friendship.
Then another day draws to a close and the
restless pastures seem to suck light
into themselves as if nothing human had
any right to it, they say, make yourselves
gods and better, or leave it alone, leave
the light out of your dark passages for good.
Do you remember Lulu and April Fever?

I remember nothing but a trace of soul
difficult to specify now in the rush
of weeks. Not quite finished, the day pulls
hard towards Stoke and gets us to the
George Inn. The food is good and cheap
the mild is strong and the hope is of
worthiness, possibly too as I walk back
finger inter finger with you on the dark road
each in performance integral, are we. I trust so.
The dark is deeper when the trust is stronger.

In the night it rains. In the tight bed
I am an earth feature witnessing a sublime
artefact. And someone in the other room
dreams language to a stone, a white
silence breaking the skin, like a mother
nursing absence as the rain on the window
wipes pretence and claim. A persistent singing
pierces the cloudy distance – tightly
bound as I am, taut as a harp in the
autumnal cyclone, I want your rest.

And nourish my fate, with little to
grow or be faithful to but what's already
counted, and set aside. I note in the night
the messengers at the window, bringing
our emanations to the edge of peace where
our bodies writhe nightly against time,
tense for birth, answer or final clause. But
I'll pack you a sandwich tomorrow if I may
and we'll take it out to the high woods
and watch the godly insects making laws.

To this purpose wake, the sun is high
and the fields are white, not exactly
white but it has snowed. The fields are
different.

III

      And the voice is broken before
the alterior face, the future is cast open
on the page. For a fideism of the heart, oh
what pastoral thing is that, what rich red
and blue border. The vastness of love is cut
to a small song out in the wild closet.
I wrap my neck, collect a frozen stone.

The mountain edge barely clears, folded back.
Surface that is a line hanging in the air
at which sight withdraws, a clarity on paper
anterior to the earth, broken by ink.
Lines that converge without touching
open centrally to a linen distance,
the whole air a time table. Light from
the blade retires behind the hill at
a slight flexing of the globe as the words
I thought this with fly to your calvarium.

I walk back to Beresford in the afternoon.
The coal tit, dyed in modern philosophy,
flits for nuts. Snow on the shoulder, sky
narrowed between hill and hill a blue-grey
tongue whose speech is far from here.
Silence lines the horizon, glowing like a lost
nation, snow-brushed fields glossing the vein
to a hole in tense, a history of light, or, moving
pain to paper an agreement is touched,
that death shall have no choice.

Clouds of pale ash drift over from
the big world, smearing the spread blades
with urban dereliction, a monosyllable
atomised on the screen to narrative, tales
of renewed vigour and washing foam.
Reception is difficult in the hills
but we make shift, erect stringy masts
on shed roofs over the moors, send our boys
out gleaming white and wash our hands again
and again and again, having no choice.

Walton's lodge is just visible through the trees
and bushes on the other side of the river,
cream stone pilasters, monument to patience
where the river turns and enters at a tangent
a more demanding geology. And holds the light
on its surface closely argued at the bend in a
systemic grammar, I mean a sort of canopy
protecting the delicate under of the human leaf
from dark dividedness or fallen ardour. Walton's
lodge is just visible through bushes and trees.

As in the oval meadow the light is gathered
such as it is in February abstract and alone:
self-supporting, concentric economy comprising
substantially the reach of language, which
is slight, and delicately toned. Toned, that
is, with failure and decay as air enters the
surface of things in late winter and light
harbours in water, a contractual figure or in-
telligence. Bow to it and cross the glowing river
on a wooden footbridge into fast-land.

As in that oval meadow, there is a light
that stands apart, without colour for it has no aim,
a pastoral substantive where the story gathers
to a close and the community accedes to what
"must be" in secret delight. Here the maidens
dance on the darkening green to the end of day,
a torse in history that rights itself by
candle lanterns, as the soul is timed to
exequies. Bow to it and cross the glowing river
on a wooden footbridge into urban despair.

As in that oval meadow the deities are slight,
their energy spreads from cliff to river and
stand in that circumference, white on white,
a silent hammer, an arch in the air, the wind
blows through it. Cosmic history in the metaphrase
of sexual reticence, but when a text belongs to
its addressee there is that opening of the heart
and finding a ring inside it, and/or a stone.
Nod to it and cross the doubled, shining river
on a wooden footbridge into prose.

As in that oval meadow I cannot speak. Shadows
of the edging trees band the lawn that upcurves
so slightly at the pericarp or tone border – I
am head-bashed against the fact of my ardour:
love takes no reason, answers no call, stands
sufficient in the light it is to bypass its
bearer and wake a line through generation,
a blindness viewing an unborn shade.
Obey to it and walk on the stone slabs of
a wooden footbridge into semblance.

So, poetry, grey chemicals on the grass
an abandoned centre which is where
we live, I and I. The price increases as the
light fails, without substantive rights
the money is a vapour on the screen wherever
it clings, the nation vanishing at its edge.
And certainly there are people in the towns,
possibly there are ghosts in the caves and
certain voices crowd me along the valley base
I walk alone in the colder and colder fade.

The cold is resistible, the news is a knife held
aloft by an over-heated person shouting Down
with bourgeois individualism. I resist it and sweat
uphill to Alstonefield, sinking with night into the
George Inn with chicken and chips, mild and
Jamesons surrounded by talk, talking the world
into a biological shroud on the mind, doing
fine, having a good time, making news tonight.
The fire burns within, the owls hoot out
in the cold I am a happy lapsing overdraw

From which the heart has departed and glides
winged over the smouldering developments.
And walk back alone between dark snowy fields
where the long-eared sheep are ever alert
and the groaning wood. I grasp an absent hand,
finger inter finger, I call it Impossibility.
And impossibility is a sweet sleep I owe
myself in a house among big trees, a wine of
world-light swirling in the skull, touching
neuter again at some pain, without any loss.

To rise to blinding light flooding
the breakfast salon and the distance
to Buxton, where there's a book fair.
I don't know why I bother. Anyone
can hear it in the skin response, and
raise a pale glass.

IV

                    Important to
check every visit that certain places
are still intact, haven't been more than
sense can stand eroded by desubstantiating
forces known collectively as shopping. More

Or less they survive: Beresford Dale and upper
Wolfscote, somewhat Santa's Grotto now with
the new walkers' autobahn and though no-one who
hadn't lived here would notice, trimmings.
Then the Manifold from the Mill to Thor's Cave
returning to the blanched uplands round Wetton
and Alstonefield where the landlady finds me
puzzling, keeps coming back here in
different company and can't work out what's
going on: Ewan, Helen, Beryl, or no-one at all.

One day I'll get Lorand Gaspar up here
or Voichitsa Tepei or the unfractured self.
Driving past Harecops with you the stresses
are few and distinct, four or five to a line,
major choices in a life, like crucifixes on alpine
passes marking breaks and meetings across
hung ground. Where lives converge, and central
vaccua aligned are the birth graves of gods.
The old stone house stands firm in its measure
grass to the door and the washing ensign aloft.

Blue hills later in the photograph that weren't
ever blue, cold feet in the bed, a true
record is a desperate thing. Indeed we are
you and I finished the moment it speaks and
lie in the village graveyard attracting
rare names from the night sky. They close
in on our plot while we sleep through the
local accommodation, night full of stones
eyes closed dark admonition serious message
your breath my script scripted burthen meant.

Ever. Serious message get on with your business.
Which is to be here in all kinds of weathers
and walk and walking trade my pulse for
notices of souldom in geophysical latitude,
spurning the news. The politics of this
carries hope like a feather on the palm:
my country tracks are crossed in oil and
its inhering slaughter. The oval meadow
trusts minds only, the broken ring-dance
humanises permanent assets to the world.

Heavens it dwells so in the hand that
might one evening grasp an opportunity
and so create warfare as the small centre
swells into speculation. The slightest
disclosure of the heart tracks a host
out of hiding and waves bright banners
north to south of power, where amor
lies broken and divided. Recumbent light
on the wind stretcher, a field of
dandelion clocks, header into goal.

Green hills why did your power abstain?
and the wrapping mafiosi cash the
benign influences at the Westminster –
I'd risk alcoholic poisoning to know, or
the big starchy dinners at the George Inn
night after night but nothing tells me this.
Where lives converge we abjure power and so
advantages can be taken and of course are.
I find walking back to the B and B with my
wife on my arm the god-grounds are equable.

We walk and talk and little notice how
some recent grasp has thinned the pasture
until the invasion is complete. But look
how the non-human belongs, how the bones of
the landscape trellis the darkness, how nothing
intervenes between the eye and its home.
Then we must be more than a condition,
a crown in hiding, a burning shade. I find
walking back to the guest house with my
companion to hand the god tracks converge.

So by the walls of grey houses with
small windows some lit in the night that
stand there like gravestones century after
century and individuals and families pass
through them and out, each making a more
or less hearted wrapper of the inside, some-
thing tells me that nothing is gained but
a vulnerable honesty bidded against death.
I find walking back to where I sleep with my
teacher the heart light is shielded.

V

Another damp Sunday morning, up and walk over
Pea Low (another distressed tumulus) and what's that
flicker in the distance? What's that convergence west
of the village? And why are the roads so busy this
English morning? – petrol flips the work-day whip
and we poor peasants dive for the verge. Binoculars.
A curlew calls far and long falling as I focus
on the fact. Cut short the walk, curve under
Gratton Hill and back down – the battle's up:
it's that trough in time, it's a car boot sale!

It is difficult to know the good in lives.
If I'd found a rare object I might have gone
chirruping to Stoke in the pouring rain
which threatens. Dull English weather,
the day stands inert, colour stops dead,
distance diffused, a green field and a shed
with the usual water tank at the back of a farm
in the mud. It would be specious to pretend
that any bit of British countryside is anything
but an agricultural factory marked Piss Off.

And people open their car boots to reveal
image destitution. But a true ring, a
soul lock, and shopping is a delight, what
traces left of tribal pain lessen in the rain
until every necessary transaction brandishes
the rose of time, triumphantly above
the stalls of love. Then the heart and the
mountain range are one. What if the inter-
vening nonsense turned out to be a small
entertainment called City of Fear?

Intervening nonsense called western fear:
anything rather than face the world-
opening it initiated. Dampening, I turn down
a plastic shepherdess at 30p and go back
to the car. And sit there waiting in the rain
for something better than pastoral, some-
thing less fairground and more circus,
something to take the truth of the west-
ern world out of its pocket and purchase
life everlasting or a well meant Friday hug.

No use waiting. Turn the key, go. Go where?
If I went north I'd live in a cold music
for guitar and steel-works and have to face
daily a narrower question over the silver moors,
the treasure chests of bird and slow thought
where the houses cling to the long ridges,
trying to preach as Coleridge that sublimity
isn't simply vertical, but carries grey
rock-juice down into heavenly furrows where
bright minerals sing for dinner, home and away.

Or to speak plainly, pennies are good shit.
If I went west you wouldn't notice me, a
Sunday fisher in the canal, a packed-lunch
gourmet who returns to a brick row with
small back window onto flagged yard and
coke-shed, there to pass the dark hours
in seasonal remembrance. It is a dream
of such fragile substance such unlaundered
currency I daren't speak, the old man in
the shaving mirror, turning the tribal wheel.

Then work is the only credit and it's true but if
I go east the whole scale of action is enhanced,
the great keep rises over the plains, on its surface
reptilian armature twined formally with affection
shield against shield, eye and ear stretched to
soul-pitch across the sky, and all the trim fields
merge into the slow richness of decay. The fewness,
the shifting drone of death, lines a shared crown
on an innocent forehead – patient scholar, mongol
child, and working ploughman, designate the world.

I couldn't go there today, the theatre is hidden
under Restoration scaffolds. I could go south,
to the heart of smooth success, deny the grit of
presence and evade the friction of self-surface
against a viable universe, don't take me there.
Please don't deliver me to that small south, that
smilybox where language oils itself constantly
in inner circles; let me wander still in the open
fields of failure, where the linnet coughs at eve
and the daffydil hides it condom, let me live

Longer in the long pain. I won't go south and
enter that gloss. But I did, I went south, why,
for a library, for fear of provinciality, as if that
meant a thing in the corrosive fog of self
-colonisation, because I wanted company.
And come back up here three times a year
for humanity. I'll stay where I am, I'll book
myself back to the bed and breakfast, I'll count
up to fifty and take a deep dinner, followed
by the wine of solitude in the clamouring vale.

So the George again (suddenly it's dark) and
a microwaved lasagne and chips, cheap red
wine a chill draught and a flea-bitten cat
scratching itself at my feet in the otherwise
empty dining-room I couldn't be happier.
I couldn't win a thing on the lottery or
the trials of polity or the small poetry
world, where fleas scratch cats. Good-bye
Cambridge and the 17th Century karaoke for
quite a while, I'm bound for the Rio Nègre.

Which is a promise I do keep, in spite of
tiredness and convenience, comfort and cold,
I walk on past the house. The corner wood
moans blue, the former sheep sizzle, I don't
care I walk on past. No hand guides me,
no finger twines with mine, no bleep in the dark
means the Education Department knows where I am.
For once no intelligence in the world has
any knowledge of this route, which is dedicated
against individual gain, to equity as grace.

The path begins to dip then suddenly drops
over the lip, and scrambles down a shingly
waterfurrow right to the base, to the very
reason, and crosses it on a wooden footbridge.
I'm there. So my family of friends, my
squirrels and pigeons shuffling into night
the heron making for roost by the river map
my little hearties my gods and insects
we share a space, and the immensity that
sections me makes for you a set of traps.

How quietly they keep their homes. Told by
the Power, the astrophysics, to seek cover,
every night they go. As I beside the river
walk in the kind cold dark an extended
moment thick with arrows. I mean I can't
see the route very well and memory-darts
fill the air: blame, shame, the world's game
I lost before it ever started and wrapped
in failure follow the glint of water, signalling
to my allies that I love their mutual singing.

And in guilty night my ordinary speech asks
after mother, how she lies now, nowhere –
just a pain in my chest. Still complaining,
that language closes the world in tight
darkness and de-recognises souls blazing
with necessity. A little Manchester woman.
And this anger is passed on, with the love,
and gnaws at my oesophagus as I walk blindly
upstream the dry leaves crackle and fall
into dust, a small owl calls into trust.

For trust is the animals' bourne, the very end
of everything they think, their highest music.
Cunning little vixen, fixing your ache in someone
else's cavity who prowls now in the secret vale
moving among trees by the river's edge
like a lost chicken, into whose breast
a sweet message sank and a fine set of teeth
so lovingly you eat me, so quietly the ants tick
in their cells and what a brilliant idea it was,
to die, leaving the answer sung but unspoken.

To lie in bed while someone else wraps
a dark cloak round them and stamps the stony
earth, stumbling on unseen roots and ridges,
always listening for danger. An experienced
city pavement mover, I sense brute resentment
at fifty yards, and routine entrenchment from
shore to shore. O the desperate strains of the
Manchester Sonatas, the barbarity of privilege,
the ruthless violin of fear. A bird's call
crosses that space a few times a year.

And bits of light get down through branches
to the river's shiny upholstery. Long reaches
and very difficult breaks are, with practice,
traversed, walked, passed alongside. I must
be somewhere near the stepping stones under
Cold Eaton and twenty thoughts from company.
A hostelry in my head accommodates this cold night
all the city's homeless and treats them liberally
to cups of Horlicks, warm blankets, dog food,
assurances that society will re-convene shortly.

A hostelry in my head with blocked drains
and a dead duck in the sink. As the homeless
satisfied for a while sleep towards new distress
a diffused moonlight on a frozen windowpane
inscribes a distance that a trust could be
bound to, that a call could come alongside and
enumerate in long song the ancestral victories
one by one; in the wall the small tick of a death
that never dies and all love's cuts be finely
worded, as a dying mallard makes a sentence.

Dying of cold and betrayed by trust as the no-
longer interested company drift away downstream
talking of success in a pub-like ambience.
Leaning into the bank and making a noise,
an understandable noise, that passes through
the dim dark air into the passing passer-by
by the ear, and lodges close to the heart,
joining the company there, of homeless singers
on a train through the night across Poland
to unthought-of terminals, kissing the wire.

Then out of cover into Wolfscote Dale in
dazzling brightness, a full moon riding
the crystal scattered sky and the great V
tunnelled before me gleaming, cold, empty,
shining unto itself against the black, deep
star-clear firmament, this whole earth-mass
holding the celestial fact in its arms
quietly and passionately by the white flowers
in the hillside grass holding the sex of a god
in gently murmuring river dale against harm.

And loud and long the constant fall
and strike of water on itself fills the air
on all sides with a continual sounding.
A river works through the night anywhere
on earth as a voice meaning a clear thing,
meaning unspecifically, that earth life
passes, thus and so and that and therefore
admit, that gratitude falls into empty space.
An educated meaning directs work where it is
wanted, and the long tones sing themselves.

Straight and proud, song and singer hand
in hand saying Grant us peace, time and space
fit for thought, again and again at day's
decline levering the voice into the sphere:
nations have mercy, give us a chance. I pray
for the future of the Ba-Benzélé pygmies
of equatorial Africa what else can I do?
but set the soul-light where it comes first
and walk up the moon-flooded dale at midnight
singing waley waley love is unjust.

And they just sat in rows on two tree-trunks
and sang (this was the Aka, in another film or
record) a kind of polyphonic hoquetting that
ran through night and day a total signal of
readiness and comprehension, of liberty and
they did it because "this is what we do now."
Also negotiating with distance, that under
these terms we take and return. Think of being
where people are tired of gain, and bored
with advantage and want to hunt down peace.

To a long valley cut through limestone strata
like a gap in a crown, where peace may emerge
brighter in moonlight than the recorded day, on
up. On and on and very gradually up. Biggin Dale
branches off to the right, the whole of history
is in danger of being forgotten. This walk
is a night walk of the world where horizons
meet. In the trumpeting of water a triumph
is sounded for the despised, who meticulously
follow their equitable ways down the dumps.

Like walking a long corridor in a hospital
the bushes in their white coats and this
shiny conveyor belt running alongside bearing
weathering solutions, enzymes, floods of tears,
back to the town. Things that reach across.
Plodding on stony track next the stream I
think of teenage lovers, Alzheimer's patients
moving to the world's edge and bearing its content.
The joining of souls is worth all the moonlight
down which eyes draw their long content.

On up, as the fall fits behind, a whole life.
Everyone has a whole life, what happened to it?
What was its final shape? I strain to hear,
above the stream, the grasses in their converse
and over the grasses the silence of air, that
silently stings memory. Failure is meant only
as a way of reaching clarity, its questions, a
life homing in the small hours, what became
of it? Did pride and guilt get it in the end,
did its fire add to the cold? Who or what

Asks this? I look up to the valley rim, dark
against the sky. Bumps on the stone walls
that follow the lip: gods and goddesses,
strolling the fields waiting for dawn,
mandarins and courtesans, arms in sleeves,
pensively avoiding the seated sheep and
stepping indulgently over their dung, thinking
together of ways to mend the world, if only.
For everyone or not at all, in common tongue.
And gather up its history, and sing the long song.

They peer over the stone walls that follow
the valley edges and see me: Look at him,
down there, walking the river path up Wolfscote
What's he doing there? What for? They can't
even tend themselves, those people. They
can't tender the faintest answer, they work
separately. I look down. The river glances
past my side, about four metres wide here.
And still the long tones succeed each other
like penitential bells, exactly on the hour.

Long vales attract extended thoughts,
from the sky or the god fields of reward.
Above the valley the fields proliferate, white
walls round them with occasional stone barns,
double fruit trees and Quaker burial grounds.
Ghostly sages walk there at night, looking
for lost tumuli, for the world-good of every
remotest soul. Down here the creatures of death
forget themselves in rapid displacement and
a sweet harmony pierces the resulting distress

Like an ulcer piercing a stomach wall,
all the stones of the body tossed in acid
align themselves to that sweet singing.
A good thought is itself a sweet song to
which the river is *basso continuo* though
my own speciality is *scordatura*: adding to the
difficulty a lateral shift thus tempting
a world register. Or the final knowledges so
tenuous and watery, *rilievo schiaccito,*
the wound a calm thing, with far to go.

As a wound lived with does become calm, all the
herbs of the valley gather round it saying
Breathe slower, there are other worlds. The lamb
agrees, and dies into distant sandwiches. Ah!
to die in earnest and forfeit your name to a
continuum of credit transactions, it is a sad time.
But forgiven while the flower fairies gather
round the well head singing (sweet) a lament
in long notes, a song partly unhuman, that
trembles through the entire economy torn apart.

Is it not so, rows of dark heads on high
walls, that I walk under, don't the days'
edges wrap the ruins in simple clothes?
And they go back to their perambulations
their night circuits on the upper pastures
humming over fragments of old folk-songs
to themselves in the search for good polity.
The valley continues, lurching this way and that,
a few clumps of trees in the river haze and stripes
of scree on the long slopes, let me go.

Let go of me and I'll give you an answer
if I have an answer to give that doesn't add
to the world's cold. The towns over the hills
are full of ills and answers but the works die
and crumble, the chimney stands at the valley head
derelict, a tower to lost patience. Not this valley,
which never suffered profit, though a negative light
inhabits it now, bearing modernity's favourite message:
No parking. Move on, keep going. No hermitage here,
no respite either. Days and hearts are torn asunder.

Well at least you don't have to pay to walk here,
though I expect the day will come. And yet the days
to come hold no terror but the world's own, how
to work kindness across the gap between one and
many in the light of the fading eye. O for a craft of
wholeness dictating every detail, finish, grace-note,
surety woven across the night and curving straight
into day, shadow's edge doubled in travertine.
Refusing collectivising aids. The delicate brushwork
of the soul courtiers proposes a republic.

Eye-bright, the inscribed line, the river's margin.
And a glow-worm at the path's edge, I thought
it was the world shining in love's desert.
I passed it by in the warm night thinking of
a republic of the (heart, mind) republic of the,
for and by the, soul-light or nothing, top
legal fact. Sitting on the marble bench
outside the Palazzo del Capitano dei Populi
I thought this proudly, and stuttered it
into the punctuated blaze on all sides.

Great pattern of healing... Though time
destroy the person, the intent shall range
the upper levels while mortals sleep, and
patiently, patiently, think-tread the fields,
coaxing lasting peace formulae out of bitter grass.
The stone barns up there get up and move
somewhere else in the night, I have photo-
graphs to prove it. The locals don't notice,
they have television. I said this repeatedly
and cursed the comforting guns but alas,

The box I stood on was of cardboard and pain
became my teddy-bear. I hold it in the night
in bed or a long valley while world routes
traverse the sky. We whisper to each other:
Remember, I was your valley, you walked me
and the black river slid past us, taking
all our vows into storage but we walked on,
keep my hard head always against yours
and our hearts will collaborate in long tones
through vast Europes of burning bones.

Pain whispers through people, and tells them
the truth perhaps walking steadily up the long
winding river dale at night. Poetry occupies its
moment completely, like heroin, it is deeply
convincing, but does it know the truth? Europe
is building a wall against Africa's groans. And you
are a stupid walker who should have been in bed
two hours ago, the world is not listening
to your solitary fantasys. The hospital you failed
to heal in stands at the north end of your head.

Favour at least, is a constant. It finds its way out
through a concealed life, transpires from the
fullest fear: here death has trampled death
and the dippers, so busy in the daytime, sleep
now under the bank in pockets of faint warmth,
as shall I tomorrow, the other side of fearful
thought. Like a hand against a feathered side
faintly warm under a cold bank and ruffling in
electric spasms of dream, I hope to win
an intellectual conviction, O faithless one.

Approaching now a boundary, edge of a reef,
where the sides descend and spread out, and
the god patches round Alstonefield recede into
cloud-land, silver hounds that serve their own
excellence. They get on with our best thought
while the working organism walks the twisty track
racked with fear and anxiety. My toy, my dump, walk
behind me and grip my shoulders in the dark. Under
the rock shelves of an edge nerve, sleeping birds
and victims of nationalism decorate the route.

Resentment rages though the black air surrounded
by transparent calm. Waves of limestone dive
into the ground and great shoals rear up
glowing pale in the night uncertainty and
riddled with caves, in one of which "A cobbler
his wife and seven children lived within living
memory." Wattle awnings over the entrance and
in the evenings they sat round a fire singing
a narrative polyphony in divided head-tones
while the weather suited itself and death hung

Suspended. At this junction the river takes
a slight waterfall under a footbridge and vapours
mingle in the air, wrapping night in the flavour
of mortality. It flickers beside the dark land,
poor waterlogged stuff owned as I recall by two
brothers in a stone fortress-farm on the edge
of the dark hill living without hope of marriage,
though a cobbler owning nothing but a certain
cultivation, constructed a fortress here against fright
where mutual favour folds the future into life.

Like a wine, like a careful Merlot folding youth
and age the night tolerates the loss of names, yours
and mine, already falling under the footbridge
out of meaning, a junction the other side of which
hope is entire. The river bends to the west and
the cliffs to the east, forming this oval meadow
in which, you remember, the fox dances
with the hare and the lamb adores its tomb;
a swollen space, mandorla in middle night,
full of river mist to chest height.

Nameless we wade in it, a Roman bath, arms
out on the conceptual surface. Histories
float past and we hum their tunes, the little
circles proving one equals zero at the highest
tone. Of what happens we know next to nothing,
but we sway in the vale, take our partners
and run a business without profit from which
a concerned eavesdropper may learn the
tariff of careless love. Relax the throat,
hold harm at arm's length and dance with it.

Round and round as night and star face
each other in the oval purpose in a
clearing of the preoccupied river, that
hurries on by. O I believe, I do believe
that I go back home. I don't think I'd ever
have started this night-long trudge if I
didn't know for sure: I end at the precise
beginning of what I am, the shared declaration.
Catch equilibria out of anonymous tunes
and believe it, the whole mist of speech.

I'm sorry I missed your speech but the rabbit
danced with me in the darkened cove and I
couldn't let his/her shoulder go we were
chest level in the seas of sleep and the air
hung curtains on our eyes. But I remembered
as I fox-trotted around that quasi-circular
pasture something in my origins that Engels
failed to notice in the back streets of inner
Manchester where various things added together
made a hope so long so real and so angelic

We waited a life for it, we got engaged
and in spite of everything raised a shout
of joy, totally disadvantaged we caught
each other at the turning-point where delight
transcends critique, declared ourselves
fully and sang our way home in the great
omnibus of the rain. We dance on, the band
shows no signs of fatigue, the floor
is hidden under five foot of fog and me and
my furry friend we flourish at death's door.

I'd like to say that again. There were
angels in the cellar that Engels never
noticed and the government inspector was
one of them. He drank with us and the night
became longer than the alienists could ever
believe or tolerate. The state in fact listened,
understood, and acted; only the aristos,
and the artists, turned up their four noses.
Am I not a plain speaking man, furry friend?
Whirl me to the end, gag me with roses.

Look, this is a serious poem why am I
waltzing with a mammal? Bright his (her)
long teeth shine in the moonlight as we
gyrate across the mead, strong her (his)
clasp behind my neck where ghosts make
their love. The land curves round us in this
abandoned place where people have always
been content to be deprived, turning and
smiling in the face of profit, dancing
the night away and no more, stopping dead.

For the masters of the earth declared (a)
there is no destination for souls (b) we'll
take all the cash thanks. So the rest of us
die quickly, to keep the machine well fed.
To this tune I dance in neck-high mist with
an earth creature at midnight. Bedridden
anxiety in the river's endless loop, red
couplets in the cave mouth squaring the ring
that nations may look at the clocks in the sky
and concentrate on creating liberal space instead.

Shared space, how we danced. Then nothing.
Just water falling over stones in the darkness.
Children left home, pets died one by one,
a voice left grating in the night, digging
in against all this dispersal, advancing in
pitch dark to the end of the meadow where
trees gather and the dale entrance opens
ahead like a hall, almost roofed. Not a
serious route since the Bronze Age. Millions
of lives simple darkness and earth noise.

A far distant voice left, on an old recording
repeating formulae in a fog of surface noise
ain't got no moma now *In cielo cerco il tuo
felice volto* divining the way to the footbridge
in the dark by memory, by hurt. The earth gives
gently under each step like an abandoned mattress.
Locating direction by wound echo, river noise,
leaf movement, residue. Import floats off behind
up to the god terraces and harvests of cloud.
Guiding myself correctly by ordered words.

Smiling, for nothing else knows how. The trees,
ever restless, cast doubt on walking creatures
who smile. I stop in the middle of the footbridge,
under me the dark river slops on and I look
back down along the curved space as if
I thought maybe a red glowing point in the
pale rock towers at the far end, and over
to the right a couple of street lamps where I
know there are no streets. But men who can't
sleep and have stopped trying for ever.

A fire in a distant cave, brilliant embers
for the end of a life radiating energy not
faint not lost. She was something of a dragon
but she never promoted fear and gloom
for elective gain. So she inherits the grace
of the unpowered and the underpaid, may she
enter nonsense with no more than a good push.
And over to the right, twin lights. All that
work, all that balancing and thrust, what's
left of it but self hatred and failed trust?

What's left of anything is precisely nothing,
trees soil and stones queuing to vanish.
A red light means hope and departure: took
my suitcase to the station and the train went
without me, an ordinary cave receding. So
the old lady converts to nil in the small hours
and the rest of us continue like street lamps or
endoscopes in the bowel of day, restlessly,
hoping to find for good or ill. And eventually
even the brightest star burns back to zero.

Red flicker where things leave us, white blades
where they advance. Out across the oval meadow
these contraries twine to the music, supplied by
strangers: gypsy on the road, fiddle in sack over
shoulder, water falling over stones, on his way
to help an old widow die a glowing death, a death
to be proud of, a death studied many years ahead
making a red punctuation in the cursive night.
Russet song-birds sleeping under the sod. I
lean on a rail over the drainage of fear and loss.

And look at the twin stars under the hill,
the two lights from the bleak farm. In those
corridors there is no death and so no joy
or sorrow. There is aim: work and structure,
masking despair. Difficulty and anxiety confirm self.
It is a long night and the electricity costs more
all the time, owls keep their estate in the trees back
of the dung heaps in brilliant irony while
the moon gets little chance before the hill crest
wipes it. These people burrow into time

And vanish into their shadows. The meadow dance
was a rare moment but what happens is water
falls over stones in the darkness and all the
kindness intimated by formality remains
dependant on a world question: a great deal
more than human if it is to return ever.
So that's the picture, and the night continues
in a murmuring of many voices from many throats
a motherly continuum in the solitary vale
saying wait for me and I'll come back some day.

I'll come back and we shall be re-united, people
who meant something and were lost and died, whose
lives made a writing and now nobody knows where
the writing is. Can I truly read it in the fall of
water over dark stones, the humanless contours of
an earth junction? Phil Davenport was one, musician
from Derby who went to Mozambique and never came back.
A few ill-recorded tapes. Wind and nests in high trees.
An old aunt who viewed me with suspicion as if the world
might not be telling the truth. I was young. Nightjars.

I could have been wrong, but I thought for a moment
over to the right in the wet fields was either a
badly oiled sewing-machine or a nightjar. Probably
not a nightjar. It is very good to be hanging around
in the middle of the night doing nothing but lean
on a rail over falling water, it shows a person un-
curfewed, a citizen not a subject, taking a certain
pride in plural space without disdain. I want to know
who's sitting sewing in the middle of the night,
in dark clumps of reed, joining what and who?

Is it the woman Elaine Scarry speaks of,
whose soul tenderly feeds the future an
improved coat and dies unthanked? Is there then
a selfless self over there in the darkness a
harmless human? The weaver on the moor spins
a solitary thread in ever thickening night,
humming the tune to the tread, a history
of obscure suffering and unrewarded pains
to which the night bird's moan is finely
tuned O Delvig, Delvig, what do we ever gain?

Pure purpose continues upstream to its point
of rest but I leave the river here, sensing a familiar
call, off the footbridge round the tree and onto
the road at the ford O Delvig, what do we become?
Nothing, a great city of it, built up from
a night point. And rain starts, that rain
of which Du Fu speaks, that "steals through
the night on the breeze, noiselessly wetting
everything." Rexroth's words. Silently screening
a truth that calibrates the earth.

I join the road running up from the river and
creep along the wall. Carefully, because there is
an electronic device here, on a gatepost, with
a light that questions the night and a button
which if I press either a lump of acid rock
blasts me out of here or the police station
at Leek is alerted. I wish it summonsed some-
thing fairer: a good wine merchant, the poetry
help line, meals on wheels, the monastery porter
(routine kindness in a hurry)'s assistant.

I step out of the small flood plain and walk
on a country road at night by pattering trees.
The oval meadow spreads out below me, open
to the sky like real space, like a Piazza del Popolo
in which meetings are real and you sit there
sipping the cappuccino while tides of hope
waft the end onwards, air currents that stir
the land, the children leaving school at three. They
play at young foxes and there's both time and need
for democracy before the whole song plunges into the sea.

No strength without purpose. Meetings are real
when just, tonight just me and the night
creatures, the badger shuffling where he must
and little owls among the leaves waiting for dawn.
They occupy their pauses above and below me
as walking slowly I posit a perilous space
called Here we succeed. Indeed I too have sat
sipping stimulants in stone towns, Gubbio, and Todi,
and I know as well as anyone how fully precarious
is hope, the singing in the empty grave.

That whirring in the fields again, like
the jack-snipes in Donegal, filling the thick
night air with messages across a vast grey
grave and it seemed at once that all the big
fast transport was flung into the sea, the slow
won every race and the patient established peace
across a republic of mitigated pain. Moving
slowly up towards the cross-roads at night a sense
of Reverdy tells me this long asking is short
of answer, at which the night birds wince again.

Half way up the slope I have a glimpse of
energised stability. It's a road, it's just
a road somewhere in the country, priests
of fear and loathing flit in the dark fields
among silent rain. It's an empty road
and the lights fall far behind, the whole hope
of Italian republicanism lies on the hills
in the form of what we are, an argument kept
alive by interjection of honesty and pride,
my love and I dancing it on the full tide.

Such stillness at the turn. White sound in
black night: thin, swirling rain, brushing and
laving the restless leaves; holding the lost form
of what we are: a struggle, from which a crystal
is gained, something you can see variously
through. A public space, a meeting-place
of conflicting hearts on limestone paving, all
the apertures in the palace facade carved with
intricate sea fauna and symmetrical fruit processes:
good is where it is forced to be, and to excess.

Conflicting purposes run together by force
of wish, working for sectional interests in an
advancing light that casts hope as a reflection,
flicker of flame on the tympanum, yellow webs
swirling on the stone above the fountain. Isn't
history such a finely forced affair? The rain
has stopped, a cloud gap opens and the moon spreads
a paste, a cream cheese of light on all the dim
rural forms that greyly glow in the fields like
a communal purpose in the missals of insight.

And who's this then? Thick rectangular lenses,
white sickly face that catches the moon and
throws it back. Hardly any lips at all, just a
wobbly line of mouth turned down at the ends,
wisps of hair on a permanent preoccupied frown –
who's this coming down the road with a stick,
what's this ghost in a horrible check sports-
jacket far too wide on the shoulders? Dmitri!
I shout, is it you? I suffer, he whispers,
from the most abominable indigestion

And cannot sleep. Why is he wearing glasses in
the night anyway? Why isn't he tucked up in bed
or buried in his fear twenty years ago? Energised
stability, how did you escape? I suffer, he says,
from people's abominable imaginations whereas
everyone knows the world is an unalterable sum,
of which we and everything we see are temporal
processes, to the strains of unlimited tangos.
Party officials float overhead howling in pain,
declaring a new age again and again and again and again.

A bowl of pain in small night. A light burning
across trackless fields, a production unit
that doesn't know how to stop. Prison farms,
concealed zones in the traffic arrangements, acrid
smoke that no one can bear to notice, drifting
across the plains. And why, I ask him this, why,
I grab hold of his shoulders, we've known each
other a long time, I don't shake him, we stand
face to face on the dark road, there's some
trace of bodily substance under the padding, I want

To know what all that was for, I don't shout,
I don't speak, he knows what I mean, where is
the finality that resolves the loss? He doesn't
answer, but the thin lips curl into a lost smile
and there's a sound in the air of his head like
what you get if you wind something up, a relentless
ticking music, as empty as the edible nothing all
round us; ghost sonata, mindless banality, a yes
from which the heart has been removed. Shallow,
O Shallow Brown, you're going to leave me.

I was interested precisely in staying put, I didn't want
to rend or bend or pump up anyone's heart, I never
traded in disappointment; the only departure I know
is of everything: Italian socialism, art, mossy stones,
wedding dances and country games on the green
it all gets sucked into the chimneys of the
meat farm leaving nothing but a space: no record
survives, no marketable loss. And this is why
I hiss and rattle in the night, and on this last
and lonely night declare finally that love is

Nothing. Love raised the death camps. The ticking
fades, trust flies up to the hill tops beyond
the fields and resides there in prenatal grandeur.
No thank is paid; we reside on the earth, we eat
and breathe it, and sing back a cold lament under
the moon, a dispassionate exercise in fidelity.
Earth's future, the whole physics, the possible
routes across it, the whole chiming circling concept
places a stiff finger on the back of my neck and
propels me up the dark road, coughing in tune.

Musician, be different. For God's sake stop
singing and tell me something! Shallow Brown,
don't e'er deceive me. It's very late: love
took its due years ago and scattered us
across the world shouldering affection like
a knapsack. I hold his shoulders, and on
the narrow road beside the long wood we are
face to face with silence. Let me fail, he says,
musically. *Luchistaya zvezda, chim ozaryon
syanyem kray, mne danny dlya rozhdenya.*

Radiant star, whose light sheds its light
on my poor origins, only from you is there any
reward. Love withers in the desperate beams, the
desperate simplicity of service, doing exactly
what is asked of you. How do you find it, then,
Dmitri, here in the so-called liberal states,
treading the graves of gypsy musicians, not an echo
in the night – what's the tune in that case alive *with*?
He never turned and never answered and was
not there, croaking untransmittable wrath.

It was terrible, there was a sick man hobbling
down the black road then there wasn't. Either
of these would have been hell. Do you think
politics explains these apparitions, do you think
adjustments at the top will change everything?
Don't you think death was all along the only
adversary and ever is? Talk yourself out of it,
pass round the red tartlets, tomorrow is my
wedding day, brown is my silky hair, where
did he go? What's the pain of an average tree?

Is in its heart, used for waste paper. I try to
call him back: Dmitri! I shout into the road-
side bushes above Barrack Farm but there's
nothing, he's gone down to the black river
behind my back and the fields shroud over again
as the moon turns in. The experts were all wrong:
musician-poets, loss merchants, marketeers of
graveyard tablets saying Long he loved and
longer died, step aside, corporate pride, here
comes Pity. The blazes with pity. "We don't want

charity we want justice." I carry my thought-radio
on my back, aerial aloft. It tells me to walk on
through such certainty. Boletus flourish at
certain times of year in the wood over to the left.
I remember this from my time here. That move
into the entire land when a couple becomes
a family, that optimism, took place in the big
stone house over there. There I leant on the wall
at summer's end far from any metropolis, and counted
the faithful on one hand, the successful on another.

For the world can go one way or the other.
There is a choice, of emotions, up or downhill,
there is a music that emphasises loss, and
another, tense with patience, *quis dabit
pacem populo timenti*. Listen to it, spell
its every move in the night, wherever you
are, daughter, brightness beyond the shadow's
edge, far from home, queen of the becoming
machine. O daughter, the green meadows that
lie between us, flecked with white bone.

So it is to reach the watershed crossroads
and be newly old. Across every field and
acreage of pasture is a life subscribed to
by will or nil, attached for ever. Loss
is then an intention, exactly conceived
and perfectly delivered, the true outcome
of desire. This was she to me and knew it,
and knowing departed, full of fear. In
that stone house, quietened now by night,
the progressive meadows opened from a point.

A point of contact. How should I know what
happens in the world? To know is an evasion.
This walk at its furthest point relinquishes
the driver's seat and stands nowhere at the dark
junction not knowing which direction to take
or what shall ever be the gain. But remembering
gladly the fires that burned in that stone house
over there many years ago and sadly the way
time rolls us onward, trouble in mind. Hell-
hound at the crossroads, pulling everywhere.

The coal-fires burning with bright snow outside
and the eastern wind. The clocks, the radio news,
the baby on the floor and safety established in
all the land. Hound, be a worthy dog, and faithful
to my side. Trot beside me through the long
night, fetching images at request. Ticking
banality, delay your despairing. Earth forces
surrounded the house beating the slated roof
with bats of forgetful air. None of it means
anything but a long track from a death to a birth.

The brightness means wholeness, the darkness
means look harder: wholeness too. Tall,
snowy beauty, year after year to look out
and see the time returned, the horse chestnut
tossing and the flakes borne up on the wind.
And in this doorway she and she returned.
And in this closure you and I survived. In
these passing violins the future of Europe
suffers a small aperture of hope, that
glows redly through the nightly smoke.

Glows pale across the fields, central affection.
Maps hoisted above the hedges, but it doesn't
matter, where to go. Don't ask, "Where am I going?",
ask, "Where does such tenderness come from?"
– right there within the arms' arc, a point
that generated a history, a nothing that ran
right round the clock and back to itself year
after year as the moment fruited the bees
took their reward and the child, that bright
instant, spoke out a new justice. Where is she now?

Where fear propels and forks the path, or delight
opens into space. I'm starting to fade. Joy
lies like a stone on the ground. Pick it up.
"I am alone in the night, a homeless and
sleepless nun, holding the keys to the city"
and talk it onwards, wherever you are. Carry
also something for the passing stranger.
Such are the demands of equity as love sinks
across the dark hills with the rain. I am
absolutely nothing in the showered grain.

The showered grain, the shadowed gain.
Complete silence at the crossroads, the white
railings and the sombre fields between the
dozy roads. North South East and West
where's the one I like the best because best
known, and get the knowing back. I drape
myself on the railings, towards a sleeping
lamb in a wooden crate. Daughter, let me be
a shadow on your fear, a weight on your
ambition, a red glow in your hate.

Let me think. Directions available are again four.
I could slide uphill south where leisure rules. If
you're tired go to bed and let the world find itself.
I could return to east and live in a document
of what wasn't except as what survives. I could
turn to north without hope of anything but
achievement. I could continue, west, downhill,
and a lot of trouble in uncertain devolutions
of the heartland curving back in. Whatever I decide
there is somebody watching me across a field.

Across every field there's someone: loved, lost,
asleep in the big house or standing there at
the far corner in a white dress, world bride,
holding a small bouquet, looking this way.
Suddenly breaks into a run and dashes along the
field wall to the left, a pale moving blur that
crosses the path I haven't yet decided to take,
over the road and into the tin chapel. I heard
the door slam, the dim light appear in the broken
window, the old harmonium lurch into All For Thee.

Such tenderness dive-bombs despair. She gets
married in the tin chapel beside the road. At this
point I bow to gravity and move off to westward,
the downhill contract into continuance. Walk
beside me on the heavy grit while the June
flower heads nod us away; I'll walk out with you
any day, O faithless one. And merrily I do, down
a starlit road, between fields where cares rest,
and past a tin chapel or meeting room
in which my daughter gets married, perhaps

I wasn't invited. Perhaps I was and forgot.
I won't disturb them now, I'll pass by.
Out through this curved horizon is an open
hope to which their promises are acrobats.
Archford Moor, ridgeback sandstone inlier
topped with poor farmland, fields of pasture
broken by small patches of marsh grass.
A lame man and his Polish mother inhabited,
as I recall, the one farm. Their promises
are a bridge to the world's long strings.

The dim light in the tin shack, two or three
witnesses, gently spoken words projecting
an optimism in which the landscape is cast
under and there is a crack or error in our
persistent elevation of the world that
time's cynicism can't fill; the moment it
lives in sweeps through the trees as their
promises take my hand and sing me to my
journey's purpose. In solemn agreement
to maintain each other, a sense of flying.

Steadily down past the chapel, cracked windows
glowing fore and aft like high windows in a
vast city as the pedestrian walks beneath, where
a healing is taking place, or preparation for
a birth. To pass so close to it, those silent
acts carefully memorised, belief unstated in
duties clearer than any verse, putting the singular
in direct contact with the totality. Why other-
wise bother? Writing books, learning a trade,
rolling in cloudy certainty down long straight roads.

Deep in the small hours (persisting through
the dark doors, trusting to the end) anthems
receding in the night as I walk on down the
long road glowing faintly in starshine and
the black overshadowing trees humming aloud
to the old refrain: If you love the world
follow its instructions. And gain an advocate,
even the spirit of truth (in the original orth-
ography "sprit"). Mulling this over again
I didn't notice I'd entered a domain.

"Explain yourself," said the landowner, last time
I was caught in this wood, which was nearly twenty
years ago, idling around admiring the blooms
of fly agaric when the person, the person entitled,
appeared askance, and explained that it was private:
private woods, private toadstools, private elves
sitting on them knitting, the whole scene as private
as a child-rape. He returns in this dark underleaf
and stakes his demand: what are you doing here? Explain yourself: "Love raised the death camps."

Indeed, they meant well, the ventured words,
determined lovers all, they all meant well
but they raised death camps and it might have been
better if they had stayed unloving and without purpose,
if they had got on with an honest trade and not
plunged to a world focus on the wings of negated
despair. My words are barely concealed thrones
for myself, my rights are insubstantial; I shall
do as the person says and return to the recently
privatised public highway in decentred submission.

My words are unconcealed thrones for my loves
right down the road, right down the right
of way. Long and straight it goes between
fields and woods like a night-mail express
bringing an urgent question: Loving exactly
what, is the question. And all or nothing
is an easy answer, a word or two. Love knows
no parameters, responds to no need, serves no
purpose but its own and refuses all languages.
Them people up in th'ills, them's dirty and stupid.

Who said that? Nothing near me but stone and
fibre, trees gathering over me as I get down
towards the river. What kind of love delivers
such messages? Some kind, certainly, some loving
home with its family values that mustn't
spend beyond its means. So keeps tight like
a pine cone in the night – daughter, forbear the love
if necessary, time like a rolling dream takes most
of it away. Leaving you cold but bound in honour
to the distant tribes who sleep in the far hills

With no advocation but the spit of truth. Left
at the junction, uphill and first right past
the doctor's house (sleeping but on-call) then
steeper down, turning through the middle of the
old mill. The little stall they put out here,
of potted herbs and lusty perennials, stands
roadside in the night. I am seriously tempted
to take one. Both to pay for it and not to,
are a temptation. But this isn't life, this is
love and war. I pay and don't take one.

50p lighter in pocket, awake and on-call but
no one ever calls, down towards the river bend
I hear the sound of it again, the soft beating
manifold tumbling of water on its course getting
gradually nearer like entering a city. Again into
edge zones, and reef miseries, again into
lowland broth. The river bass thumps it out as
the road skirts the river bend past a silent cottage
and a side road where there's a public telephone box,
which starts ringing as I approach.

About 1 a.m. River bass humming alongside,
miles from advancement or delay on a small road
in a geology of violent disruption happening
very slowly over vast stretches of time, like
the dream of a nationless economy (Italian, say,
or sub-Saharan) beginning slowly to assert itself
across the northern plains where the worker at
day's end sits in real time. All the questions I ask
pass unanswered behind my persistent foot-
work when suddenly a phone box rings.

"Explain yourself," half a voice says. I'm sorry:
wrong words, failed nations like old soup, they
meant well but congealed in the cold world's fear.
Ironical clicks to this, and an electronic drone,
a channel adrift. Then a kind of purr which means
you're on your own, mate. But I am never alone.
Look here, it says, that demi voice, those people up
there in the villages, are foul and mean. All I can say
to this is that the only trustable percepts are of
detail and whole. Hug me Mr Mole, I'm home!

*Oh I'm so glad to see you, sit down in front
of the fire while I put the kettle on. Where
have you been all this time? I was worried,
I was...* and he sorts the cocoa and drops
a match into the ring, the dear old fellow
with his heart in a sling: Old Mole, hesitant and
polite, connoisseur of sheltering arcs. Gently
in the cosy grave behind the waterfall he
offers his slippers to a total stranger and
hums lamentations into the azimuth of war.

I drifted into a certainty, a hole in the sands
of my head dug by middle-class children on holiday
led to a night shelter at the base of knowledge. There,
small-scale conformist anxiety sprouted a belief:
virtue is what people return to. Virtue is original.
Soldier Mole closes the circle and intones the office:
*Here's your cocoa, are you comfortable, let me put
this shawl round your shoulders and I'll sit down
here to the side. I'm so happy that you're back,
I really am. The world is a hateful place.*

In a rock shelter in my night mind a retired worker
mixes a bittersweet cup and encourages further
warmth from a glowing log by poking it with steel.
Sparks rusticate the night sky. Full knowledge
is surely love's bible and the people are the lexicon.
I go this way and that, straight and crooked, my
daughter passes across the sky in a Chagall copula
and the artisans of Zaïre set up a whole-night rhythm
screaming for peace. But nothing unites the im-
possible choices. We solve into bits and pieces,

We heal into death. We vote ourselves out of
democracy again and again. The earth offers
suffocation. The tumbling water echoes in the great
cave-shaft by Apes Tor, water folded over water,
falling beneath water to the underground wheels
pulling water back from its earth. Is this a music
to dance to? Or to sing true and complex, like Seán
'ac Dhonncha in his old tweed jacket, floreation on the
walls of the ancestral cave, singing fate into a caul,
with tales of industry and long slow fall.

In a night glimmer in a slowly descending syllable
I heard an elderly gentleman welcome me to
his humble house and offer me the earth.
I settled the headset back on its rest for an end
to questions, I pushed open the door and
re-entered slow thought, dark road, happy
to shed a tear for the unquestioning souls
of cosy moles, now coasting homeless in the
fell mists. May the adventures they renounced
leave them wise to the world's twists.

For really, the smallest scale of kindness
steps out of history and stands on its own
floorboard against corruption. How real is that?
Here I divide into two travellers. One goes left,
up the hill and over Ecton on a hard slog to Wetton Mill.
The other carries on with the road as it is,
reaching the same or similar point on the level,
twisting this way and that as the river valley goes,
letting the question pass. I intend no lessons,
I figure policy by the cramp of my toes.

The slow song unfolds earth's theatre
at a dark scene, of bitter sisters, cruel water on
the shrinking leaf. Then no one way to go: no
success without harm. Now there are two of me,
one each side the great hill, and the hill between us
full of vast winding hollows, immensely deep
pools and falling noises – long abandoned
copper mines, spasmic histories. Each of me
takes the industrial echoes to heart like the last
waltz: good night to yous all and God bless.

Well we need our anxiety. I follow the river down.
The folding here is spectacular and rightly
text-book. In the night it stands as a thing
of millennia while school parties and solitary
selves pass below with their notebooks and
note in their books, "This big arch of black
rock made me think that the earth is a thing
merely witnessed by me and all my kind, miss."
I test the path at night as if I were blind, I release
my free selves to the old world's mind-stress.

Dr Williams, whose house I recently passed, if
he's still there, was a good doctor, he knew
the limits of his science and rested a hand on
a thinning arm. Maybe the war was a good war,
it made us belong, and live to a singular purpose.
Now we live outside that small home for ever or
destroy everything. The world changes piecemeal –
it multiplies its answers. Can a dark valley
with a swift stream can a walked value in a
riven dream teach outer solitude to the home team?

Can I teach a fish to swim, or bird to die? I
pass by the old adits along the foot of the
broken-backed hillside. Noises resound within,
of someone striking a match, of icicles falling
onto stone floors. But still I hear that singing
in which everyone joined like a wooden ship moving
out from berth. They sat round a fire in the night
(the Aka again) singing need out of the original
compact for safety while the girls fastened papaw leaves
to their bums and swayed to the absent light.

I wasn't there. I never shall be. I'm some dreadful
concoction of various trading possibilities, I was put
together by church-goers on a Saturday. Tennis courts
on the southern bounds of Manchester were my pre-
natal sunset. They traded happily there, tit for tat
and well within their means. So what went wrong?
And here we are fifty years later haunting the night
of some derelict valley dreaming of a slow sad
Transylvanian music to lull the heart from fear, or
an African rap to wake the soul from sleepy war.

The blind sleep of real war, which is never far away.
Yet a madrigalian sobriety on the other side of the earth
nurses the feather hope, the Aka or was it the Dorze
in their pauses from laceration chorusing the prize,
the netted death. A music to heal the not-yet hurt. I hear it
in the night hush and marching under the copper spire
I notice clearly how it speaks woe to the city
and solace to the single life, with great relief.
Softly under the rustling berries at the river's edge
I stoop: fear and loss become agents of peace.

Which brought the edges of the sky nicely
knotted to the hearth: there was a law at last.
And O the ease with which she sails those top
notes! Saying that death's welcome is not
an individual skill, or self-heart stadium, but
a mutual cognition, a history. The bushes
on the valley sides ejaculating maroon berries will
confirm this to the letter if approached officially.
The law is my passport, and after many years of
shirking trade I walk lighter for a shared skill.

I walk beside an empty hill, its stomach
rumbles to my left. It's like the news, or
what's happening to the world, how it gets more
complex and the language breaks up. Actually
it lies quiet until someone provokes it. I walk
beside a thundering emptiness, a truly enormous
fellside hits the base just here in a scatter of gravel.
Looking up at it I know it ticks within, I know
supply takes most of the energy, I know my right
is fallen through surface, O my son

Absalom, would I had died before the warlords
began to rule the earth and robotise the fair contours
of the human map, our many ways of falling.
At the bridge I turn left, and scrape open the gate
onto the old winding road that hugs the hill's
foot and so avoid a bureaucratic directive which
pushes itself into most corners of the geography.
I'll stick to a narrow track that grants me the width
to accompany my child, still conceptually hung in
the crook of my elbow like berries in the previous May.

In dark night there are always lights, little glimmers
at the edges of vision, sudden streaks by the roadside
when you look again it's black. No one knows
what they are. Perhaps one of the millions of
the dead, had a bit of harmless energy left,
perhaps mineral friction. Or the plain inability
of the human species ever to know exactly
where it is or what goes on— that such a thing
should shine! if only for a moment, an elsewhere
flutters on the verge, and the far stations merge.

I am in favour of that merging, and the dispersal
of claimed centres. Simple gifts delight me, wishes
and distances set in the certitude of recognition,
the song cupboard, reliquary of the self locked
in the world's thusness. At the bridge I turn left
into the quietest section, a mile of the smallest
of roads, just about car-width and riding the
undulating hill-foot through hawthorn thickets
and oak sets where in the daytime small birds
constantly connect, and small hopes collide.

Before me the night's strata recede, occasional
tunnel entrances to the left. How's the other one
getting on over the other side, I wonder, maybe
on the top now? Would he dare to walk up there among
the summit ghosts? Would he unpack a sandwich
in the night courts where only the future stands a chance?
Would he greet his own fear on the bare mountain?
Down here in covert I share thoughts of quiet health
with sleeping birds. Coal tits and nuthatches
dream me through their territories towards light.

The graceful daily furs they wear are the scores
of a constant music. And isn't there again
a distant choral singing in the air? Dead miners
carolling under the hill, Dervishes turning
under blackened domes, evening in iron-age Africa
where puffs of white smoke from clay smelts
drift across the village to no-one's disadvantage
and the ring is struck, the wedding or shopping ring
is sung right round from zero to nought
echoing in delight or the whole fabric breaks.

Charcoal-burners deep in the English forests, high
as kites, singing through the night, turning and
turning in the distinct life, choir-boys dancing in
the side-chapels of Italian cathedrals, under frescoes
by Simone or Cimabue by candlelight, poetical histories.
Carolling hurt. Coming home from hurt and calling
out to a remote tenderness in the deep mountainous
minds and mines of the people in remote clefts between
accidence and malice. "I asked one of these blacks
where they get these songs, *Dey make 'em sah.*

"How do they make them? after a pause – *I'll
tell you, it's dis way. My master call me up and order me
a hundred lash. My friends see it, and is sorry for me.
When dey come to de praise meeting dat night dey
sing about it. Some's very good singers and know how,
and dey work it in – work it in, you know, till dey
get it right; and dat's de way.*" I think I hear it
in the far marriage shed of this trembling night,
rustling in the woods behind me as I walk on,
silent and alone until I reach a café-bar.

Which would seem unlikely here, disused country road
in the earth's darkness, gates to open and close,
sheep droppings on thin gravel. But there seems
to be a light ahead. No buildings on this stretch not even
a barn, pray God someone hasn't set up a hope camp.
No, just a light, that substantiates as I approach
into the hatch of a white caravan, with a person in
cooking clothes leaning on it, waiting for custom.
What would you like? he, or she, asks. Very little
actually, in the obtaining politics, but suggest a cocoa.

A hiss a gurgle and there it is. *I must owe you
something for this.* You'd think so, she (or he)
says, and nothing else. I sip and get stared and
grinned at and hesitate to ask: *I don't suppose you get
many customers along here at this time of night do you?*
In ten long years, sir, you're the first. But "many
customers" is an ailment I have sought assiduously
to avoid. It is better if the night passes itself
sleepily under the dome of leaf friction, than
vast promises that no one ever believes. Then

leans over, presses a bony forehead against
my temple and whispers in my ear. *The principle
is very clear. To construct a space in which
worth is realisable and whatever anyone is bears
its meaning forward so that the time lived, always
at an end, holds at any point its own prize where
the transaction is returned across hope. This is simple,
is virtue, is the act of the unacknowledged giver.*
I know, but my heart shakes for the cold world.
I turn my back and listen to the curled river.

The night is full of holes, our lights
destroy them. *She nurst him back to life
and coverd up her hed, not to be known or
seen.* Black holes that maintain us. Love is
fragile and deep, I cannot cross it, I
cannot know what it will do: she chooses, she
is the darling of my heart. So the night's
gaps and ditches fasten my collar to its
bone and this slave of wholeness brandishes
a fork over a plate in thought's morning.

Actually I think a well toasted sausage at
this point would be entirely redemptive. Right
you are guv she (is it?) says and the whole
sizzling thing gets under way. But what do you
do here in the long night, I ask (thinking: what's
the source of supply?) these ten years past (what's
the subsidy behind this bounty?) *I turn, sir,
in the simple life* (where's the hammer that
halved your heart?) O canny at night, bonny
at morn, where's the victim of your scorn?

The sausage however is in no points lacking.
There is no problem with the sausage. The back
of the caravan seems to recede into the hill
and the small birds keep their distance singing
Lemady O Lemady what a lovely lass thou art
in their sleep, which is safe yet. I ask again
but get a re-run. We sketch a zodiac on the counter
which we never travel, we turn from our quests
into a work-pot. The stars on the edges of rock
formations call time and the trees grow tall.

Thank you and please accept this potted herb. S/he
doesn't hear me, revolving in the kitchen fume to an
old tune like a hilltop heretic in pre-France, soon
to be fumigated right out. Innocence is so
dangerous, and the leaves of the tall trees
fall one by one to the ground. Don't you know,
I think, the danger you put yourself in wanting
only to love and give? No you don't and I
love you for it, but the dark world in fitting suits
blasts you to a caravan called nonentity.

I tread off without farewell. I was never convinced
this person existed. I look back and sure enough
the whole stage set has vanished. O Schubert,
build us tempiettos of our fears we are all very
close to not existing. Long tunnel mouths to
the left like other people's long talking mouths,
in which we recede to zero with the news.
I say it's not history and listen to the dark, listen
to its speaking moment as the dreaming martins
offer themselves to each other on quick wing.

Moon, where are you? There hasn't been a hint
of elucidation since yesterday but a lamplit room
in Cambridge and a slow bottle culling the dark for
fortitude, where are you moon? Busy somewhere else,
watching other grassy slopes, real heroes and villains
hiding in the shadows clutching guns and Bibles…?
Once when I couldn't sleep, I was about ten, I crept
to the window moved aside the curtain and looked out
onto a plot of suburban gardens transformed, turned
to silver, the sparkling glass of someone's old age.

And my delight was in the theatre of what is
not yet languaged, clearing apart from harm, cryst-
allised night in which kindness sleeps coiled.
There, it seemed, is the real world not yet coded,
not yet reduced to its own good-byes but lying there
glittering in the night. In that brief space we could
ask the answers, re-set the terms and bear a bright
currency into day, the guarantor of truth before
the moon sets and the entire stage of lawns and
rockeries dims and the mind returns to its daily sleep.

So sleep, Bo-peep, walking sleep and talking sleep
dreaming of an electronic pastoral which bypasses
the industrial conurbation saying: This is not history
and this is not a city, a city is a slighter structure
finely engraved at the heart of a commerce, a liberal
and rewarding centrality. Not a growth. The tide
of night runs back, the dream of equity breaks on
the dark valley-side under the elected star-heads
confirmed at a series of hi-tech fulcra or ganglionic nodes.
So they sing, and die, delicately across the earth.

There is no other lamp to this grinding walk, but
the purple protein and flickers of bombed cities
reflected off the cloud-base as I feel my way
among the boughs of the lonely ash-grove, thinking
of you. At the dormition of my greed the saintly
passerines gather round, ringing in my ears.
"Nothing is certain," they say. I wouldn't dare,
in Cambridge, say such a thing, though it's true.
But I do, and win some time that death won't ever
get back, and clutch it through a shrinking track.

Reaching Wetton Mill on tiptoe because people do
actually live here. And think back 31 stanzas to
Apes Tor where Self Two took off to the left. He
has no time to fall with the leaf he is dialectically
driven. He accepts the cocoa and while Old
Mole's in the toilet dreaming of lost seductions
helps himself to the life savings and slopes off
silently in the night, leaving the door open.
I expect to meet him here about now. I expect
to kiss his brow, I don't know how.

Leaving the door ajar I return to the stately night.
And hating all this affect take the left lesser and more
demanding road onto higher ground that bears
the great hill towards the vale. I feel ill. But I always
feel ill, I've felt ill for as long as I can remember
night and day and night again and haven't kept
quiet either. Another fond familiarity, another star
on the Christmas tree, to you I describe the aura of
my decay as I would to few others. Schubert, build us
tempiettos of our fears, containing martyred brothers.

It's easy enough at first and I think when this is all
over I shall have two eggs for breakfast. Wrapping
my future in a napkin I go softly under the cottage rows
clinging to the hillside, without waking a dog. The shoes
of this text, recommended for poetical discretion, are
Clark's, with firm soft soles. And the little lake still there,
down to my left, former power to the mine-weirs,
and the fishing lodge at its corner which I once wanted,
knowing I couldn't stay here, wanted that hold,
wanted a corner when everything else was sold.

Wanted it, a roofed room on the corner of a reed-
choked lake, one big window over the water and
a loft you could sleep in though God knows
what you'd do for a toilet. Anyway it wasn't for sale.
And I hadn't got any money. I mention it in passing
as I pass it and it passed me in 1973 and we all pass
the world's small and peaceful places with a touch
of despair. Perhaps I could have been happy there.
Perhaps I could have gone out of my mind in screaming solitude
and hypochondriac mania without troubling a soul.

All quiet then on the downland side. But a distant
roaring from the ridge top as the little road zig
zags along its flank creeping gradually higher:
sharp right, straight up, sharp left, on, I don't know
why I put up with it, frankly, this dark and overscaled
topography pulling me over the contours and the trees,
what few there, are alive in a new wind. The only thing
I know that keeps me to this demand is I suppose I know
it can be met, I know we have made things to equal all
its banging doors. One of them is Fretwork playing Lawes.

I think so, as I recall, I think that would answer
this aggressive night-pitch, this relentlessness.
I've got arthritic fingers, back-ache, a sliding
hiatus hernia, frontal headache, chronic bronchitis,
periodic nose-bleeds, tinitus or something in my
head that sounds like a tape-looped starling and I
love the whole set-up, the vast biological space-
pitch that holds living in a constant tension of
one death played against another by inaccessible laws,
like Fretwork playing William Lawes, like inflamed tendons

Burning in the limbs to illustrate the earthly form.
This paining by which to earn life I do adore it. I
wouldn't have it any other, I wouldn't pitch a note in
any other scale. I'd paint this procedure as a
cross of heavy strokes, of earth-colours riven with
occulted light, blood traces on a working surface,
pink and orange tones overpainted by an increasingly
violent night. It would stand single as a sign
on a small road, a splash on a wayside stump,
where earlier haters moved to love's strict design.

And move I do: back there I crawled or was carried
between home and office but this is striding country.
Legs, one of the few sections in good working order
impel me up the ridge side, clown on a unicycle my
head spinning with sinusitis or whatever it is (what
is it? is it me? or is it it? is it that dark knocking at
the door again?) O Doctor Doctor you'll have to run
to keep up if you want to conclude this consultation.
I am after all the living image of a god, the winter nights
are coming and my duties not yet done.

My body is a screen of the world's progress.
It hurts, it fights itself, the mind contradicts
itself and the cold sloping stone burns all of it
in a righteous fire. Author of unsent complaints,
to the government, the police, the broadcasters, God,
the nearest businessperson – that's me, burning in a fire
of defiance and fear. A fire in a hole. Then nothing left
but thin sticks of bone in hillside grass, bits of home,
twitching with wanderlust. When the whole takes over,
when I'm driven to earth, remember me if you must.

On this side the hill remains sealed. I don't hear
any singing, no inner space resounds, all I hear
is the foul rush of air. All the fools who died,
soldiers, miners, worked themselves to nothing
for nothing and now sound like nothing ever happened
as the wind sweeps over the ridge from westward
and hisses down the stony fields. I turn towards it.
I have to settle this. I take a small stile in the wall
and go straight up the hillside to meet my bride,
gather ye rosebuds someone paid for all this.

I'll tell ye what befell me: Cupid pressed
the rosie niplet of her breast and the cream
of light fell to the dark earth writing walls
and contracts across the fell ground rising and
falling. So these pale daylight markings on
night pages where all the lives involved are passed
into nothing, every living thing. One such
stony sentence leads me straight up the hillside
through a small quarry and onto the top.
On the top is a mine ruin and love-strife.

Knifed ground, I struggle onto it. And try to
stand up but the wind blasts over the top, tears
my hair, pushes the snot back up my nostrils,
I can't stand it; I duck under the wall and fists
to cheeks crouch under the holy border. Then
turn onto my side clutching my legs on stones
among stone mounds and close my eyes as
the force of force tears above me – let it.
Let it howl and win and work us until we're
finished. Then crouch and roll into the great bin.

And die working, die at pitch. I'm saying you can
have me, astrophysics, biology, industry, war, what's
the difference, do what you like with me. And
a faint flute tune carried in my head which if I
go now I'll take with me, a whistle in the night,
a tone-row held in the cracks of my skull. Shrink-
wrapped head to knee I swirl it round my brain
and roll on the barren ground. Damn you,
the silence I contain here and the musics
circulating in it are all I ever found.

Then realise I'm quite peckish and sit up to
unpack an egg sandwich. While quietly munching
this and minding my own business I am aware
of a strange whistle in the night over and
apart from the wind's desperate barrage. And
wonder what it is. A whistling might be expected,
but that it should whistle the final chorus of
Act II of *The Triumph of Time and Truth* is not.
Perhaps it's just a gentle burdock in the barren field,
a numb sentry carolling she knows not what.

The tune remembers what we forget and carries it
from one life to the next, the Scythian word-processor
in the stone mound wrapped in blue silk, repeating
again and again the story of the beads, the grateful
lining of the trade routes across mountain ranges.
Only a remembering person could move on such tracks,
secured from harm as reward relayed from self to history
burns roadside palings into the night sky. Now also,
to die were sweet and I bend again to my Beaker
posture for the ice of day lodges in my sigh.

The high wind pushes the clouds away and
the fearful stone-heaps on the ridge-top beam
their stasis each to each. I was cruel to both
my parents, I denied their claim to live forward
through your children which was all they had
after the war. Mother in self-pain howling for exit,
father seeking a quiet answer in despair. I'm clenched
knee to forehead rocking like a Russian doll.
About 1953 prosperity and comfort stopped in their haste
and became mental torture of directionless waste.

And I sing as I roll like a Peruvian mummy, *I thought
you were true as the stars above.* But the stars bend and
break our heads. Something like a dead crow shoots
across the sky something like a worker's soul *What
have you to show for years of working? Worn-out boots and
damaged lungs, children in flight...* Out on the minefields
long years of slowly cultivated resistance, a chorale
sung under great hills, lessons fixed in the heart
through mutual deliberation and confirmed in the
couple-dance, geology and flesh, all suddenly nothing.

Slow formation of a structure of substantive rights
maintained by discursive education and realised
in active solidarity with periodic knees-up. Cancelled
overnight, outright, and for ever. "Behind the times".
Public good translates as Business interests there is
a strange sense of déjà-vu as we creep home, and
the economy is saved, hoorah. But the economy
is not what we live, the economy is our enemy,
casting us into a future of empty tombs, grey
prairies scattered with Disneylands eating their own

Flesh for lunch as if a market could be its own motor
and spin itself to the top privilege without someone
somewhere footing the entire account. We refuse to die
into this economy. The songs carried in slow centuries
bear purpose larger and more singular than state, and
turn the benefits back to earth, offering an escape route
to central distances where despair and love build cairns
on the horizon and passion lights bonfires in hollows of
bankrupt night. Throw the book into the sea, the balance,
and applaud the metropolis crumbling into its own goal.

I might have said something. The sky blasts the ridge
-top cairns, throwing every fertile particle into the vale,
a deathly movement of air protects us from the
stars we see distorted through its tide and crouched
under the nearest leeside arbour I moan into my ankles
and await the interlocutor I know is expected, indeed
invoked. I wince and cower and offer for the third
time to roll into history and be forgotten. My stomach
twists itself sideways in the philosophical onslaught
of ultimatum and shooting pains herald Urizen.

But no one comes. My left temple twitches,
finger-lock on ankles burns, can't hold this
foetal position any longer. Release myself into
relaxation exercise 24: breathing very slowly
out as the shoulder muscles unclench. Will
this prolong my life at least past four o'clock?
Down by the docks I bid my love farewell
as the slow boat moved out like a piano study
in triple arpeggios *don't you e'er deceive me*
and eventually return. If you will, if you dare.

But no one returns, no one turns up, up on
the godless terraces there's nothing but a raving
wind and dark ground with pale stone forms tracing
the night's vacancy. I anticipated at least a sphinx,
I wanted to learn something, I thought I could be
asked difficult questions to which the answer is
sheer presence, the cup we hold the world in, relayed
through lives, always complete. But resistance
meets nothing but resistance, on barren peat,
or the pale street-lights of a silent estate.

I feel like a NHS heart specialist who suddenly finds
that the enemy is not death but life. Lessons of the
1990s. All those slow centuries, livesful of teaching
and practice and sudden vision like a Duccio madonna,
care engineered to a working process: *de Humilitate*
gold-worked silks pressed to the ground before
the human fact – all suddenly nothing. Someone
creeps up behind you and says, "Hey, I could sell that"
and does. Soldiers, managers, are sent into the hospital.
To break it up. They do this out of love.

Not for themselves, that's the point. It's an idea,
it's a vision. It transgresses death. But death
is always welcome. Cappella Pratensis singing Josquin
in a dark church in north Holland against occasional
foghorns on the vast foggy canals, sing in the very
jaws of it, dance in a line as the happy mouth closes,
continually on an island in harm. Blood flecks on
the pillow, *ploravit in nocte,* powerless as the tenor of
the plainchant or the complex song. I'm prince of life
but I shan't be worried long.

For death is always appropriate. "See: he has escaped
the whole thing" and lies in my arms weightless
as a college leaf, completely forgotten. But else-
where calcium and phosphor take the same chance
again, the skull grows like a midnight mushroom
in the proactive womb. What was that call he gave?
Before he left? A white shout that span across
the black fields like a furtive bride, white ribbons
on his bonny waist – hushaby child, your cradle
rocks on the hilltop, your cry calls to arms.

Meaning I depart voluntarily but for heaven's sake
do something about these holes in sense these
darknesses in the world's diction. These sombre
suits that cash any crisis as soon as. I crouch here
in bureaucratic terror like an Inca summit child
awaiting the social spasm and a motherly homunculus
in my stomach is the only messenger of history,
barking at the head carousel, saying Come down,
child, from those fancy wilds. Come to the sable
spread where what we love is asked for. For

My days are full of fear but my nights are joyous
bouts of nonentity. Unavoidable questions of value
engender the fear which twists my shoulder blades and
pushes its thumb between my eyes (have I mentioned
this symptom before?) until the kind god scoops
me up and lays me in a selfless enclosure of use-
less calm. Rocking like a beam engine in the wild
night under the windward stack, what have I
to bring? I notice again that even tune whistled
below the force, as something far from this hole.

And sit up again. And shout: *Don't you know it's
bad luck to whistle in the wings during Macbeth?*
No reply, unless someone whispered *Could you
spare some small change?* In this tearing wind
I can't make out a word, in this darkness I can't
distinguish a separate demand, in the density of
population I can't find a home. I'd live alone
in a caravan on the edge of a Welsh field if I
believed in God. Did a voice come from a hole in
one of the stone-heaps like a song from a craft?

You can't make a cave in that one, I shout, *it's
the shaft mound! You'll burrow into nonentity.*
No answer. Is that a depth there, or merely a shade?
I lurch towards it but cyclonic pressure allies with
bronchitis: I'm silenced, lose my bearings and fall
among loose stones which rattle down, and dying to
answer can only ask: Where are you? What shall I
do next? If I locate your homelessness and dialogue
through it shall humanity in my breast bear
a lighter burden, a dawn of trust in the streets of Durban?

One thing exchanging for the other. A dawn of frost
in field and garden. You can keep your homeless
certainty, your privileged plea: I'm out here
in the entire length of land and won't be drawn back
to a social problem, I'm looking for the template error
that leads harm on through worlds without need, and
yet if I could locate your hand I would certainly
press a coin into it, if I had obtained one recently.
One thing for the other, a valid token for the touch of
recompensing flesh, and the voice it nightly manufactures.

I hear it now: Look at you, it whispers, all got up for
the fight in the hilltop pulpit and someone hands you
a note: "Please excuse Peter from games today,
he has a slight cold and doesn't like having his face
stamped into the mud…" And rage, against the dousing
of your light in easy terms, your logic in selfish
metrics. And a messenger you can't hear, an ally
or adversary you can't locate laughs in the darkness
at the closing of the gates (of the heart. Clutch
what's left your innocence and depart.)

And go content, for actually (the whereless voice
continues) this is indeed the top tribunal, this is
what you asked for, the question at your feet. You're
not in Cambridge now – pick it up and ask it. I do.
I tick and tock under the broken stone and bid for
straight answers: *What about the lives? – if the lives mean
only to this limit* (tapping the surface) *what
completes them?* Shut up! the little sphinx murmurs,
go away. I don't care. I want to programme quicker trains.
I want to daft us all in bigger and bigger drainage units.

It could be that I won that one, though the few plants
on the exhausted slopes quiver and cough through the night
and I hate winning anything. That was also my last chance
to mount a hilltop theatre. But I never was much
of a college kind, I was never a village fellow. I grasp
the world by its corners and shake it in the wind
which hoots over me like a new year greeting. And three
lines short of a stanza suddenly realise that the dragons
of earth are all round me. Their silence, their fear,
their no-theology, is what tears my heart to death.

For we fear the unfearable from breakfast to year's end.
I stumble to my feet grab my hapsack and slope
off under the wall. How like the populace I am,
crouched against threat, paying the lords, waiting
centuries for a justice that never arrives, ailing
downhill sheltered from thought. The dragons of day
breathe behind the stones as I slip off the ridge-back.
I hear their piston talk, their adversarials. I fall
Down the night pleading silently for the souls
Of those who caused hurt in a rushed quest for peace.

Down the grass track, sheltering wall to right down which
produce of that miserable bit of superseded industry
would once have been dragged by horses to line
someone's pocket or poison someone's bread and
onto the road. Even on foot tarmac quickens the pace
and like the owner of a dry-cleaning firm in Oldham
heading for a motel date I zoom down the smoothed way
as if I were going to live. I'm not. Neither is he. We both
fool ourselves into momentary eternities while
the dragons of result smoke behind our backs.

The road however soon shrinks, twists and drops,
and ejects me onto NT land below the manor house,
in which someone by luck or privilege or just possibly
rewarded labour, lives. But it is a simple place,
a valley-head junction of rounded hill-flanks with
a three-storey 17th century towerlet in grey stone
presiding over the routes thus formed at the feet
of the slopes while the working dragons cut comfort
to fillets on the far moors. And rough as it is
this tufty terrain is welcome home from such wars.

Welcome home to a fiction of rewarded labour.
But what a house to die in! What a lay-by in
which to abandon the hopeless machine and
stumble off across the fields among the slightly
interested cows begging eternity for a clay bed. Or to
wake up in the morning on the top floor and see
the white light between mullions, the snow-coated
hillsides and the telephone ringing with a message
from a daughter in Durban saying it's safe here but
something of a bore, the cars again and the hatred.

And how bright these other hills, so far from dawn,
leapfrogging before me, left of south, whose heights are
pure reason and whose flanks are crowded with earnest
surgeons whose bank-accounts are the laughing-stock
of every accountant in heaven. Look at their white coats
dotted over the bounding slopes, whose heights are
the triumph of memory in days of managing, where
cosmological princes study the lie of the land as
a strategy against harm, to the throbbing roar
of the balancing engines on the opposite moor.

These hills where there's plenty of time, you can
search all night for a stray crotchet and arise
not a whit wiser in the green morning but a
continuance to be continued, a fragment fitted
to a future formulation bypassing in sufficiency
the constant failure of advantage. But exactly
fitted, exactly fair. O you black-eyed Susan,
you made me love you and left me standing here
in excess of make-believe, trying to dream
the real into a fiction in order to forget it.

A five-piece brass band appears for three seconds
across the pasture where the valley head starts to dip.
They stand on the path beside the stream, raise
their instruments to their lips, get through the first
upbeat of the Rákóczy March and vanish. It means
I can't stop, it means I can't forget, it means
two hundred years of industry brush the grasses
down the fellside. O you black-faced coalman
who dumped the earth in a heap with a crunch
and woke everyone from a dream of desert.

The glint of metal in random night. I saw
a socialist statement scissored before it
could become a nationalist sentiment. I saw
the shortest hope as the truest. *Blush Roses
in a Glass* (1905). Everything I saw vanished
and I walked on under the somnolent arcades
of night. I felt like Ivor Gurney, to whom walking
was a necessary music, audible in darkness,
eating the miles, consuming the place. Ah that!
with chips would fill my best face right now.

O you white-faced clown, blushing under the powder,
you surface of earth, where have you put my brother?
I walk into the top of the valley where the stream
comes shaking under the hill like a tizzy girl
such as I was in 1957, mincing across Manchester
to the tune of Drainpipe Shuffle (O you pink-faced
bloom you blue-bummed baboon you earthly fear,
when will you finally relinquish me to the five winds
of total forgetting?) This wayward distractedness
is entirely typical of middle-aged war-children,

Remembering the drone in the sky (you red-faced prefects,
don't you remember this?) the bombers moving in formation
towards Manchester with the concerted irrevocability
of a sextet by Lawes (William) the big grey balloons over
the houses and Death walking the bounds of the playpen.
Do you think we had need of gender remodelling?
Such wars are always with us, the old enemy and the old
fear and the shining of hearts in mutual trust,
passing mugs of tea into the bunker, setting a hand
on a shoulder, listening, listening all night long.

You listen long and eventually you hear, the
enemy approaching, the slight wind shifting
the bushes and the delicate stream beside you
chatting into gravity, the enemy earth whose
disguise is such delight. Take me by hand or
shoulder, son or daughter, and we'll walk together
down a long street or short valley decorated with
meaningful bushes. Easy walking, no harm, years
passing, I shrink as you grow. And the nearest thing
becomes the most difficult to remember, a hidden glow.

A lightness in the tread. Something happened, I
don't think we'll ever know exactly what it was,
it was like casting off high culture for ever and
locating instead a common desire that shed heat
and light from the centre to the atlas index like
an anchor chain, though it wasn't exactly that either,
for it was sad enough dancing on the earthen floor
so far from power; but the hope in this thought was
practical, the strictness was a far sustained voice
and the bushes this year loaded as never before.

It takes some courage, actually, to inhabit survival,
to set the burden of technology aside like a wet rucksack
or the artists with their fingers up each other's noses
and locate a human adequacy speaking only of the world,
only of the green road, green by night and green by day,
that gently falls, I'm opposed to a universities poetry.
As the valley deepens, faint hint of day on the moon
coated tops, let us instead be a people, let us be
zonked out on people wine. And sing like Roza Eskenazi
of the peculiar joys of sustenance, the daily fine.

All over the fellside the bushes sing to me clad in
fruit. They sing in the night of what they learned
in the day. The lyrics are truly African: "Education
is the only way forwards / I wanna hold your hand /
Look for peace on the gathering road my children".
They sing variously in a choral landscape so that
an accord runs over the valley from edge to edge
and revolves with the stars like something by Obrecht,
folding and refolding on itself in the dark distances
and finally settling almost into nothing on earth.

So answering we die. But the green road continues.
It is itself the death we are in. As are the berries
hanging in great red clusters on the dry hawthorns.
As I pass down the valley each bush calls my name
and clearly states its thesis in the available space
of the night, when the light tread of the old man
walking to the sea rings out clear as a bell.
Ways of doing good in the world. I try to hear
what they say though the self-music of a proud longing
pulls me away and all the bills I'd like to pay.

Bush 18. I keep a bar down town. Get the best music,
hi-life guitar bands on tour, or some old guy up in the hills
does sanza like an angel, I get to hear and in two weeks
he's on. Local nonsense too, got to give them a chance.
I pay proper, they go on all night, people really listen.
The kids start fights but they're kids, soldiers, most
soldiers are kids, and get a good time out of any war.
The trouble-makers hide from the music round corners.
We sweep up next morning. Stick my claim to virtue
on the back-wall slate: I got them singing together.

Bush 27. All I do is work in a shoe-shop and hope
one day to get married and have children, perhaps
in one of the stone-row houses in the hills I always
rather fancied that, they'd have breathing-space
and fewer temptations. I could talk to them as the rain
banged on the slates and shifted the tumblestones
down to the stream, telling them how to live, how
should I know as if I'd get bright in the brightness
and perhaps I would too. What more did you
ever do, artist, claimant? Make us a chair to die in.

Bush 32. I like to speak to the patient before I
operate and give as full an account as possible of
what I'm going to do. And afterwards I hang around,
witness the slow revival, talk, join in some basic
nursing. I won't be rushed – I have after all quite
possibly saved or extended a life or made it bearable.
I like to see it revive, that's all. The life, not the person.
What I've mended doesn't belong to the person and
my act must be understood as an episode of a work
driven into the whole world's unrolling darkness.

Bush 33. Bells on her ankles, that descant when the sun
divides. Little bird, when you've woken up and had your
breakfast, fly to her, my knot of sorrows on your back,
and remind her all her paths are peace, say a stone heart
will crack, a wax heart will melt. Then good-bye to the
circuses, goodbye to the soldiers, let a holocaust of nostalgia
and love spread all around us! Edge-being, await my message
of post-metropolitan resolution and take it to the earth's
end for her I adores, ignoring the stuffed shirt on my left.
Never could bear a successful gorse.

Bush 57. I have devoted my whole life to a careful study
and meticulous translation. I have collected and preserved
many artefacts and natural objects and have taken hundreds
of photographs of the people and the places. I have taped
the singing and notated the dancing. I have listened to them
talking and transcribed what was said into fifty manuscript
volumes. And I hope to have understood, or what could not
be understood to have faithfully set out as it was done and said,
for the sake of a wholeness which informed everything about them.
What kept me going was the love that grew slowly towards me.

Bush 60. I cuff the kids around here about the ears. They act
as if their nose tips are the heart of hearts, come off it I say,
use your eyes. Me I never read but half a book but I know
from somewhere it's not going to work, I can see them at 80,
pitiful relics clinging to bits of pride in the roar of death
saying I did it my way. Come off it is my answer, share
your sweets with her they can't afford them and feel the better for it,
give yourself a sweet sleep. Look her in the eyes, I say, as I
wallop them, you can't get too close, watch the mouth quiver.
The half book I read said something very similar.

And fifty others and a lot more over the next hill,
making a calling and a whispering all over the landscape
through which a fox might snake a route at ground level
or a lamb tremble under its mother's flank or a wise
southern songster cry at the vista of separation. Half
sentences and stray words torn by political advantage,
cast and lost in the night air, here and gone, fully trans-
scribed and dumped in a skip at the next library chuck-out
and scattered to the winds. I particularly liked the Irish
shepherd who'd found a new way of squaring the circle.

And as the lost claims shoot across the small valley
they network together and make a chorus, a gathering
conditional that takes my arm like a faithful relative,
ways of doing good and the world tightens
and clarifies into a pure lament, the song the
four fairies sing at death's door: *Si je n'étais
pas captive, J'aimerais ce pays.* I thought I
caught it but the valley of chanting bushes comes
abruptly to an end, the last accord floats off north
I am left facing a grassed bank for all I'm worth.

I'm worth what I'm called. There's a small path
through the branches that climbs to the right,
over the bank and down some concrete steps into
the Mill yard by the tumbling water where my
lost twin waits for me. The kind compliant me I
cast adrift for the sake of upper questions and what
did I or anyone gain? A very late bush (79?) calls
over the rooftop, "I catalogued the five joys in order,
do I get a reward?" Smile knowingly, raise
an arm and merge into each other silently.

And walk over the bridge splash across the ford and
tramp on the easy road under the cliffs – uneasily,
surrounded by dangers, but relying on common sense,
trusting in trust: somewhere the world's credit
is good and a crackling 1920s 78 from Dallas still rolls
its sad echo down the mind's question, for there are
no sureties. Virtue scrolls from eventuality. Take me
with you, Dusky Meadows, and we'll walk perpetually
in darkness dear, as I do now in darkness drear
and ever threat of error guided by own fear.

Fear of dark water. Fear of apparitions, like
a bunch of skinheads rolling down the road twirling
chains, shouting GO HOME to the homeless, ready to
pounce on the faintest glimmer of difference on
anyone's face and stamp it literally into the ground.
Safe in the knowledge of doing good, for the future,
absolutely pure. Fear of skinheads, fear of walking
into a river in the unfenced darkness when you can
hear it falling around you. Skinheads falling into
purity with big thumps. Hear the thumps and weep.

Chubby infants fallen into error, weep for them, weep
for their big trousers, the chains round their wrists,
weep for their premature baldness and loss of adventure
in ersatz certainty, weep for the bold ungiving kids they were.
I do, I worry and sob in provincial helplessness while a
financier in Leeds casually spends the night stripping
Korea of what prosperity it has. So the darkness closes
round, the valley deepens, the river sound shrinks to
a gurgle in the museum of fear. I sniff to myself under
rock formations that spell dread (thump) completely clear.

I pause under an overhang, skinheads falling to earth
all round me like lambs dropped by eagles, skinheads
changing their minds and offering sweets to Slovak
gypsy children – O what a fall from ideology was that!
(thump) what loss of image what sudden and true
messages A to B in a flash of kindness, nothing is
faster, nothing more common, give the earth for it.
The eagles' nest was long deserted and the bones of
trusting lambs decorate its margins, souls intact
and speaking messages of thanks across vertical thumps.

I weep on the small winding road (far thump) and again
hear a singing somewhere. "The musicians follow the dancers
down the main street towards dawn, playing and singing,
My tears fall and soak my shirt, they make a pool in my lap…"
Musicians ushering us back to our real conditions
by the morning star, drawing us out of the dream
*Autumn comes, the nights grow cold, the leaves fall off the trees,
the young men are taken into the army.* The sadness reveals
a rightness (near thump) and the cold skies watch us
making a rightness out of what we can't prevent.

But people learn, slowly, that they don't have to
send their sons to an early grave, don't have to
live badly for the sake of the national economy.
Don't trust the music if it isn't attached, if it goes
wandering off up its own track unlikely to come back,
pirouetting on the ridge-top and leaving us helpless
at the end of the party, hopping and stumbling
back to our empty houses, from which the children
have been removed but a small flame perpetually
burns in a jar. A small flame burns in a jar.

We also get older, and mysterious bumps appear
here & there, the artists wave their nose-bags and
skinheads thumpetty-thump in the bare fields,
but a small flame burns on. If it goes out here
it revives there. The old flute hangs by the hearth
waiting to be repaired, to trill out over the darkness
and burdens of sorrow like the lark in the morning
soaring and trilling above doomed farms, singing
*Last night I lay in a good feather-bed, this night I lie
in a cold open field, under a gypsy laddie-O.*

For this I gave up the earth, and my baby and
life itself. Full of result the virtuoso lark trills
in the sky, tied harmonically to a history of hurt.
Trills in hunger and slides and soars in fear, this
bird I cannot hear, for it is still pitch night
and no birds sing. But a dreaming murmur from
nestlings in pockets of the pale cliff says
tomorrow will be my dancing day. Tomorrow
the rights of man are reconciled with the earth
in an open field with the slim dark faithful boy.

Signalling the end of the metropolis, redundant
to communication production or distribution.
A few lost souls left dancing by themselves
to a full-blast machine-music, a few mind-suicides
on a night out. It preaches, and it threatens, it says
We shall not be moved, it waves a red flag in the
darkness but it's too late. Slowness has won.
Trees invade the centre and flourish among desks
and machines, all claims to status are so much
tinnitus and the owl mocks the benighted politician.

I know perfectly well what's going on. The river
gradually disappears into holes in its own bed
and clefts under the white cliff, with a slightly
horrible gurgle. As far as I'm concerned the whole
works goes with it, the great conurbation that never
distributed anything but despair, this is where we pull
the plug on centralist coercion and turn to each
absent other in the pitch silence, people remembered
at their best. And shake hands with that shade, welcome
the beast in its eye and the bioplast of which it's made.

The no longer feared stranger who pats my head and
scratches my back and pushes me on my way merrily
without saying a word, black person on dark road,
someone my daughter met in Mozambique who helped
her on her way and out of nothing gave a small meal
to two young whites… memory of days not lost, not
sad, not here. The just, who from their labours rest,
shine in the heads of poor travellers. What other reason
is there for travelling, walking the night, but to find this
justice, and the roadside constellation that carries it through?

And wouldn't so much as contemplate a war, but
fights for peace: a space in strife in which things are
born, and die, and dance, and work through a quiet
or turbulent life to further the promise into the future.
This must be what I believe in, a trust open to any-
one, in whatever text of work they operate, so long,
Babylon. And close the gate behind you. A strange
silence after the river has sunk away, lifting attention
to the top horizons and what they hold in their cryptic
script: hints of light, movement of air, final reward.

So very long, Babylon. I remember walking here
on New Year's Eve, must have been about 1977 just
after the child was born. It was well below zero and in
the frosted air the pale cliffs glowed fuzzily either
side of the dark trough in which I walked, it was
the moon's stage and my speech on it was cut.
The river was very slight and a turning point in
a life was a treaty with strife. That must be why
it sticks. Again that Senegalese singing wrecks my
business-float and the proud breeze blocks dissolve.

Lessons for others: advance cannot be virtue. Yellow
cowslips hide their heads at night and the roadside
cup-bearers keep so still the meniscus of the wine
is like glass. Advance can at best be necessity.
Some skinheads are all right actually: great lollopers,
Shropshire lads on a night out, surfers caught in
a wave they didn't propose – I've known meaner and
more vicious types on the far left, and high academe.
Uphill is where we advance from here, me & me, and fast:
the poetry police are at my back: You Been Statemented!

The road crosses the river and shoots up the hillside.
I really can't manage it, I'm almost treading the spot.
I creep the first stretch and pull myself slowly round
the corner under Thor's Cave. I can't do it, I sway
from side to side and stop, laughing. The old men
dancing, that Ciaran Carson speaks of, their whole lives
stood behind them in the dance as they summed the courage
of being exactly where they were. I'm stuck. I don't know
where you are, I'm sitting on a sod in the dark facing
an inverse moon with my heart beating a different tune.

Hounds behind me, echoing their calls across the vale:
"Get the tell-tale!" and I'm stuck, a stranded whale
puffing on the verge. My failure to climb this hill
is the funniest thing and the moon sails on the sill
of my heart, casting brightness to the night sky, lost
into space. And there, receiving the acclaim of the host
of distances, Thor's Cave lords it over me, who can only
fall to the edge and laugh at his weakness. It could be
I have hidden reserves, it could be my entire history
is drawn to a hole in the sky for what it deserves.

Teach me to see, hollow eye, to hear, blocked tube,
into the distances that hold the solution to fear,
an arm round a poor man's shoulder, a widower
in the scents of night, the rustling broom on the
sloping roadside. A listening trumpet that calls
into the far reaches of the climate messages of
wholeness the far earth turns towards, setting
a cloak of aromatic air on a poor man's shoulder
whose bad eye sees the furthest and whose waxy ear
catches an echo in the rustle, pronouncing a name.

Names change from time to time. I breathe one in and
prise myself to my feet, I must continue. I nod to
the cave in the sky, lord of the heavy sentence whose
trumpet blasts anger over from the industrial estates,
silent at night under needless street lamps. The anger
challenges a long succession of undeserved gain
for the sake of the labourers whose loss makes
the entire dictionary, whose loss is continual. For my
heart is always trembling, from clear day light to dawn,
at the warnings that must stay silent

And the loves that must fail. Person much missed, how
you call to me in the capitalised pause and your
scattered ashes float above me like patches of mist
on the dark slopes drawing me up the hill. The night
collapses nightly into this loss, and someone has to
walk it into day through the dark of dreams, scratch
the writing across the sloping desk-top over the
furrows and ink pits Much missed person my hope
is always there where my heart's capital is sunk.
See it through, I tell myself, to the end of the book.

And I no longer hear that music, that partialises the world
and the rich silence I hear instead specifically lacks any
call, any claim or region. Yet your story made all these
hills and how wonderful it would be to hear a few bars of
S.E. Rogie's sweet baritone voice singing *Nodomei Neneckpa*
the sweetest, most beautiful, powerful thing: singing
simply, there is a best thing. The comfort needed
at waking because we know the night gap has been
betrayed again. I wonder where you are tonight – don't
pass me by don't spill the sky's translucent wine.

Or the soaring contralto of Munadjat Yulchieva holding
all our answers to unkind fate, our sky clothes, our
few night jewels. And the birds have already heard
the news and are passing it on. From tree and bush
in barely a trace of light the old questions are beginning
to be asked, high up the throat: What chance now?
What choice? Are you still there? Do you remember
Caruso at Belle Vue in 1953? Yes, every turn every
restitution every final farewell, nothing is lost.
It all gathers to the great chorus of hunger.

The best thing, but all I can think is complete thing,
get up this murderous hill under the frown of
judge rock with hole for face, get this night over:
step step inch inchworm cold pre-dawn when human
tide is lowest, might be. Forgotten why, forgotten what,
working/walking, for. Left (over) poetry forgotten.
And good riddance, however many or few human
souls gather at the river one day we'll cross over
and not be disappointed. True expectation, of
astral liquor, exactly where we succeed.

The road eases between banks (flesh crumbles into dust)
pace quickens, head up again (Dies Fleisch, das
in den Staub zerfällt) up onto the plateau, the fields
edged in dull stone, the dust brewed into humus. Tod!
Wo ist dein Stachel? Usefulness is freedom and here's me,
travelling on, rich in a currency nobody recognises
and quite prepared to chuck the whole (whatever it
was) enterprise over my shoulder (Dein Sieg, o Hölle!
Wo ist er? / Unser ist der Sieg) like a hibernating toad
but I have gone the wrong way and there's a knight in the road.

I went on towards Wetton turned south in the sleepy
fieldsides to get round to the Alstonefield road
and it was normal except when Shostakovich's head
suddenly popped over a wall saying, "Furthermore,
every time they play me now they preach about Stalin
as if that's what the whole thing was about. All I
wanted was to forget Stalin…" but it seemed the music
had forgotten me and all the trouble in the world when I
found myself at Long Low, desolate and cold, where
hope meets pain and I think there's a knight in the road.

I was walking on with my head full and noticed after
a while the road was getting very dusty and developed
a central grass ridge, sure sign of impending impasse
and it began to seem to look quite likely to me that
this road was the wrong road, that it led to where
I didn't want to get to or indeed didn't lead to
anywhere at all but stopped at a field gate and
a sense of death as failure, as everyone's own indi-
vidual failure to continue, as a relinquishment of
energy and purpose and a knight in the road saying so.

In, actually, some light now, some pre-dawn squabble.
Out here at the end of the road where the gods hide
behind the field-walls and watch their monuments:
"battlefields to the right, hospitals to the left", another
abandoned mine following a vein towards the valley
edge, heaps and holes; and to the left a linear tumulus
unique in Britain. These lines cross my path and I
stand alone in a mitigated darkness still bound up in
stillness save for the groaning birds the wind and
the heaviness of the load for there's that knight in the road.

False knight in false dawn, like a gibbet by the track.
You sought your self. My head hurts, I can't breathe
properly. *What's that you're carrying?* I don't want
to go to school, the teacher's got it in for me, I try my
best but I miss the questions. *It's a teddy-bear isn't it.*
It's late, I'm going home, everyone will still be there.
Nothing you do, nothing you say. I just wanted to pass by
I just wanted to die. *I don't see that there's any alternative*
to a constant strengthening against the powers of this world
and any who can't/won't is a lost life I haven't the time

For, falling, The world falls and you jump on board
you share the world's lapse but it doesn't lapse half
enough for me with you heartening it. It was bad enough
and now there's you too, humanising it back into time,
selling itself for a song. Look how wetly it glints in its
wrapping, this you-world. I won't have it here I'll thwart it
out of you I'll stop your eyes where it lurks smiling –
right back in there it lurks, your love of all this being.
Take your pet and go. Go failed, go subdued, go weak,
go self-blamed and go now. I'd like to say three things.

(1) Hard falls the rain on the lip that bites its owner.
(2) What is anyone ever going to make in this place
but a brooch of honour in the covering darkness,
an ornament passed to a future friend? 3) You may be
right but at least I never prioritised resentment.
He's gone. Was it a he? It vanished downwards with a
hollow tone, I'm alone at the road's end and the stories
that made these hung fields hollow me out like a bell,
like a churchyard bell calling the gods to their hunger.
They are hungry for the day and shadow me wherever I wander.

At the road's end you turn round and go back home
but I stand here in acute smallness, a life spent in
a dream of verbal redemption while the *polis* fingers me.
Something, not a bat, flits from the mine ruins back
to the passage grave. The steel-grey fields wrap both
of them in shopping, in slumber, in healthy tissue.
Nothing moves. These scars, heaps, works, these long
forgotten stories, these accusations, stand there like
tanks by the roadside and a small bird makes for cover
with a quick flutter. We must stand by our own stories.

Halted at almost-dawn far but not so very far away
and certainly still within privilege. In eastern border-
-zones centuries of failed diplomacy continue to blast
shells into living-rooms and every night is a question
of waking. The peace and mind-spaces we enjoy here
were hard won and rare on the earth, at a price of distraction
and disappointment. The mind runs on its vocabulary
to the end of the road, what it finds there is a shadow
of itself, no use blaming the government if it runs guilt into
our living space. The harm done is actual and irreparable.

The grey fields barely emerging into visibility,
the laying of diffused water on the land, the leaves
throwing open their shutters and switching on
the radio for the morning news: distant stories,
threats and promises, all quietly. And moving into
the calmed land, not yet measured by work. Somewhere the maidens dance on the green at break of day
arm in arm in a ring and nothing from an idea to
a tubercular lung can break that tuneful process
or mitigate the pain that showers final light on those subtly

Deferring messengers. Final dark is dimmed indeed as I
follow the way the tall sign points, down the grassy fields
on the style path to Hope Dale brushing the dew and
the singing accumulates from hidden quarters as the colour
fills in, shadows retreating before me and the birds all
up in arms. There by the lower pond and up across
the fallow slopes the backs of soldiers under instruction
to silently vanish from sight shrink into the darkness
that clings to corners. Armies in retreat with their new
recruits and the long wedding is over, the band follows

The last revellers down the road singing *My tears fall
and soak my shirt,* the early wind breaks little hollows
in the hedgerows and pastures and the leaves flit past us
as we make our way back to our quiet houses. To sleep
and be ill, and retch up mucus from the lung, and
call it a day, forgetting our children's names. Blanked
by the music, like Amédé Ardoin, one of my heroes,
who lay by a railroad track in Louisiana punished for
serving, punished for fidelity and never knew another
thing never played another note and called it living hell.

And got out fast. Which is a long way to go with the songs
of longing beating in your head and the accordion for ever
removed from your hands. I go on over the tumbling
peneplain, the road mounting humps and scooping hollows,
shadows everywhere departing, red lights on their bumpers.
Back of night or receding armies, creeping along hedgerows
clutching trophies. That man who sang out sweet and plain
is no longer on the circuits. But his answer cruises strife
and strolls from the known to its fore edges. *He do the song
about the knife. He do the walk, he do the walk of life.*

Excuse me sir have you got a licence for that singing
says politely a police voice behind me I'd forgotten all
about. I know nothing of this I was brought here against
my will and stuff my mascot under my blazer as the tall
trees call their laws over. But I'd like to say three things:
4) They are working people, the musicians and plasterers
who guide us back to where we live in a dawn halo
of old and tried devices – see how they walk with their
consorts on the sweet paths of earnest learning and learnèd
earning. You who die be my compass this curling morn.

A young woman in a nurses' uniform leaves one of
the scattered cottages, gets into a car, the first car, and
drives off towards Hulme End. A sleep-over, an old man
dying of lung cancer, a daughter. I wish I had been
like you and never tendered the artistic excuse. But to be
even in this thin light a working agent and the very ground,
the dawning territory itself, is won back. Back from what?
Sleep and adventure. To what? The real. These failed
missionaries in black robes running under the road's
edge from day are but your dwarfs and do what you say.

I'd like to say three things: 1) Where does such
tenderness come from? As I pass by Hope the
singular thing pours, the morning star, the lark
on high. There it goes, like Nusrat Fateh Ali Khan
on one of his shaking ascents and the sign of
tomorrow is a fat man shrinking into the sky,
rising into the precise location of a known star.
Cold mornings, it's autumn, the leaves fall from
the trees, the young men are taken into the army,
half of them never come back, the bark of care.

I wish I were entering a land. Rattle of the death-
camps in the stream-bed, carried away – a music
you can't have or bear back home, you can't
have it, they say, it remains ours. He don't say
nothin, he just keep. He roll. I gets weary.
Water clocks in the sky, little owls in the trees,
shadows of dispersing armies. I thought I heard
in the swift dawn air a nursing person shouting angrily
at the ideological accusers that segregate our band.
I wanted to live, she said, in a land.

And you shall, I thought, coming up the slope into
Alstonefield, still sleeping. And passed along
the deserted street to the starting point, the village
football pitch to the left of the road, site of the
boot sale and what I collapse into isn't the B&B
which I never booked myself back to anyway, but the
cheap red car in the village car-park. Soon the farm workers
will be out in those mobile telephone booths spreading
hip-hop music on the land. The earth's movement never
stops. I've had enough of this, I want a record shop.

Yet the laying of stone on stone, the careful nurturing
of pot plants in a lean-to, are as much signs that people
find life worth having and are prepared to do something
with, in, by, and for it, any day. Let's call it a day –
a tired man motionless in a car thinking feeble thoughts.
Where are you going, dove, this pale wine
of new day? Bundle of nerve calling over the slates
and pausing on the wires as the echoes conjoin, where
are you off to now? I'm going right out of this world,
and I'm taking your love with me.

Notes

Alstonefield, sometimes spelled Alstonfield, is a limestone village in North Staffordshire at OS grid reference SK 132556.

PREFACE

p.152. Estimate Brown (not to be confused with either Capability Brown or Shallow Brown): John Brown, 1715-1766, writer of essays and guide-books, early promoter of the enjoyment of wild mountain scenery, influenced Wordsworth.

ringed in darkness...: The Peak District is encompassed on all sides by: (a) gritstone moorlands to west, north and east, producing darker landscapes, (b) large industrial or ex-industrial conurbations from north-east clockwise to north-west: Sheffield, Nottingham, Derby, Stoke-on-Trent, Manchester.

PART I

p.156. Mansfield: town on the Derbyshire/Nottinghamshire border to the east.

PART II

p.158. "The sky will not help you..." from one of Martin Luther's sermons.

p.160 When a meticulous light... two and a half lines here were written by Helen Macdonald.

p.161. Thor's lip: reference to Thor's Cave in the Manifold Valley.

Lulu: a popular singer in the late 1960s. She never, to my knowledge, did a song called 'April Fever'; nor did anybody else.

PART III

p.164. The mountain edge... Most of this stanza is after André du Bouchet.

Beresford: Beresford Dale, on the River Dove upstream of Dovedale, on the edge of land which used to lie within the estate of Charles Cotton of Beresford Hall and still contains (inaccessibly) the stone fishing lodge used by him and Isaac Walton, author of *The Compleat Angler* (1653).

p.165. a more demanding geology: at the top of Beresford Dale the river passes from a sandstone inlier (open and undulating countryside) to carboniferous limestone (a gorge cut through white rock).

PART IV

p.169. Wolfscote: long tall open dale of the Dove Valley north of Alstonefield, and hill of the same name above it. Occurs several times later.

walkers' autobahn: long stretches of the riverside path in the Dove Valley now take the form of evenly laid beaten gravel about two metres wide.

Harecops: isolated Georgian stone farmhouse on the ridge of land between the Dove and Manifold Valleys, with a view towards Wolfscote Hill, inhabited by the author and his family for four years in the 1970s. It is passed again rather more slowly in the middle of Part V.

PART V

p.172. Pea Low: Locally to the Peak District "low" means a rise of ground, usually a prehistoric tumulus (Old English *hlaw*).

p.179. *hoquetting*: musical term, from the French for "hiccup" – a sequence of tones constantly passed from one performer to another, in its simplest form a melody using two tones in which each of two participants only ever sings or plays one of them.

p.182. *basso continuo*: the supporting bass line of 17th and 18th century European music, with chord structures above it indicated numerically.

scordatura: the practice of changing the tuning of (most commonly) the violin.

rilievo schiaccito: extremely shallow relief engraving on stone, as practised in the Italian Quattrocento.

p.183. *Palazzo del Capitano dei Populi* (and similar names): a kind of mediaeval Italian town hall, signifying self-government, republicanism and democracy of a kind. The Piazza del Popolo (p.44) would be the square in front of it.

p.185. my toy, my dump: both of these are also the names of instrumental musical forms current in late 16th Century England – short, dance-like, entertainment pieces, the latter quite sardonic.

a cobbler his wife and seven children… This is Frank i'th' Rocks Cave, between Wolfscote Dale and Beresford Dale. The cobbler is mentioned in several local guide books.

p.189. *In cielo circo*… In the sky [in heaven] I seek your happy face. Ungaretti, *Giorno per Giorno*, 7.

p.192. Elaine Scarry: in her book *The Body in Pain* (1985)

p.192. *O Delvig, Delvig*: This is a foreboding of the apparition of Shostakovich, quoting the title and incipit of the 9th song of his Symphony No. 14. The poem, by Wilhelm Küchelbecker (b.1797) is addressed to Baron Anton Antonovich Delvig (d.1831) (both were members of Pushkin's circle) and asks what reward an artist may expect promoting freedom and justice among villains and fools.

p.193. Leek. Town in Staffordshire, just off the hills six or seven miles to the west of where we are. By crossing the river the walker has just stepped into its administrative zone. The "good wine merchant" was also in Leek.

p.194. *jack-snipes*: This bird sometimes emits a strange "drumming" sound in flight, which is not vocal but produced by the tail-feathers; it will do it at nightfall and the sound can seem to come from the air all round you.

pp.196. Shallow Brown: title and refrain of a sea shanty, extant in many different versions, the gist amounting in some to "You're going to leave me," and in others, "I'm going to leave her."

p.197. *Luchistaya zvezda...* translated in the next three lines. Russian version of Michelangelo, 'Dante', set by Shostakovich as the 6th of his *Suite on Verses of Michelangelo*, op.145a.

p.199. *Quis dabit...* Which gives peace to the frightened population.

p.200. "Where does such tenderness come from?": Otkúda takáya néznost? Marina Tsvetayeva, the second of the six of her poems set by Shostakovich in his op.143a.

p.202. Archford Moor: The walker has now crossed the watershed between the Dove and Manifold Valleys and is descending to meet the River Manifold at Westside Mill.

p.203. original orthography: of the church anthem by Thomas Tallis: "If ye love me keep my commandements and I will pray the Father and he shall give you another comforter e'en the sprit of truth..."

p.205. time like a rolling dream. After verse six of the Isaac Watts' hymn *O God Our Help in Ages Past*: "Time like an ever rolling stream, Bears all its sons away; They fly, forgotten, as a dream Dies at the opening day."

the river bass: I have myself noticed, precisely at this spot and at night, a steadily repeated bass tone caused by the movement of water in the river as it rounds a bend when quite full.

p.207. artisans of Zaïre: refers not to Zaïrean commercial pop, but to ex-tribal amateur urban music for celebrations patronised by the poorer and more recently urbanised groups. See *Musiques Urbaines à Kinshasa* issued by Ocora Records, France 1986.

p.207. Apes Tor. The rock formation at the northern point of Ecton Hill (see note below). There is a large mineshaft in a cave here at road level and formerly a conduit brought running water to here from a reservoir further up the west side of the hill (mentioned later) which fell down the shaft to work the water-wheels of an underground pumping engine. So falling water was employed to raise water.

Sean 'ac Donncha: Singer from Connemara, in the style now known as Séan Nos, an elaborately ornamented solo singing.

p.208. Ecton. The two figures into which the speaker now divides go one each side of Ecton Hill, a ridge-shaped end of high ground in the western edge of the Peak limestone, and meet up again at Wetton Mill further down the Manifold Valley. Ecton Hill was formerly one of the biggest copper mines in Europe and is riddled with underground spaces as a result of this, its surface scattered with mine ruins, spoil heaps, shaft tops and tunnel entrances, most of them now absorbed by age into the hill's worn and bleak aspect. The mines all closed before the 20th Century.

p.209. I follow the river... From here until further notice the voice is that of the one who takes the road to the right, and walks downriver along the foot of Ecton Hill.

folding: horizontal rock strata folded by geological action into acute V or zig-zag shapes such as are exposed at the north end of Ecton Hill.

adits: horizontal tunnels driven into the hillside to reach the copper ores.

p.210. the Dorze: not another pygmy tribe but one in Ethiopia, also given to polyphonic singing

copper spire: There is an eccentric stone house with a copper spire pushed into the side of Ecton Hill here, built for the owner or manager of the copper mines.

p.211. O my son Absalom...: David's Lament for Absalom in the second book of Samuel, part of the text of two English anthems of the early 17th Century, by Tomkins and Weelkes, "When David heard that Absalom was slain..."

bureaucratic directive: At a number of road junctions in the Peak Park there are signs intended for touring visitors, which send you to the next village by the most circuitous route possible.

p.212. Dead miners carolling under the hill: When Vaughan Williams took down what has become known as the Corpus Christi Carol from a Mr Hall of Castleton Derbyshire in about 1900, he was told that every Christmas Eve the lead miners of Castleton would descend to the lowest part of the mine, and in an open space there set a candle on a piece of lead ore and sing the carol sitting round it in a circle.

p.213. high as kites: charcoal-burning produces narcotic fumes which are said to have been one of the few delights of the life of a charcoal-burner.

choir-boys dancing: not at all an unusual feature of the mediaeval cathedral.

I asked one of these blacks...: a passage spoken by a freedman to J. McKim c.1850, as quoted in *Negro Slave Songs* by M.M. Fisher, Cornell 1953. (The same passage is quoted from a different source by Geoffrey Hill in his essay "Language, Suffering, and Silence" (1998).)

p.214. She nurst him back... A lost quotation. It could be from one of the female cabin-boy songs, except that it doesn't seem to be in lyric metre.

p.215. O canny at night... From a Northumbrian traditional song addressed to a child. canny = clever; bonny = beautiful.

Lemady: title and addressee of an English traditional song, one of those (like the previous) set by Benjamin Britten. There are several other phrases from mostly well-known English songs in the three stanzas of which this is the third.

hilltop heretic: the Cathars at Montségur.

p.216. *tempiettos*: I understand this word (which occurs again later) to mean a small temple or chapel or a model of one. The famous one is that by Bramante at S. Pietro in Montorio, Rome, which is a circular memorial chapel in a courtyard.

p.218. leaving the door ajar... It is obvious that the speaker from this point onwards is the other of the two selves into which the protagonist divided at Apes Tor, and the scene returns to that point, taking a route on the other (western) side of Ecton Hill.

little lake: This is the reservoir for the Apes Tor shaft detailed earlier. The wooden fishing lodge at its corner was of course added after it fell into disuse.

p.219. William Lawes: English musician in the court of Charles I. Fretwork: name of a currently active viol consort.

p.220. On this side the hill remains sealed: i.e. there are no tunnel-entrances to the mines on the western side. Due to the disposition of the metallic veins they are all on the other side.

pp.220-1. Gather ye rose-buds... is of course Herrick and "I'll tell ye what befell me..." is adapted from his 'How Lillies Came White' as set by William Lawes.

p.221. on the top is a mine ruin: I have not discovered the name of this mine but of all the remains on Ecton it is the one which still stands out from the surrounding terrain, with bright ungrassed stone heaps, on the shoulder of the ridge-top.

p.222. *The Triumph of Time and Truth*: an early oratorio by Handel, originally Italian (1707). In the English version (1757) the final chorus of Act II begins "Ere to dust is changed thy beauty, Change thy heart and love pursue."

Beaker posture: i.e. tightly crouched knees to chin, like the inhumation burials of the British early bronze-age "Beaker" stratum, commonly interpreted as foetal.

p.223. What have you to show... adapted from an old coal miners' song.

p.224. Urizen: figure in William Blake's late long poems, held responsible for the restrictive condition of earthly life.

p.225. *de Humilitate*: from Madonna de Humilitate – one of the formats of Virgin and Child paintings in mediaeval Italy, showing Mary kneeling on the bare ground before the baby Jesus.

Cappella Pratensis: Dutch choir specialising in 15th Century continental liturgical music, which sings bunched together in front of one full-size choirbook. Pratensis: of the fields, as in Josquin Despres. (Plorans) ploravit in nocte: (She) weeping weepeth sore in the night, *Lamentations* I.ii.

ribbons on his bonny waist: marriage or betrothal tokens, as in the song "The trees they grow so high."

p.226. Inca summit child: it has only recently been proven by excavation that the Inca really did slaughter young children on the tops of mountains for ideological reasons, after making them walk up barefoot. Physiological evidence from frozen corpses has shown that at the moment of "sacrifice" the children were terrified.

p.227. it's the shaft mound: i.e. it is a mound of rocks cast up around and over the mouth of the vertical mineshaft, the top of which will now be concealed somewhere within it.

p.229. poison someone's bread: white lead, a by-product of lead production, was used in the 19th century to bleach bread.

p.230. Rákóczy March: This would be Berlioz's version, and the band probably Salvation Army. The march itself, said to have been composed by the gypsy musician János Bihary, was a rallying-point of the 19th-century Hungarian struggle for independence from Austria.

p.231. Blush Roses in a Glass: by Fantin-Latour, in The Fitzwilliam Museum, Cambridge.

Ivor Gurney: English poet and musician, 1890-1937, who habitually spent a whole night walking in the Gloucestershire countryside (and not sleeping in the daytime) until imprisoned for schizophrenia.

Drainpipe Shuffle: possibly Lonnie Donegan, but extensive research would be needed.

p.232. Roza Eskenasi. c.1895-1980: singer of Greek-Turkish ("rembetika") urban popular songs, mainly active in the 1930s.

p.233. sanza: west African term for the mbira or thumb-piano.

p.236. *Si je n'étais pas captive...* Victor Hugo, 'La Captive', set by Berlioz, opus 12. "If I were not a prisoner, I would like this country..."

pp.238. "The musicians follow the dancers..." This and the following references in this stanza and later are from the Hungarian-speaking population of Transylvania, and refer to the "dawn songs" which used to be sung with full instrumental accompaniment to mark the end of a night-long festivity, sometimes, as described here, as a feature of a processional back to home and normality.

The mention of recruitment here and on pp.247 and 249 is from the same area, though it happened in many places and probably still does – a regular season, in this case October, when recruitment teams went round the villages, taking away most of the young men to an uncertain future. The recruitment song, a kind of lament sung in the voice of the departing recruit, was one of the forms sung as dawn songs.

p.238. Last night I lay...: adapted from the ballad most popularly known as The Raggle-Taggle Gypsies.

p.241. Ciaran Carson: in his book on Irish music, *Last Night's Fun* (1996)

p.242. For my heart is always trembling... dawn: These words seem to be sung by Joe Heaney in a rendition of The Rocks of Bawn.

p.242. Much missed person... adapted from Thomas Hardy, 'The Voice' (Satires of Circumstance)

p.243. S.E. Rogie: "palm wine" singer and guitarist from Sierra Leone who settled in England and died in about 1995.

Munadjat Yulchieva: Singer from Uzbekistan.

Caruso: Italian operatic tenor, who died in 1921, so the memory is an error. The tenor heard in Manchester was probably Beniamino Gigli (1890-1957).

Belle Vue: former pleasure grounds in south Manchester including a large circular hall used for recitals, concerts, circuses, etc.

p.244. Dies Fleisch, das in den Staub… and other German in this stanza, is from the text (by Karl Wilhelm Ramler) of the oratorio *Die Auferstehung und Himmelfart Jesu*, by Carl Philip Emanuel Bach. "This flesh that crumbles into dust…" "Death, where is thy sting?" "Thy victory, O Hell, where is it? Ours is the victory."

p.245. a knight in the road: cf. the ancient ballad called by Francis James Child "The Fause Knight upon the Road". No. 3 in his collection of 1882.

p.247. Amédé Ardoin: Louisiana "Cajun" musician, died 1941 in an asylum, possibly as the long-term result of a violent racial attack.

p.248. *He do the song about the knife…* Dire Straits, 'Walk of Life' (known to me in a swamp pop cover version by Charles Mann). *song about the night* in previous editions was a mis-hearing.

towards Hulme End: i.e. through Alstonefield and on the road to the north, towards Harecops.

a sleep-over: in the sense meant when a professional nurse or carer watches over a patient at his or her own home through the night and is provided with accommodation for sleeping.

p.249. Nusrat Fateh Ali Khan: Pakistani devotional musician, singer in the Sufi Qawwali tradition. He died in 1997, which was towards the end of the writing of Part V.

He don't say nothin…: imperfect reminiscence of the song 'Ole Man River', from the musical *Show Boat*, which was mounted by Stockport Amateur Operatic Society in about 1953.

I want a record shop: a reminiscence of a poem by Frank O'Hara

XVII

Two Setts and Coda

(2005)

First Sett

(Of the hermit's cave at Cratcliffe Tor, near Winster, Derbyshire)

*

Crucifix and lamp niche carved in the wall
quiet breathing, slowly devolving thought,
wine corks and olive pips in the ash heap,
soft singing, dry earth, global home.

Prevent me from disheartening, spread
my thought into result, seal my song
in a small pot, my heel turning on the ground
at the centre, where the sky sits.

Night closes in, heat lifts from the valley floor,
the stars reappear, the grasses part
and they enter the earth, the sung men,
the traders, burdened with a constant elsewhere.

*

Crucifix and oil stoup
in the gritstone wall
a floating wick, turning
shadows. The book
sings itself into the sack of grain
the owl at the door
and the washing-up to be done.

Gladly, willingly, free of guilt,
free of not-guilt, fixing
sequences across
distant points, where
shadows gather, where
the living trade, and sing
their lives into the earth.
Everything I do is that song's descant.

The broken pot in the grave
outside the front door,
what you might wish to become:
shadows on the sea,
stronghold safe and sure.

*

Cross and cup scooped
in the living stone
in the earth, elsewhere.

For equity, for spread of gain
raise the white stones, the red
light on the shore when
the merchant ship rounds the headland.

Two pale lines on the ground
over the hill's shoulder.
The returning workman catches
the song in the night
from the wooded hillside
a faint light among the trees,
owl and badger signalling
beyond their species.

Intimately, in the village, turn
the dance, the baby's head towards.

*

Face gazing down, rush-light flame
marking eyebrows, inscribed into
the material as if through it,
from somewhere else.

Singing teacher, from somewhere else,
come and sing to me
down the ploughed fields
where the lapwings gather,
the incline, sing to me the elsewhere,
the outcome,
make it plain for all.

The incline, the outcome, I mislaid a life.
But the happy lads on the way home
notice a small light among foliage,
slowly falling to earth.

*

Human image, arms outspread – sign
of welcome, pain, abandon, chiselled
into hard earth and held in the cup
a floating light. Hierusalem, slaughtering
ground, turn and see.

I should be modern. The transport passing
overhead in the night, bearing trouble
to the ends of the earth. I cannot
be modern.

It remains with us,
everything we did that mattered,
everything we didn't do that
might have helped. Pasts accumulate
upon us like shining clouds.
We nourished a deaf white cat,
Adrienne and I. When it died we

*

The pictures on the wall, I can't
remember the pictures on the wall,
you shadows, reaching into life.

Every day at six the mill girls passed the window,
their clogs clattering on the stone streets,
calling and singing, six-day week.

Walk with us, take your part,
the need that cannot perish
that no plenty can ever sate
perches for a second on
the welcome tree and flies into the dark.

The dark land wrapped round us,
the shame of injustice and exactly why.
Nearly said so, but didn't, flew.
A life spent avoiding saying

And it says itself, the thin glass around the flame,
the final contract, dawn on shop corner.

*

Small light in a cave wall
floating flame in a pool of oil
above it some joker, some
punished man.

Love's punishment in the tall tower
what is it? to see the world stalking itself…

The men come home over the hill
carrying wood for the fire, toys
for the baby, the women do so too.
It is considered right to laugh and fuck.
By the owl too, calling
out of his food chain
and the nightingale all day long.

With my singing hand I rummage
echoes in the burnt archive, the dust of
forgotten signatures. There was
fair term in the original prospectus,
the welcome that constructs a town.
Phosphorescence in the sea, and the sky
open overhead. Same old tune,
we yearn for a fair and honest earth.

All the birds know it by heart.

*

Chiaroscuro. Not a luxury.
A labour, picking at the rock
for years, slowly realising
a quick thought. That there is
someone.

But there was no one.

Thumb-sucking question. They
move fast on all sides, the fat workers
tiring themselves on the land and its outcome,

Its incline, naturally. I love
that faint lack in the air when
the light stoops over the trees and
shrinks to a pale rectangle.

And the actively innocent,
the victims, for whom there is no one.

*

Shout of joy in death dump.
Cross and point, as on a map.
Lights converging to a town.

The image stands out from the wall,
solid, indicative, moves
almost. The earth moves.
The body fades. Is helped
into the earth.

Sheltered by yew trees, and below,
by the track, damsons. *Ten
thousand years, drinking of the wine.*
Messages of hope from besieged caves.
Poppy, moth, and candlelight.

Swish of car tyres passing in the night, in the rain,
minor A-road over a Suffolk heath, light
beams into the leaking cloud base and folds back down
and over they go for home, one after another, thousands
of homes, somewhere or never, refrigerators, hope.

And above, in the head arc, frightful machines,
in the speculation zone, above the clouds, star calipers
sharpened to a point, closing. Shout of joy or pain where
Africa turns back, and Arabia weeps
for her lost children. Clipping the heart.

*

Christ against the living tree
cut in stone, sunk
into hardheartedness.

A few olives in the late evening, and red wine,
saying the word, Africa,
into the night.

And starting up the song, that forgets suffering
completely. My poor mind, it says,
turns on the spot, in the glow of the world,
my alcohol and daisy brain.

Then says that other word, Rwanda,
into silence.

The hard heart breaks, the wax heart melts,
the final heart uncoils.

*

The terminated man, ghosted by light,
realised by night, thin taper
in a niche in the wall, Y-shaped shadow.

At night the stars gyrate on the axis
of the village plan, a cluster of poor huts
in miles of scrub. Sleep secure,
night bird on the roof-ridge
proclaiming common fate.

And with day, cloud chambers,
blue light ushering us to work,
the great milk-stained skies youth walks under.

Prolific, until the transport rolls up and
breaks the truce, and, full of hearted fervour,
names the victim, collapsing the sky props,
turning the black domino on its side.

Calipers and wedges. The future.
Poisoned the fields, and the sea,
slaughtered the livestock, only
Africa survived, singing
"I'm on the road again".
And the past widens before us, saying
it is love, it is love, that breaks the world.
But I wouldn't hesitate,
at any price.

*

Crucifix and lamp niche
solitary spirit in temporary accommodation
at home with the lynx and the bear.

Dark, you came and sat beside me
I lost half my wing, on waking
the sky was a dome in the rock, the wren
screamed past its entrance.

The hired men, bashing at the rock face
and walking back to the villages, singing
slow old songs. I believe
passionately that steady work
to a good purpose is true love.
The wren knows it exactly,
the moth expiring in éclat
no one called it art.

*

Cave wall crumbled into human form
arms outspread and the world is restored
to what it is, children playing in the square
under the coloured lights, thumb-nail
turning the screw-head.

Sings love into the roads and
up the steps and over the threshold
of the house, where we sleep each other's sleep
and mark to the inch the star measure
in the neighbour's eye.
And pray, and demand,
to be thus, at least.

No it is not granted. Doherty on the roads of Donegal,
wind and rain, a fiddle in a sack on his back. Arabia
howls. Tuning the earth.

*

By the thin light, watched
by the dead man, writing
new words in the old book.

The travellers' wagon passes over the brow
singing, scattering words into the fields.
Clown father pushes syllables together like
plug and socket, belches and falls asleep in the hay.

Gender merchant, with icy breath, love
hesitates. But knows no other inclination.

*

Years fighting bureaucracy, and finds
love is an ordered thing, requiring
good light for reading at night, little midges
squirming on the desk top.

There is a knock at the door. A small boy
stands there. "I have nowhere to go.
I'm hungry and I'm cold."

O steak-eating modernists, the lamp
dims and fails. Slowly, over centuries
the fourth estate advances. And where
are you then?

*

Desk top, death top. Sandstone inlier
yielding readily to the chisel, a watch-point
over the trade routes, guarded by a stranger.

To retire, to turn
face from world, ashamed to weep so,
being a king.

And those who return in the evening
know death is debated in caves in far
crannies of the forest hill, and nod so.
And grip the spade like a sceptre.

*

The stone man
sees all, the light enlivens his
frown, concealing the vast
animal resource, the golden wings
buried in the frown.

Everyone's wings, the wings of everyone,
shadowing the plain, descending on the hill,
the accusation, of the great wings, Yes,
you meant well, but did not open and beam.

Indeed I did not, I harboured resentment,
the children irritated me. But I go gladly.
Lay your last feather on me
like a dolmen cap
as the army rounds the bend.

*

So the image gets erased,
hope sunk into rock,
grasped.

We go but we shall be back, we shall
return here. Everything will be
as it was before the war. Walk up the steps
and enter the house. Same old
address, same postcode, same subsidence.
Say hello at the bar, yes, we're back.

The world is peeling apart but
it'll be over, and we shall be back, sporting
the uniform in which death is dressed.

Butterfly on the lemon balm,
gentle drumming,
my worst fears, my sweet rest.

Second Sett

(Of the villages of the Mara Valley, Maramureș, Transylvania)

*

Heaps of fruit piled up against the houses,
grandfathers piled up in the ground,
churchyard fruit, pears, cherries,
travellers selling small bags of hazels.

If all the world is to go the same way,
all one empire, all serving the one broker –
a thin sigh in the fields, baby
where did our love go?

The house in the fields
breathes, its timbers
flex in the night changes,
the star wheels churn.

Piles of apples outside in the yard
yellow and red in separate heaps
slowly, under careful control
rotting into the music.

*

And all our promises
                        Dim light beaming
into the dark street through a doorway,
shadows passing, many shadows, blurred
into the night and the soil of the road.

Kindling stacked up in the yard,
quiet talking behind the wooden fence,
shadows passing like smoke in the street –
familiar journeys across the town: questions,
about seeds, electricity bills, the exact wording
of a fourth verse, carried from door to door.

Shield us from the arm in the sky
the glittering scar badges
when the hand drops the cash.

Partners, workmates, door
to door, guard your
hope, columns of shade.

*

Guard your offer, the trust that spreads through the towns,
the open door, the carved double arc
catching the shadow at morn and eve.
Strangers welcomed, departures wept, a real town.

I, or whoever this language pauses at,
pause again, where the railway crosses the road,
the slow fire threaded through lives,
the aromatic smoke above the roofs,
the dusty hands that hold hope forth.

Meadow light on the iris
and the microscope and the bauble, turning
the market calendar, shunting the days,
the doors that stay open.

*

Late afternoon, a layer of wood smoke
hanging over the village
like something asleep.

Far away across the world
the corporate voice dries to a hiss.
A malicious hiss.

And in all this country, these thousands of households
there is an annual fair of all the pitches of the heart,
house to house in sub-zero temperatures the true love
chalice is brought with singing, clear, direct, locked
in its form, echoed from the hard earth. It is
the only corporate voice. The only defence.
The red cusp at its centre.
The rest is a dry hiss.

*

Stratum of wood smoke, pale blue over
the village roofs, the beasts
returning from the fields
walk down the street, turning
each into its own yard.

*We thrust our hands into dirt and grease
and fray them against rope, but we
hold the crown of the years, it is we
who sew the calendar into the sky.*

Night arrives, the smoke disperses, the sky clears
and the plough, the great plough above
signifying nothing now,
but a far greater nothing
than any President.

I thought so, in the small room
made of wood
the flies veer to the light.

*

In the stillness an evidence, plain
there in the air above us,
brother, sister,

Mud on your shoes,
standing still in the tides
of expansion, and the wreck
of the communal tone –
markets strung on fear.

Your steady patient walking, sibling,
in the rain, among fruit trees
and dark haystacks, laughing
at the new rhythm.

*

A ceiling, translucent over
our anxieties and calm,
someone walking by the river, casting
a shadow into the air above.

The anxieties knitted into our calm,
us someones, walking under our thoughts,
the light hovering where we stoop.

We stress the condition
but the fruit is continual.

Leaning against the wall.

Old man with a little plum-wood flute.

*

Curtains of onions and maize strung up
on the verandas to dry, the smoke rising when they
fire the yard ovens in the late afternoon
for tomorrow's bread.

The car mechanic sits on the doorstep drinking beer,
the mountain behind him turns black.
He is the mechanic of all moving things,
he is not in a hurry and he doesn't want to be paid.
The mountain is wooded to the top.

The work lies there like a song, waiting.
The lives sing their completions, constantly
infolded resolution, daily work
of the whole valley, singing out tomorrow's fear.

*

The white smoke layered over where and when,
over the name, and the day, over all of us.

In that day the renewed agreement,
the empty river bed full of red leaves
winding down the pastures among
haystacks, and small trees full of
small red apples and no leaves…

Yes, we are willing to stay around
for a while. We believe.

And say, good night, *noapte buna,*
smoke rising to the star base.

*

Columns of smoke rising
from the 5 o'clock fires
all over the valley, tomorrow's loaves
waiting like moons, like slow clocks.

Roads of wet earth between the houses.
"Look at this miserable place I live in,
look at this mud, this filth."

Look at us, developed, perfectly smooth,
perfectly dry. Listen,
where did our bombs go?

Our love, our bombs,
our loving bombs. Our contradictions
waiting like mines, in complete silence.

*

Open land, then forest, then air.

Leonardo Bruni said that the harmonious
workings of the institutions of Florence
derived from the beauty *and geometry*
of the Tuscan landscape.

A thin track, a line in the grass across
the pastures and over the riverside humps –
everywhere worked, the shape of the place
carved from work, lines curving to meet,
leading ultimately homewards.

*

The forest walking backwards
far away that other land
green eye in the branches – *this fear
protects our children from our success,
and the astronomy from our failure.*

I am nothing to this place, a
hole in it. But the tears they cry with
reach my lip.

Compatriots of the unimportant spaces
slow backs that bear the entire geometry
carrying the can to the bar, mending
the bicycle, tuning the viola,
as the hills swell into night again
and another wedding tilts
the earth into sense.

(Dawn Song)

Evidently, the world, and
the pine twig, the process.
I have held this hope for years.

A pain to the left of the stomach
another behind the thigh,
hair that was once black as night.

Will I lean into you
at midnight, will I
see you from a grey fortress

On the long worked land
washed in rain
not looking back.

Coda: 14 Poems

(Of driving westward across central Europe in an old Renault Espace indulging serial breakdowns, fleeing winter, with interventions from other journeys at other times)

The Towns along the Tisa

The towns along the Tisa, the flaking walls, the ragged squares, Habsburg halls and communist concrete eroding in the river wind. Border towns stuck with closed borders, broken bridges over the Tisa, holes in the roads, buffalo carts ignoring the traffic lights. A shepherd with staff and cloak stands outside the Hotel Tisa, gypsies in orange skirts and wide-brimmed black hats cluster on corners. People wandering the streets hoping to pick up some work or leaning against walls on market day holding in front of their midriffs the one object they've got for sale, a model house or a packet of tea. The last offices in the west, heated by small woodstoves, desks heaped with impractical directives, as the first bits of snow descend and everything gets dark together.

Kalotaszeg

Low hills carved into terraces
neglected now, wild grass. Trans-
sylvanian air, a music
as of saddened royalty

Who became migrant workers, drivers
of long-distance lorries
with the same patience, the same
gateway, sun and rope

Moon and string. We forget slowly
the star's aim on the bare hills,
remember in a different script
the answer of the heavy beast
snorting behind the gate.

Consequence at world pace,
slower than the death birds.

The Crowd Yelled Out for More

Suddenly, in a cellar bar in Oradea badly heated in late October, coats on waiting for dinner, a few young people drinking beer and the Romanian edition of Who Wants To Be A Millionaire on the screen behind us with nobody paying any attention. They should know, the uselessness, of riches to poverty.

I realised what was coming out of the speakers was A Whiter Shade of Pale, Procol Harum, 1968. I was alone again, Andrew Crozier was leaning over the billiard table in a pub in St. Leonards. I was recently married, I was doing summer language teaching. The future was something completely different from what we now inhabit. It was all over, the death-dealing state, blasting the necessary outsider, the furious rage that maintains vast privilege, it was finished, we had hope we had normality before us. I was back in my cell, quietly singing the nonsense.

Pilliszántlaszló

Forest paths in Autumn
columns of sky "heavenly blue" between
brown trees with orange leaves.

The wind moving slowly
through the tree tops
on long legs.

Frustovento

The wind walks the grass. Bee orchids, crickets.
The good, solid house, the stone house on
a platform rising from the brush of the hillside
under Monte Subasio. Clover, trickling water.

The closed house, platform for an angel's foot,
an angel from the paintings over the hill. Voices
gently in the ear of the mind, negotiating
a temporary pact with the gravities of the world.
Crotchet of green leaf chained to the solar system
where the angel's foot descends, and lightly rests

For a moment, on a roof tile, or neatly avoiding
a buttercup, and is gone. Does the hero's heart
burn for something grander? Or the earth beg release
from hearts with no time for such smallnesses?
Begs and pleads, for the tear to fall as due.

Schiele

The skin also marked
where the foot landed
or the tear fell, touched
blue and green, faint
bruising, thin membrane
letting through
the shades of society. Eyes
staring out in alarm.

Stuck in Vienna for Two Weeks Watching CNN Every Evening

Of course we inhabit decisions not made by us
or anyone we can trace, decisions threaded into
the streets and forests from impossible distance.

Forget Tuesday, forget Vietnam,
day to day, door to door,
bomb first, forget later.

Walk the streets, forgotten children,
dust of burning villages on your shoes,
walk the forests, learn to live.

In this house
Franz Schubert wrote
An die ferne Geliebte baby,
was our love not here?

In these clean streets
not made by us, this
integral distance, the ghosts
that walk it.

Room 40, Frühstückspension Caroline, Gudrunstrasse 138, Wien 9

The courtyard tree swaying in the wind.
If the business is still going strong
how can you bear to die? If the space
owned is cleansed of failure, the walls
impeccably bare, the one tall tree reaching
beyond the courtyard roofs and so
catching the wind, how can anyone
bear to live? What is there to forget?

As if every block didn't proclaim a history,
the pink arches, the eagles with straight wings,
the world's savagery always ready.

Withered flowers.
You are rest and peace.

A Cold Room in Granada

A voice calling in English under the trees
of the square. Already they are going
for their newspapers. She has
arrived safely, go back to sleep.
The news ends where the story begins.

And we shall dress our minds
in all the hope of the story –
the hill covered in white houses
the long story, the carefully turned
corner of alabaster holding a piece of light,

The measuring wheel, carefully turned,
the electric fire hung on a coat-hook,
the water as it flows over the sculpted edge,
agreement between things and people,
the trees at night full of birds.

Chattering heart, turn finally
to the end of the story in clear cold light:
the moment achieved, snow on marble,
people living in caves, singing
bodies fruit and die.

Terezín

The world stands. Visitor, reader,
be quiet, learn to die. Lover of sleep,
learn to fall, into a small space
with a plaque on the wall saying: HERE...
This place, this grassy ground where it swells
here against the wall. Was brought here.
And forty thousand more, one by one.

Sang, danced, acted here. Worked,
as people must. Killing work. Nobody
is disqualified from the duties compassion
exacts, nobody is privileged by this suffering
and the vastness of resource it sets in motion.
Vast Europe, breaking circuit at a small
garrison town, the mountains in the distance.

The mountains in the distance, breaking Europe
across a small child's arm. The small child left
a crayon drawing and what the drawing said was,
Agree to suffice, not to surpass, agree to be
the actual person, nothing else will break
the circuits of plunder. The drawing was of
two beds and a coat hanger.

After Terezín

So on the bus back, mountains
in the distance, fading fields,

Compassion without privilege or guilt
peace over Judaea,

The stars signing their
light into shrines in the desert.

O that your state power
were buried in those shrines.

The bus rattles, I hum
songs to my bones.

Withered flowers, you are
sense, you are light.

Alstonefield, After Dinner

Leaving the George Inn to walk down
the small road to Milldale
it is so quiet as the light diminishes
pale things begin to glow on the ground.

Each tree makes a slight whispering,
bat flits overhead, gnat
attempts to enter nostril – solitary,
you are free to let your emotions expand.

Light peels off the downy slopes
green to silver. Someone has chalked
DAD HURRY UP on the steepest
part of the road, and this grand

Sense expands, towards
people living in their structures
everywhere against each other
in a common fall

Turning at the day's end
into the movement of the earth.
Entering sleep, knowing nothing,
the one moment free of harm.

Across Central Europe

How much more is there to add to what
we can never forget, and what
will happen to it in the end when all
the memory goes out like a light switched off?

Forest and mountain without end.
Night falls, clustered lights, of villages
and small towns on ridge tops or the sides
of big valleys, deepening green.

Ride on old car, *bockwurst* at the services,
snow squalls, what is the future of memory? –
keep it rolling towards us, the road under
and the dark over, all coming down together
to the cathedral lights of Limburg.

Zum Weißen Roß

To shine in your eyes like
the cathedral lights of Limburg.

And in the morning watch the frost
rising from the river.

XVIII

Poems and Prose,
Cambridge (ii)

(2000-2013)

Pieces written at the time of writing *Excavations*

1. *The Songs*
When the dead awaken and lament the condition of the living, the failure of language that cannot say what we are or what we do / a sound in the streets, a smear on the rim of a glass / someone passes by carrying a bird cage through the streets of London looking for a removal van because a *non sequitur* is an unbearable thing so follow it, follow that forward van as the old man said. The old man is laid gently in his grave, to join all the other old men. Where are the songs we were promised?

Biting the tongues that feed them, rising over the fiery trees to die above this calm land full of instruction.

2.
Write from henceforth, blessed are the dead and suddenly here they are, sitting under the pine trees playing cards, with musicians and dancers, with wine and food, ceramic tallies at their elbows. The moon reflected in the dark stream, the stars among plum blossom... Tuning lutes and zithers, these homiletic skeletons under a grey mound on a northern moor, *in cortesia* / setting us dreams of abundance to challenge everything we know, making poetry, the scoundrels.

3. *From an abandoned alley*
Hands claw at newsprint as newsprint claws at minds, force shoots from finger-ends. Whose hands? Whose minds? Where does disaffection become creation? What messages lie in the rubbish, the uncaring *disjecta membra* of the construction industry, the illegible numbers? The homeless in the streets, the sleeping-bag bed in the closed shop entrance and these are not fragments or waste but entire meanings at which the captains of the earth blink.

Hands and faces embedded in black surfaces, traces of people, faint outlines, dimly glowing quarters, profiles of wrist and shoulder, indistinct lettering... Buried in/ projected onto/ black tarpaulin banners rampant in decay. Traces of life in the tarry surface, movements of small winding shadows. And shall these one day speak, or is it an attempt to regenerate a society buried for ever under tarmac? The sleeping heads in the shop entrance, outside this turmoil. An anger which is / is not political.

Broken, failed, or unformed limbs, people become graphemes burned and printed into fired surfaces. Death floating on the sea as a flotilla of small lights. Little bells, like goat bells, tinkling through the night in the harbour of a small seaside town, floating eyes under closure. We wave the flags of poverty and obscurity behind the hill and fall nightly into the dream of belonging, anxiety and peace, death's musicians. For death isn't the beginning or end of anything. Death is the central edge.

"How slow the wind [that blows these things away], how slow the sea [that calls to foreign shores], how late their [banners] feathers be." Q.E.D.

Note: From an exhibition by Peter Kennard at The Darkroom, Cambridge, 1995. Ends with the quotation of a complete poem by Queen Emily Dickinson which was set touchingly by Howard Skempton.

5.
A step forward and the past clarifies. Geometry of the heartland, moon marks on the ridge, the river stepping down the vale... What we work for lies here in the decided risk, the speech saying yes, on, yellow feather at the world focus as the chest empties into [song] bursts into [help].

Later is the silent river enclosed in night, the ferryman leaning on the pole, later is sleepless dream. And why so far from the earth and its light, the beautiful earth? The black boat on the far marshes, no one knows why.

But that our story brings us here, to darkness and silence, broken by the slight push of water against the bank. And is completed, formed, a cup set on the shelf of a corner cupboard where the mouse p[r/l]ays at night.

6.
The clue to the Neolithic star-farmers is song: they were mainly interested in singing. So all we know of them is their tombs.

The music that sets a valley in the mind. Up which we ramble, you and me (who are you?) hand in hand… up the valley over the pass and down to the town. Towns are for us being buried in later.

7.
The man in Jack Yeats' little water-colour (in the library at Sligo) singing his heart out in a village street in the middle of the night *O Sailor Rose of the Parting Seas* stands still and sings, his mouth a round O in a fat face, the flower tossed in the wind releases its pieces one by one. His heart stands round him like a stone column.

Blind Lemon in some whorehouse, waiting, shuffling the epic phrases back and forth, two matches left, don't you leave me here. A cigarette, a column of smoke ascending.

"They had these emigration parties, when the son of the house was to go to America. And they lasted all night with the music and the dancing. And at the end, before it was dawn, the young man would pick up his sack and go, and they would all stand outside the house and watch him walking away. And the custom was that he would have a box of matches, and every now and then as he walked down the valley he would strike a match and throw it into the air. So they watched these little flares descending the valley until he went round the corner and there were no more. Probably they would not see him again."

The vinyl decays, the magnetised molecules on the tape coating shift back to the earth's fields, the laser marks on the CDs break into rust. The original voice heads out from the harbour past the metal man, rides the corrugated shining and sails for ever the arriving oceans.

Messenger Street
In memory of Douglas Oliver

I.

In the harbour, in the island, in the Spanish seas...

In the hospital, on your death bed, which you suspected it might be,
you became again the beautiful boy your sister painted:
very thin, wide eyed, hood of grey hair, bright and inquisitive.
"It's as if," you said, "some god has decreed, this writing
has to stop." You explained about the cancer, and Paris
turned its back on us, the Paris of wine and poets and
southern seas had thrown us out: we were cast into the world's
cold fields together, you and I, to wander away from all the love
we'd ever known. You wept, as you should. You had plans.

That night I crossed one of those steep, tiring footbridges over
the Canal St-Martin as a return to the uncaring mainland we
construct for survival, but with a new badge close to my heart,
a cameo there of your new image, focusing the whole tenor
of your work on a helpless creature sinking into its cot.
But bright of eye, and bearing that brightness on to a future
somewhere else, of which we know nothing, taking that
brightness away from us for ever, to some other purpose.

And the god who decreed this writing had to stop suddenly
whisked you away, over his back like a baby in a sack and strode
off beyond the outer suburbs into a vast outer darkness
in which a tiny light shone, a foetal worm gyrating
in impossible distance and this was you and the entire city
of your enterprise, a star-thought diagram, a rose in night's eye
as the months pass and small flames descend.

Messages, which if we can reach them strip us of our privilege
and leave us like old babies dazzled in the new day. They
lie around everywhere – in our hearts, in your books,
in the air and the streets, in the very gutters of Paris.

I pick one up outside an Algerian cassette shop. It says,
"I must seek the goodness appropriate to my flawed life."
It says, "Thus would we pass from this earth and its toiling,
Only remembered for what we have done."

And what have we done, what is the best we have done? –
spoken the truth, sown the seed, which opens somewhere else,
where someone knows nothing of this name, this death, this darkness,
the future of our words and deeds a line of light on the horizon
towards which a heron flies, slowly, beating from the heart, slower
and slower. Stately bird, messenger bird, bird of good omen,
guide us to that gap in harm.

2

Douglas, listen to me, there are people in the world
with real hope, whose lives cannot be an incompletion.
I have seen them dancing and singing
and sighing in the rain and going back
to where they live, in small flats above bars
somewhere beyond Gare du Nord. "When will Algeria
ever know peace?" they sing, and we who
cannot know their secret joy cannot answer.

With what fullness they enter the dance, is that
the measure of your death? Is it so far to a meeting place?
I don't know. I believe in a passionate transcript
that engages the whole place, the whole city stirring
in its separate sleeps and winding into the dawn,
where after a long night an arm goes over
a neighbouring shoulder, and the doubt folds into the love.
We are at our best when we reach that edge of stillness,
a line of light growing at the end of night
writing the ancestral store of kindness into the day
where we make perfect sense – shared,
and its failure, with the lost nations, don't we?

3

We are at the source of the music, which will always,
like water, return to where it once has been.

Yes, we are going home, we are ahead of us.
We have nothing in the end, which opens the door
of the first house we ever knew. Tears flow
down your face to know your welcome there,
in the final closure of your enterprise to find
an access back, to where you started.

And the evangelists are singing and dancing
in the cavernous street. We stop our ears,
we don't want to hear that, we know better.
We know nothing, and the heart sighs for such
plain hope, sighs for the one thing it can truly know:
we are in death with fields and purposes

Whose light spreads over corrupt spaces
and lightly kills them. We have a strength
in this clearance, deaths clearing death.
Mahlathini died too, and Rogie, I don't know
where any of them is now. Such lives
form a building site in the possible city

Where all the failure gathers and offers the world
something, something to engage with, a way
into a future, a thought that opens a door.
Listen to it, that distant singing, through
the mist on the hospital window, the gleam
in the glass that burns the heart out, the completion.

And we'll go together, arm in arm we'll go, in some
format of the world the world doesn't recognise,
and sit by the river and watch the cathedral
on the island and the light passing over the water
and sort out the whole bloody mess. Two old blokes

dead and alive, talking and silent, dreaming
of betterment, eyes full of common sky.

4.
HALF-LIGHT OF DAWN
A translation of Baudelaire, 'Le crépuscule du matin'.

The reveille sang out in the yards of the barracks,
and the morning wind blew on the street lamps.

It was that time when a swarm of harmful dreams
makes the dusky youths twist and turn on their pillows,
when, like a bleeding eye that throbs when it moves
the lamp makes a red stain on the daylight, when
the soul, fretted and heavy under the weight of the body,
mimics the hostility between lamp and light.
Like a face full of tears that the breezes wipe clean,
the air is full of the tremor of vanishing things
and men and women tired of language, and tired of love.

Here and there the house chimneys began to smoke,
the women of the town, their eyelids pale,
their mouths open, slept their stupid sleep.
The homeless old women, dragging their thin cold breasts,
blew on the embers and blew on their fingers.
It was that time when, what with the cold and the dearth
the pains increase of women in labour.
Like a sob interrupted by a froth of blood
the far cry of the cockerel tore apart the misty air,
a sea of fogs washed the buildings
and people in pain in the depths of hospitals
let out their final rattle in uneven hiccups.
The party-goers walked on home, wrecked by their efforts.

Dawn shivering in a green dress with pink roses
advanced slowly towards the deserted Seine,

and dark Paris, rubbing its eyes,
reached for its tools, old working man.

Note.
Douglas Oliver died on Good Friday 2000 in Paris. Messenger Street *quotes several times from his poetry, and also from songs sung by L'Orchestre National de Barbès, Coope Boyes and Simpson, Mahlithini Nezintombi Zomgqashiyo, and the Seventh Day Adventists Students' Association Chorale of Soweto.*

Alstonefield Part VI

The value of common emotions concerning
the passing of time. The counting of joys,
and changes of love, the sad persistence of the days
dragging our hearts out of us – more than the world,
more than the silence of work these things
convene our powers. Pain and promise move
the hand to sign the contract and we are again
engaged, reader, by a factor of the earth bowling
between us. Quickly on a warm day I walk up through
the smell of moist leaves to a sheltered summit.

And all the people in the land, as the clouds clear,
without priority, the fruit of work, all pain and
sorrows over. These are the ghosts in the white stone,
written in the strata: Go down, you blood red roses.
And all the work in the land, as the stars fade, doesn't
bear more result than a leaf reaching the ground, all
its joys a history. Such are the songs that surround us,
near and far to comforting me, shadows on the sea.
So with some sense of purpose on a thick morning I
pass by empty fields to a tree-crowned pinnacle.

Today there will be a wedding in the village. This
village here, grey houses together like a cemetery.
And those other villages, full of people, busy working,
crowding the streets all day long moving, talking,
leading the beasts, bread ovens smoking in the yards,
everything out in the open. And other villages,
as the soldiers depart, human corpses in the street,
the houses heaps of smouldering ash, women some-
where behind the trees wailing. And the cuckoo in
all these places signalling its everlasting troth.

And the first swallows arrive, diving the ridges.
What is there beyond this knowledge but death
and fear, what is there to learn in the cyclopaedias
of failure? The morning lark haunts the
falling air sweeter and gathers from its throat
the whole armoury of the possible as a practical
course: known result, true outcome and
strong memory, when the gates open,
the creaking wooden gates without which
the gates of the mind will never open.

Those words first occurred to me (the last 20)
while listening to the group IZA in a smoke-filled
cellar underneath the Metropol in Cluj last May.
I wish you had been there, gentle observer
of these preparations, moving like gossamer
over the far fields. There is something sweetly
definitive in the grasshopper's lament that sinks
deeper into the possible world than any scriptural
displacement, any designated topping. They played
from midnight to three without stopping.

And the place rang and the rafters sang and those
who remembered the villages got up and danced
the dances they were born to. Something had survived.
Now back in the opaque world I clutch my lunch
and walk across the fields looking to left and right
for there are no paths here and security devices
have been purchased at high prices almost everywhere,
making us all feel rather insecure as we bear the burden
of the endless creation of markets from cradle to grave.
One day we'll work a way out of this costly safety

And attacks of peace-of-mind. But I got here, I walked
unobserved (fearing the shouts of angry farmers) over
the stone-walled fields and climbed up Steep Low
and settled in a niche with my packages. And here I am.
Down there the village lies doggo, like a coin
in the earth, like an illegible stone, this village here.
And those others, full of life and death, full of
continuity, continue, somewhere beyond the line of hills,
beyond us and our parental ills, beyond guilt and favour,
the vast labouring populations work their wills.

The universities of the western world are full
of people in highly privileged positions making
great moan. While in those villages incessant toil
bursts out singing. Sadly too, of the bird winging
away for ever, the hopeful messenger, but held deep
in the throat wither all returns. There we have it,
there the maimed and the oppressed unite in a sleep
truer than the narrows of day. Indeed it is our habit
to sing at day's end, in the light we have preserved,
all the prizes the soul has ever deserved.

Sing, rise, turn, advance, offer, kiss, dance.
Do this for me, wedding villagers, before I go.
Spin your question on the stone hub: *When
shall we ever know peace?* In the passing
of how much time as bird after bird life after
life ruffles its body and leaves the ring and another
wedding is declared, the musicians are again notified
their assistance is required in the attempt to chime
a future out of nothing. And we do: acts of hope out
of ruin, gather, turn, kiss, weep, shout, dance.

Our good songs have their melancholy ring
at the heart of procreation. *My rose, think well
of the beginning and the end, with whom you will cover
the world before your eyes. For it is not borrowed bread
which can be given back, neither is it unearned money
which can be spent, nor is it a hot pillow you can
turn over. You have found, rose, your life's partner,
winter blossom, fallen bud.* So they sing,
and dance it, in the dying villages not yet dead
to which increasingly my heart's dance is led.

Through the streets of Europe in the metal dawn is led.
Streets of northern Paris in the rain, under the railway
at Barbès selling fruits and spices crying *When will Algeria
ever know peace?* and working for a real future, which we
can never know, which is neither hope nor dream but
a movement, towards a space opening. And the whole
of the past is drawn into it. Then death cannot be
an incompletion – all the people in the land, all
pain and sorrows over, turn their heads to the east,
as if to the faint sound of maybe a wedding band.

The view from here is difficult, the village down there
somewhat round the corner, I catch the north edge.
The view towards Paris from Belleville one misty morning:
small parks and white apartment blocks clouding
into the sky, the city in its opacity. You don't see it
but you know it's there. That vast sea of lights, throne
of promise, the surface of it. Douglas Oliver, with
a brandy and a cigar on the top floor of Tour Montparnasse,
or sitting on the slope of Montmartre at night, in pain,
his work silenced. Talking to the rubbish man,

the man from the east, the man from poverty. Not,
though, the only man. Poetry, impossible beast,
lifts on the wings of everyone, every lost alcoholic
camped in the central reservation of every roundabout
every forgotten island in creation, the heart of
every American soldier. Has no choice in this. Sets
the song in the air that forgets suffering completely
and turns in a momentary space of truth and safety
thinning at the edges, where the town opens out
and I sit on a hump viewing the vast hope drawn.

Unsettled because when I arrived in Alstonefield
I found the B&B had gone out of business, combination
of fatigue and Health & Safety regulations and all
the rest seemed to have gone "up market", combination
of greed and pastoral nostalgia. The water still
springs at the foot of the hill, the root still grips the stone,
those who can pay more inherit a rubber duck, and a star
scorches a path through the grass for a neighbour's sorrow.
I'd lost my rhythm, my recurrence, and ended up
at The Greyhound at Warslow.

And from there get in short time to the top of Ecton
in the late afternoon, in the dull light, and lean
on the summit post. The great hill scattered with
tumuli and mine-heaps. Such hopes for the world
as old socialists entertain belong here in bleakness
and raised distance. Where the devil's toe ripped
the earth the future angels sing. Lend them aid, anyone
with half a care, take your part in the silent chorus
spreading over the forsaken grass, spoil heaps, plastic
buckets and sheep shit. Gargle triumph to the age of debit.

I lean on the trig post. This really is my place, an
historical landscape completely unknown to the
heritage traders, a ridge top to deter all seekers
after loveliness, but beautiful. Crouch under
a thistle here and catch the verticality of fear.
Fall asleep on the downward slope and hear
the world cussing itself in stones and moss.
I sink into the wind, I squat on the tumulus, I
spy the stark stone-heaps on the far edge where
the last theatre closed. I am at least my own boss.

Rough pasture and mine mounds up here. Fallen
ground, crumbled stone, rusty barbed wire, red
yellow and blue plastic buckets among patches
of sheep shit, O God this earth is given us.
It is ours. And what are we to the godly book-keepers
but plastic buckets that hold something for a bit,
something nice, something nasty. Something that needs
to be disposed of. Shan't we each eventually
fan across the landscape like spreading lights
like lost kites in the wind of multiplying nights?

A strange sense of being observed, from the next hill,
from the small back window of a stone farmhouse half
a mile away, from the Christian despot himself. And
always that sound in the air, a groaning
that stretches from city to city across the land,
under the burthen of fear, for there is more profit
to be made from fear than anything else and easier.
It is our moan for the end of Old Europe, our
secret song, that gives delight and hurts not,
our unsellable souls vibrating in the overtones.

It was stronger on Morridge. I drove up there later,
at twilight, and stopped in the lay-by where
the phone box used to be, since liberated,
and looked out over miles of edge-land merging
into low Britain, as broadcast. Tiny sharp points
of light sprang up, gathering to a swollen
cluster down the vale: Leek. And that sound, more
than ever pressing down from the sky to tell us
we are run by those who gain. In a sense it is true
of poetry also, and paradisal homes. I think

it is time to stop, mid stanza mid flow mid
nettle-patch atop ugly hill, sensing the song wrapped
in the overtones of the common complaint,
a song of pure delight with no justification,
orchard colours sprung from the metal files. Posit
this as a human constant and stop, demanding nothing.
Hum it down the hill, leave it to the world.
Walk on the bones of the dead, start like a bird.

Notes to *Alstonefield* Part 6

This is a separate poem, but which retains its title because of its continuity from, and references to, *Alstonefield*. A number of things not noted here will be found in the notes to that text.

IZA. A Romanian semi-professional group of musicians named after the valley of the Iza in Maramureş.

Steep Low. A rise of ground in the fields near Pea Low (*Alstonefield* page 172 and note on page 252), a rocky outcrop crowned with trees but sometimes interpreted as a burial mound.

"*My rose, think well...*" quoted from a Transylvanian wedding song. See the third of *Four Transylvanian Songs*.

Ecton Hill: site of the "sphinx" episode in *Alstonefield* Part V.

Warslow. A village to the north-west of Alstonefield beyond the Manifold Valley on higher ground, thus off the edge of the Peak limestone dome, on gritstone.

Morridge. An edge representing the far (west) side of the gritstone moors from Warslow, site of the telephone box mentioned in *Lines on the Liver*, Appendix. The movement here is as if the choice of direction made at the crossroads in *Alstonefield* (page 201) had been re-thought and a decision made to proceed westwards, towards the conurbation in the distance below.

The Glacial Stairway

In the summer of 1956 John Stanley, the art master of Stockport Grammar School, led a group of boys, including myself, then aged 15, over a mountain pass in the Pyrenees, from Tarascon-sur-Ariège in France into Andorra, by a little used route which he had discovered. The distance walked was about 50 kms horizontally and 1 km vertically. The vertical part was done in one hard day-long slog near the beginning, to get over the pass known as Port de Siguet and into Andorra. In June 2004 we repeated as much of this walk as we could manage, given more difficult weather conditions with a lot of snow still lying on the upper slopes, and streams which had to be crossed badly swollen by meltwater. Partly by subterfuge, we did gain the upper slopes on the Andorran side and I was again descending the great valley through El Serrat, Llorts, Ordino, to Andorra la Vella, places well remembered but significantly changed in the intervening 48 years.

Part One

This is me 48 years ago, this is 48 of my years, the same valley
the same sky's water crashing down the gully the same
striving uphill, taking the strain, bearing the weight.
48 years, something happened in the world, what was it?
Intentions conjoined and dispersed, soldiers died.

Then I was young and in company, now we tread the steep paths together,
two experiences conjoined. And we note as we did not then
the flowers all around and the valley full of the sound of falling water,
the fleeting hopes as the air opens before us. We form from this air
the names that stand behind us: birds, flowers, insects, villages,
everything we know, and the dead of seven wars.

To walk with thought in the very muscle, of answering, thought of
Un mundo mejor es posible, taking the strain of disappointment by the thrush's
peal of pain in the dark wood. From which we emerge into the open valley
and thought of a possible speech, one that must be true, and open, and must
do good, where good can be done, and where's that? So rarely here.
Clear river shooting over stones, where is our power zone?

All of the present and all of the past, good-bye. Ahead of us
our strength is trailing away. My eyes hurt, and legs and back,
and the news places a sciatica across my frontal dream, a burning thing,
a mask. We look up to the concealed seeds, the invisible day stars
as the ground plunders our energy and the path vanishes into a stream.

Vanish with it into 48 years, excavate the air for signs of hope.
There are such: the behaviour of a beetle, the communal will
when it is free to breathe. Grass, stones, help me will you – think!
What's the answer, what are we going to do with the world?
We're going to forget it. And it us.

Had I brains and courage, I would chuck all this poetry into the skip
wouldn't you? If you thought you could actually do something to the good
that would last. Beauty may last, that stands in the space between
stone and hawk, sheer persistence on the painful routes,
where the land turns thought into its own substance, of rock,
of rhododendron bushes, of pouring water, of heart beats.
And the turning dance on each step, of modernity, the search
for inhabitable centres.

Guided by the mountain's shadow, the rock planes, the lines
of the hibiscus leaf, sight breathes a defiant longing for peace at large
in the emblem of two linked arms, spray driven off waterfalls,
pencil thin on the far slope as the leaves wave from side to side
and the wounds do the couple dance, sharing their blood.
The defiance and the love bleeding into each other, over a dark stone.

A neglected track over the mountains from Ariège to Andorra by Port de Siguer. Muleteers' route, smugglers' route, escape route for Cathars fleeing the Inquisition, and for Jews and Resistance during the occupation. Merchant caravans, wide-ranging professional shepherds with flocks of thousands, seasonal labour from the French villages to the mines and forges at Llorts and Ordino, summer wood-gathering in the high Andorran valleys *I have trodden these paths,* special goods to and from the al-Andalus courts, manuscripts in astronomy and music, slaves, dancing girls bringing treatises of ekstasis to militarist citadels and kick-starting European poetry *I have not trodden alone,* bread daily in season from Tarascon and Siguer because of Andorra's lack of cereals. Bread and Troubadours. Also a minor variant of the pilgrimage route to Compostela. All these high passes considered dangerous and only used late spring to early Autumn *and I have now trodden twice.*

Some place in these mountains made Baudelaire think we are innately virtuous, at first: "…en parfaite paix avec moi-même et avec l'univers; je crois même que, dans ma parfaite béatitude et dans mon total oubli de tout le mal terrestre, j'en étais venu à ne plus trouver si ridicules les journaux qui prétendent que l'homme est né bon [*hiatus*] et un morceau de gâteau suffit pour engendrer une guerre." You could step into the hiatus and break your leg.

Far below us are cave systems where people have inscribed the meaning
of death many times over, how it gather us up among our objects
into the dream funnel, the last focus, every hope and every gain
converging on the sides of the vault. That route is with us up here,
we feel it through the soles of our boots from far under, patience
and persistence, further and further from anywhere until
you meet the earth, and cast your being out from your hand
onto the wall, the closure, the surface, where it hovers and howls.

Stones and gravel underfoot to the bright music of streams
taking human weight on the turning heel. Who is this elderly man
struggling up a Pyrenean valley, how many more years
has he got of draining strength not 48 for sure. *Who are you?*
And the bright water turns round the granite base as it will and it will.

Je suis le veilleur du Pont-au-Change, I am the watchman
of the stone bridge in the heart of the city. I hear the enemy
creeping through the streets at night uttering the words of a binding
that I can't untie, an enclosure I can't break. I am trying to cross
a swollen stream in the Pyrenees by leaping from clod to clod
wrapped in the surround, wrapped in privilege, daring to hope
for victims of power by trust in human resource under limitation,
tears flying over the stream, curses mobilised into the sky *Je suis
le veilleur du Point de Jour.*

Water banks above glacial step. Fear and sorrow, creeping
towards the death void, the death ignorance. Loneliness, failure,
inadequacy. The world destroying all the work we've done.
The music stilled, the music wrecked, the company dispersed.
Ibn Arabi turns his back and heads for Anatolia.
Alienation from reality, disappointment, voicelessness:
unmediated, unmitigated, and largely unmeditated.
Considerable possibilities for expansion in this section.
Luchar contra lo imposible y vencer!

Overworked muscles, mounting the stairs determined beyond
any possible doubt. A good is possible. I am entitled to elide

geological and moral structures. The good is where the bond serves,
between thee and me, wealth and labour, care and desire. Denying voices
in the wind, accusative hungers grasping at collective advantage.
Perhaps they are right, perhaps the world is a pit of gains.
Violets, anemones, and narcissi living in small enclaves. It's terrible
what happens to people's brains. Blame and hatred by category,
confirmation of own safety and progress by hurt and halt to other.
Water banks above glacial step to a curved lake
with floating reed beds, the mountains dip their feet in.

On up, tired, lacking sociality, forgetting how they sing together a common
melancholy, harmonies not easily replicated in modernity. Forgetting
how they warn against these heroic ventures. *Fair knight setting
out to war, cowboy angel, what will you do so far from home?* Bèth chivalièr
qui partitz tà la guèrra, T'on vatz enqüèra Tan luenhe d'acî? Non vedetz
                                                                                               pas que
la neuit ei pregonda, E que lo monde N'ei que chepic? don't you know,
that the night is deep, and the world a load of pain. Thus they sing
in small bars far behind us. And in palaces of contradiction they construct
thrones of difference. But difference is only one of two things.
Pick the little leaf and whistle.

The water runs down the hillsides and strolls among stones and grass,
dropping into the stream. So easily down, like a market-led culture
down into nothing, nobody interested, nothing matters, let it all fall.
Uphill struggles are for the pre-defeated. That's us, you and me,
we shall be eagles and crows.

Agents of war also trod this track, and their blind servants. Alpenroses
thick among pale scree and boulders, with their bloody flowers.
We used to live in a land but it was denied. We live
where the crow chokes and the world has betrayed us.
So shout at it: Sun! Sun! where are you? Come out and shine
on those who have nothing to eat. It's your duty, it's your job,
come and shine on the betrayed. *Nesci nesci suli suli, ppe la luna
e ppe li stiddi, ppe le povari picciriddi ca non d'annu di mangiare*
for the moon and the stars and the poor little ones with nothing to eat,
children of war, masses of anemones and valerian and stars concealed in light.

Which war? In 1943 they never got this far, they were stopped at Siguer
and shot against a wall (there is a plaque) *Mamma, la luna comu gíra
e camina trapassa i monti lu mare e la marina* And the moon turns
and travels over the sea and the mountains like a hawk
singing, I shan't change, though the rock breaks and the earth changes I
shan't. Though reduced to dust and clay and the brown leaf turns to
ash in my hand, I shan't quit this body *ti 'vo e' tton affino 'utt'òrion soma.*
And George W. Bush will not mould my soul nor uglify my poetry.

* * * * *

At night the stars occupy their river, blazed along the skystrip,
stars pulsing like babies' mouths in the night like something calling
and calling. What does it want? Desires and thoughts mate
in the darkness around us, shadows of the things we live by
moving among the dark bushes, creating new terms while
the beautiful replete stars throb over the grey mountains
and ceaseless streams, guarding our clear eyes, that see through
the darkness beyond the shapes of night, to the world's progress,
tomorrow's necessary demand.

Sitting on yellow plastic outside the tent. A night creature coughs
and heaven marshals itself over the peaks, over and above their snow streaks.
Beyond the mountains the usurpers' fingers reach to the edge
of the culture zone. On distant plains armies clash in the night,
and not a single one of them represents or in any way defends,
the human reality. On this we sleep, amid a continuous crashing.

And in the morning on and up, the final stretch
to the summit, Port de Siguer, a slight dip in a high ridge.
The planet turning, water spilling on stone, the earth
'suspended in its canticle', gathering a circuit of light around its victims,
exalting the humble which is a thought, to stuff in the rucksack,
a thought to carry up the mountain packed between the toothbrush
and the tablets. On the paths of love and war the poor heart hesitates,

beating double, begging the earth to relent. And the prince of all my pals
is the good-willed citizen who doesn't count.

Steady work, like carrying a child on your back in a sling, coming up
to another glacial step, a mass of pale stone blocking the valley.
There are ways up it, and streams coming down it. Age carries youth.
The child remembers: Look, father, this was where we camped in 1956!
Above the third step, grassy humps on the edge of a mountain lake.
Where is that goodness we were seeking? Is it in the height and the labour,
does it trickle out and back down to the town, is it like a clear water arriving
in people's homes? Or is it more like a living creature and if you
raise your thumb on the long road will it give you a lift? Is it an agreement,
not to take advantage of poverty, and not to jump the death queue.
We'll stop here for a while and refresh ourselves for the final strike.
It's beautiful here, a fine place to be, good. Youth carries age.

No one has ever lived here. The lake fills the valley floor,
early morning darkness lies under the eastern flanks, first sunlight
picks out raised knolls and brightens all the western slope,
that the water comes to touch. It looks as if there is no possible way
but a narrow path skirts the water's edge and will take us over rock piles
and scree slopes along the side, round the corner, out at the feeder.
Often it seems there is no possible way. Into the top valley. Every
defeated move is a step forward, a message passed on.

Up here the river divides into three or four and drapes itself across
the valley base, rattling on stones. From all sides
a constant rustling of water in motion, like thought
forming in the throat from an inner event conditioned by knowledge
and 'riddled with the sensible' and that could be a form of love
or the only form. The not-yet programmed voice, the clearing.

Up here the river divides and rattles through spaces. A sky of small clouds
moves over, a fresh wind comes down the valley in the morning.
The river to be crossed, three times, wading on the stones, the path mounting
the fellside towards the col and fading away among boulders. Stop and
look back.

This is Nowhere, where No Name lives, in all the weathers of altitude.
A private person intrudes here, awkwardly attempting
to dry socks on a boulder in the sun. Slipping and falling against a rock,
cutting a lip open. So bright so deep the red show, like the flowers
of the alpenrose bushes all over the hillside among the pale scree
and shattered rocks an announcement of vulnerability,
a wreath to wear, of common fate, you blood red roses.

Umbrella and walking stick, rucksack and tent. Bags under the eyes.
Muttering under breath, I can't go on. Soaked ground between granite
                                                    boulders,
and snow banks ahead. Looks like time to stop. World, wherever you are,
it is time to stop. I know you won't stop. Reaching a far point towards
                                                    the summit
beyond which you cannot go, like the far depths of an underground river
                                                    system,
a rock shelter, the pilgrim's goal, a logical conclusion
at which the liars walk out of the meeting, a show of result.
A small office in the suburbs, a seat in a quiet library. Stop there,
and think, and watch the forms of earth clenching into images,
forming a crust of language at the surface of experience, where virtue coheres,
the threshold, of death as of act. And eat Alpenbars and drink melted snow.

The violins of the wind praise our slowness in double stopping, our equality
of exhaustion, the flashing, equitable whiteness of our teeth
and the red rose within them. Fruit of slow growth.
"I saw a man writing on his bones".

48 years. It's good when things don't change too much. If the world
is a false place, there are other places. A mountain valley crammed with
knowables, a library of them, descending back down towards the shops
and factories out of sight. Can we bear this knowledge on with us,
can we work on the earth's table? The parts of the world are truer than the
whole. There are other wholes, and up above everything the dancing
                                                  slippers shine
silver over the grey folds of earth. And one day to join that dance
at the incorruptible bound. Forwards and upwards to life in the crystal blocks!

Part Two

Descending now on south-facing slopes, the warmth drawing soil minerals
up into flower heads, that nod and flutter. Anemones, narcissus, a few
wild tulips mostly not out yet, yellow streaks on the ends of green stalks.
Desire in attendance to eyes, and up where it's cooler, gentians,
blue gentians in the grass of ridges. *Let me guide myself with
the blue, forked torch of this flower down the darker and darker stairs
towards Persephone's throne, who is but a voice and a darkness invisible.*
And the small dog-violet in its vast home enters into no competition,
barks at no one, its democracy is pluralist. Nodding in the breeze
it grows like words out of lumps of sensibility, signaling consent.
Couldn't we stay up here, in the precise economy of need,
do we have to go down there into all that wastage?

Wandering among the upper slopes song-struck, coming
to a refuge, a stone hut on a shelf, looking out over
shadowy masses from a flowery mead, a glacial step.
Wash hands, curved grass under the stream, lands we never claimed.
Inside the hut a smouldering fire, a first-aid kit, a broken axe.

To know by the sweetness of the new Ab la dolchor del temps novel
as the grass shakes in the wind sitting on a rock outside the hut
listening to the streams and reckoning what we have:
la boch' e-ls olhs e-l cor e-l sen – mouth, eyes, heart, mind.
A first-aid kit, a broken axe, and a smouldering fire. Which is plenty.
For I shall not change, my wish is singular,
Ades es us e no-s muda is one and shall not change.
Walk downstairs and answer that voice in the night.

Nurse and feed this wish like a falcon which shall one day be set free
and fly over the currents of forward desire, and call to the comrades and
swoop down to the cut. Call this falcon 'Learning' be it no more than
a street-corner meeting after the bar's closed – but in public, in the open,
not hiding behind language weaving threats. Say as things are,
open the hut door and set the bird free, that pecks the private self.

It is difficult for a man to save himself from cobwebs in the heart.
de tela al cor c'om no.s pot defendre, and claims on the world.

Now the inverted flower shines among sharp cliffs and hills
Still hanging round the 2300m contour, reluctant to descend,
passing by snow-bestrewn lake basins, looking up at cirques,
all the waste lurking behind the ridge. A fake country,
cut-price nation, feeding off the corruption of its neighbours,
entire towns of shopping malls, the high hills wrecked by ski resorts,
the valleys thick with apartment blocks that no one lives in,
tax evasion addresses for the rich, the poor suffering old rich
who worry themselves to death. A 'fiscal paradise' called Andorra.
Just out of sight of this heaven, pausing at snow, testing its crust, sitting
uncomfortably on tufts of wiry grass by the lake with cheese sandwiches,
icy blue water among black slopes. Noting a strange hirsute nodding flower
that hangs. Why is the lake called 'Tristaina'?

If I were a hawk I'd sail over the mountains and the cities beyond
getting messages on the wind from outside my territory.
And I'd bear my tension across the air, balance on the gale
and swerve across the current and under to my base, my heart space,
under the world. Where the calm people drew pictures.

Water pours from the high lakes over shallow ledges
and trails down the valleys, accumulating substance from side streams.
Constantly balanced, it rattles the stones and excavates a route,
the shortest possible, through rocky landscapes unceasingly.
Linear arenas unfold, long troughs of grass and pale bedding planes
with a stone hut beside the stream, the door unlocked.
The water passes on and over the next step to flowery meadows
where horses graze, and small marshes spread
to the sides among trees. We go there, we agreed to fall.

Increased volume. Increased speed. No gain. Hold on to what we trust,
simple connections, result, truth, words we still use. Clear water in channels
falls down the valley, tumbling among trees to El Serrat,
which I mis-spelled in 1972 and has since been removed. I think I cope

better these days than I did then. Cosmic scope and epic trope
no longer trouble my sleep. They never meant anything
but power, but grabbing a space. The bottle is half full we share it.
The man behind the bar doesn't know where he is. "Yes, I think
there used to be a village, they knocked it down to build the hotels.
I just work here in the season." It is something else, the failure.
It is not us. Nothing can stop the war merchants now.
Clear moving swiftly water sliding down.

Pouring down the valley between the magnetic mountains
we fall alongside, easy walking, fate grant us to float
many years yet thus along the earth holding a future in our eyes.
In 1956 there were peasants working in the fields here
who looked up and waved at English schoolboys, the road
was earthen and a passing car shrouded us in dust. They won,
outright, the cars, the professionals, the dream fabricators,
they tear through the world. We maintain a vocabulary and a future
glimpsed through cracks, globed in tears at the eye rim,
waiting to descend. We shall not revert writing back to writing.
Llorts (next place) looks like a village but isn't, is all new,
and not for working people. Not indeed for anyone.
The higher professions take up the space and never use it.
Tax evasion draws an iron wall over the distances. We, what
are we among it but passing results of cheap oil?

If I were a hawk I'd rouse my red feathers and not be allured.
If I were a raven I'd sit on the roof of the new apartment block
and sing 'koax koax' to the empty rooms. If I were
a lammergeier I'd just hang around in the sky waiting for lunch
thinking "Do what you like with your beautiful mountains,
but try to fear only the fearful and spare a thought for the fallen."
Then I'd swoop and tear.

Amors de terra lonhdana, long-distance love, brought us here
and sustains us through the toil, of long-distance walking, of
short-distance confrontation with modernity. Let us therefore
open a bottle of Spanish wine we deserve it. And let us open it

at the breeze-block restaurant of the campsite at Ansalonga
with roast rabbit and chips. There we are safe from our own accusations
and what we wish sleeps in an inner pocket. It is a little cold
but the ambience is nested. Can we go any further down than this?
Is it really possible to reach the Capital, the biggest megastore of all,
the Tesco of Divine Wrath? The bottle smiles, we haven't got far to go now.
The cook wishes us well and the river outside escorts us to our tents.

During the night bangs and a roaring, but the small thin walls of a tent
protect us from whatever is outside. We survive the night, as some don't,
and emerge into day. Sometimes you meet a bright person in a lowly job
like the woman running the camp office, who tells you exactly what goes on,
how this country has no society. "There's nobody much here
but migrant workers and absent owners." An unreal structure, but
very expensive. Who pays for it? In the high hills yesterday
it was more than real it was the planet itself. It comprehended the city,
the forests of columns, the starred vaults under which true governance
improvises. Coffee at the breeze-block shed and on we go,
gently reluctantly downhill towards the Century of Massacres.

* * * * *

Of which we've had one and it looks like we're going to have another
for nothing, for nothing can stop the war merchants now,
with their little smiles, mouthing a dialectic. I remember Ordino
when it was a place. Our building is a razing, our concord is a rift.
What's left of Ordino doesn't seem to work, though it is
twice the size it was. But the air works, a mountain air coursing
down the vale like silver hounds and calling our thoughts back
to the unforgettable zones, where quasi human ravens
make their nests and croak freely the madrigals of love and war.
Outside the surviving food shop it works my hair into spandrels.

The mountains are still with us, we still bear, dry now,
the wounds they inflicted, the pain of the sensible,
the memories strung to it. The little town still mounts
on pedestrianised streets towards the sky.
[Eros] "shook my heart like the wind flying down a mountainside"
into fir trees, aeolian harp of the earth, songs of yearning. Not
an emptiness, not at all an emptiness, is the wilderness song
that follows us down to the town but a florescence of many lives
from which that thought grows, which "doesn't stop at words, but flies on"
into the veracity ('blue') of the sky.

The plants on the tops of the mountains flower on our breath
the gentians and the tulips, when we breathe the language clear
and benign, *media vita*. Also in the middle of a small town in the hills
every feature of which would wreck the vocabulary of pure poetry.
Come with your cappuccinos and your bus stops and your many
many empty flats and be a compositional impediment from which
to launch ourselves into metropolitan ardour, armed with alpine petals,
small and friable mountain cups. In brief, we catch a bus

towards retail immensity and immense indifference
to the bloody wars that pull at our centres.
Foc te ardă, lume-amară – Let the fire burn you, bitter world
and burn away the dreams that cling to your surface, image deals
for the walls of your empty homes. The bus rattles on, concerned, politely,
to get us somewhere. The valley opens to a vast theatre of earth,
ridge upon ridge towards Spain, soaring over the wires.

A 'fiscal paradise' lies before us. What will you do, fiscal angels,
when apocalypse comes knocking at your door, and there's
no one in? The valleys tilt, the churches turn blue, everything
slides to the left corner and falls into a hole
(which is but a voice and a darkness invisible).

* * * * *

The central zone of building and development, the growth hole. The capital.

There's no one here. Memory of a voice round the corner, silence of the tall blocks. The city is our wilderness. Shamans transport human souls to the arctic hells of the finance market, to become an animal.

Tallness has erased everything. Things stand alone, in masses.

No one has written on these walls *Sonos eternos jóvenes rebeldes!*

Music hidden in stone.

Leaning in fear towards the threshold of the Arab world.

Again a bright person in a lowly job, managing a small coffee-bar under the tall walls, who explains the place is run by migrants, and bought by visitors. Is this the dark voice at the foot of the stairs? But brightly she explains that in some way 'the nature' keeps us going and a future ahead, a work to be done and a pact with sociality. A dawn thing, when all the dreams fall off. A hard time for the heart, but "We are proud of our tears". Then how do we face the spread of harm? When our hands reach out to the power glades they grasp a vacuum.

There were ethics, among all classes, maintained from generation to generation by the means available to the group, to acknowledge common humanity and locate blame precisely on the structures of harm. Neither the European wars nor *The Daily Mail* could entirely destroy them. There were discussions on street corners in Salford after the pubs were closed, men in flat hats and white scarves deciding not to sack the Jewish shop and not to listen to the media campaign against Muslims and not to be afraid.

Heart, how can you not break down, that your love
is shrunken to four walls, and everything outside is delivered
to the empties? They have taken over the whole public world, where desire
planted a garden, and they have built a car-park on it
and nothing can stop them now.

But the airs and the electricity circulate on the mountain tops and things are remembered that protect us against destructive certainty. A slow history accumulates in those parts of the world that remain true to themselves, and forget the whole.

The tall hole. *Heart speak or die.*

Give payment and thanks and go. It is time for some sanity. We catch another bus, to El Pas de la Casa, which is completely insane, and another, to L'Hospitalet, where French shopkeepers struggle with enormous sacks of cheap goods on the station platform like the damned of the 4th bowge, and the train goes through the mountains and across the plain, to Toulouse, and dinner. I notice the word *Ospita* contained in L'Hospitalet as I sit at a pavement table with cassoulet. It concerns me. How could the world think without its soul? Always if you look for it there is something curative, the words held in the seeds scattered on the mountain slopes, far away, waiting patiently for winter.

Music released by stone. Fully declared whatever the options.

The threshold of the Arab world, if Lebanon could be saved.

Ordinary and orderly, acts and failures, tipping the heart cradle.

Notes to *The Glacial Stairway*

1. *Words in foreign languages not translated in-text*

Part One

un mundo mejor es posible
a better world is possible

Baudelaire: ...en parfaite paix avec moi-même...
...in perfect peace with myself and the universe, in my perfect beatitude and total forgetting of terrestrial evil, I even went so far as to think not so ridiculous those who claim that humankind is born good... [*hiatus*] ... and a piece of cake is enough to start a war.

Je suis le veilleur du Pont-au-Change / du Point de Jour
I am the watchman of Exchange Bridge / of Daybreak

Luchar contra lo imposible y vencer!
Struggle against the impossible and win!

Part Two

media vita
in the midst of life [we are in death]

Sonos eternos jóvenes rebeldes!
We are young rebels for ever!

Ospita is a word I invented as title to the poem sequence. It stands for some kind of healing structure, or the will to one.

2) *Things quoted from substantially or leaned on heavily*

Baudelaire, 'Le Gâteau' (*Le Spleen de Paris*)
M. J-F. Bladé, *Études géographiques sur la vallée d'Andorre*. Paris 1875
W.G. Hill, *The Andorra Report: an undiscovered fiscal paradise*. 1991
D.H. Lawrence, 'Bavarian Gentians' (the quotation near the start of Part Two)
David Lewis-Williams, *The Mind in the Cave*. 2002

Michel Maffrand, d'après A. de Musset, 'Le cançon de Barbarine', sung by the group *Balaguèra*.
Peter Riley, *The Linear Journal*. 1973
Robert Roberts, *The Classic Slum*. 1971.
Troubadors: mainly Raimbaut d'Orange.
Three songs from Calabria in Italian and Italianised Greek performed by the group *Nistanimèra*
Slogans (in Spanish) on walls in Baracoa (Cuba) and on billboards in Havana, noted in March 2006.

Pyrenean

The little valley in the foothills
tall birches and twisting stream
snowy crests beyond in sunlight.
A marten runs across the road,
first thin cherry blossom in the fields
a bell-tower at the crest of each village.

Later sitting on the station platform very cold
suffering pain from an oesophagal hernia
surveying the council houses beyond the track
so like home.

Cathar country, how people survive
or don't and leave a trace in the mind
that survives through centuries, a trace
of defiance, that the world is open, a blue book
wrapped in wool, clutched to the chest
over high and snowy passes.

This House…

This house on a Greek hillside with its geckoes and millipedes
wind bringing rain down from the mountains, the shutters
closed at night. Me with my mill-talk quieted, lying here
in the night and weather trying not to remember
failed claims pains of inarticulation and true attachments.
I don't forget. I don't remember very well.

There were never any gods of rain, peasant of the elements
who gets on with the allotted task and washes the white stones
on the red path, slides them down the hill. That rushing sound.
That particular brow. Unerasable intimacy. Far from here
northern town cold night wet streets curtains closed glow
of radiator red in dark room, illuminating the hangings.

Anywhere, a coming together and making a voice, a god's work,
a voice for ever, a voice at large, in the mountain sides
the small mills in stream clefts turning their wheels at night, that
rushing, hollow sound. A double voice of solitude and connection
melancholy and ecstasy writes itself into channels of the earth
as we dream between walls at night of distant points of contact.

This house on a Greek hillside with its geckoes and millipedes
and painted walls. The vast wars raging across the earth
the law of the heavier weapon… When the heroes come we run and hide,
we peasant faces, irrelevant elements, we are lost and done for
and kick stones in the road, the dirt road that winds up
into the hills. Our sighs run back down the meadow.

The god's eyes looking suddenly up to us in the carved stone,
the warm air wafted up from the heater, stirring a few cobwebs
on the ceiling rose. Two fires signalling across Europe. I'm
twisting my voice out of its body to rescue a glimmer of recognition
from the blasts of warfare. I'm working hard at this:
I'm not singing and not shouting. I'm looking for a stone.

All the pebbles I've picked up from the desolate shorelines of Europe,
a worn grey stone with a straight white line across it from Denmark
I press this stone into the world body, the dark mass,
to make there a small silence, in which we can hear each other
and the faint sounds the insects make, the grasses hissing in the wind
the unrepresented voices of the generations. In the hard edge

Of this sphere the dead also speak, massed seeds in flower heads,
and gain a recognition, participate in a chorus which strips
me of sad particulars, if I could begin to address the issue,
with stones, yellow flowers, CD players, anything that works and say
that in the orkestra my guilt will modulate into the collective.
Well it may, or some other voice while the sun sinks under the earth
and we tune our voices to its echo. Voices working together,
for an honest peace, for sense in the structure,
for tangle threads that connect across the indigo.

Loutro

The daily ferry pulls into the harbour
as the shadows expand. Next time you look
it's gone, down the coast, sailing
soft seas full of light, normal living.

There is no other access except footpaths
which are hell without a mule. The mountains rise
almost from the shoreline. The sea spilling
light proposes equity across the land, as usual.

Poseidon groans in the dark medium, the wash
against the shore in the empty bay where the ships came
in 1941 to rescue an army. The runners turned their
backs on the sea and headed for the summits on

almost vertical goat tracks, carrying radios on their backs.
Their fears are not ours. We await the news,
the pain of the languages. The ferry lights
come round the headland again, on earth and on time.

Bits and Pieces Picked Up in April 2007
or Six Days in Tuscany with Roger Langley

Sunday
The depth of incision into the stone: the degree of power exercised.
The balance and turn of the perceiving body, in attendance,
carved, light or deep, by the nervous system. There
shall be no rulers. We shall make our own ways.
In the middle, the three attendants hang their heads.

Monday
O world world, you disappoint us.
The gentle green hills and the forced labour.
Later reassured by
I gettatelli, the abandoned children,
the bronze angels that carry you into what you can be.

Monday
Sienese: free play of detail within market-led formalities.
Perhaps not a very good idea.
Some of these Madonnas are nursing dolls or piglets!

Tuesday
Paradisal sight, which extends to infinity.
Arcades, stars, shadows, the eyes staring through us. There shall be
no more wars. The light in the blood, the promise
kept, out there.

Wednesday
No mystery, no symbol.
We hope for messages.
The birds flock across the sky.

Wednesday
The great forehead, the downcast gaze,
the head held high, the rich lips,
the interior pain, that never dies, of this,
queen of this.

Thursday
Paradisal sight, halted at a wall
of blue-streaked marble.

Love as focused as my eye muscles can make it
to a sky-streaked terminal.

Thursday
A landscape which is a state of mind
but not always the same state of mind.

This evening a proud antagonism
an anchorage, in dark green grass.

A pause in anxiety,
A painting.

Friday
Elliptical settlements on hilltops with small churches.
Alternate bands of white and red stone.
Pigeon flutters in the tree-top,
serin sings from the thicket. Somewhere else,
sad dancing, in couples. There is
Only one end. A circular window
in a chequer-work of white and red stone.

Airs at Furthest Accord
Listening to Fayrfax in Haute Provence October 2007

Beyondness growing from the thin skin, a call
to earthen distance awaiting a response
   Swallow, earthen dart, return
   air-broken, lashed to the crystal that
   turns round the earth. We are locked
out of death until the message is delivered
and our progress settles back into the moment's
wild spin. Can't you hear it unfolding from the palate
sweeping over the white rock of Europe
the cities that cower and inflate, doesn't the swift
wind on the crest call us out of hours doesn't
a far fetched thought of calendrical pact
settle on the meadows after harvest? A call
   in the far fields and we turn as a returning
   swallow turns in parabolas among the roofs
and grazes the dog's head marking his
faithful progress on the dusty road,
locket at his throat for it is in the end
the true dog that trots the length of the road
bearing the account, a European story or
long song that the children will sing
at the turn of their days, summing all the wrong
they have to own, all the knowledge
and shame of the proceeds and all the jubilee
of a rewarding peace. No one else bears it,
there are no substitutes for the dog, the dear
devoted dog who walks the road, the linear dog.
The thief doubles back behind the angel
the ministers of hatred divide the flame
the hills wrapped totally in small oaks
take a yellow edge towards the ending of the day
that pulls our hearts sideways into question
but only a steadfast mongrel passes by.

And presumably one day the dog's journey will end
with a pat on the head and a scratched ear, as we
cannot end, but sweeping a hand over Europe
as if to calm the world, pass into dream, the last
spray of seeding flower-heads flung into the air.
And families broken and scattered
by war or paranoia travelling on the plains notice
a swallow returning with no message
but its self, the arrow of its being.
The dog has the message, plain and
articulate directions towards the world's
furtherance, and walks on among trees,
between people's legs on market day
up the street and over the hill and beyond.

Best at Night Alone

version of March 1st 2017

In 2007 we stayed for several days in an isolated house in Haute Provence near the village of Montsallier. I spent most of the late evenings there sitting at a table near a window, reading, writing, and listening to music. The window showed only darkness and faint sky lines, with some lights from the village in the distance. The next week we moved to a flat we had hired on the edge of the village of Faucon, to the east of Vaison-la-Romaine. The window I sat at here in the late evenings looked down onto the road at the base of the village with a few lit windows and small vistas of the stone of the village rising to its hilltop centre before me. From another window there was, in the daytime, a view of the north face of Mont Ventoux. The writing as it continued drew in various other places where I have sat at a window in the late evening and the person sitting at these various places writing bore signs, from the start, of not being entirely me.

Nightlong over fields and hills the dome turns.
Lit window, figure bent over table, forest edge
star traces contracted on a point of harm,
biting the bone. Where are my people?
Cowering under desert shadows.
Children laughing and frightened.

* *

A distant street lamp suddenly goes out.
My vanishing point. Dark wind
and the thrashing of branches, rain
on the glass. My home's validation.
Sitting here in the night complaining.

* *

Me with my alcohol and fat. I remember better days.
Why are we living out here in this shadow land
driven from our pasturage or choral fate, our tale
a thin script thrust into the night
across fields of lavender, ecstatic proteins
burning into our lives. My sweet poison.
My working timetable.

* *

All our resources gone to
waste in the desert, these people are
wrecking the earth.

And nowhere but here in these patient groves
will an eyelid be opened to the earth's curve
at dawn or fall of night.

No, I don't want a sandwich.
I don't want a valet case.

**

Street, street, banal street
paved with promises the mind
walks you in the middle of the night,
and a hand is held out, cupped I am
busy with my insects, truth and
hope, hand reaching for hand.
A knock at the door. Two
children run away down the street
laughing, hand in hand.

**

Upland slopes full of spiked plants, October
skeletons rattling themselves in the night.
A message forms at the lips' limit. What is left
of our liberty but a scatter of aggressive bones
and very disgruntled populations liable to
paranoid acts?

      Moths at the window.
The home that survived resentment.
The home that survived alcohol and fat.
The home that survived encrypting.
Needing help to climb the stairs.

**

The great mountain forms erased at night,
no more lights, no more houses. How could there
not be paranoia in such a time as this, threatened
by the world brokers at every act? Shouts of
Freedom and Democracy, shattering bones.
Beacon darkness through the fields, where
the children are hiding.

* *

Moths on the windows, serious and symmetrical,
moths with purpose. When I open the windows
the moths fill the room the pillar
of alienation suddenly opens like a winter rose
and all the company of song.

* *

(after Deguy)
Singing old songs together in the evening
like nomads round the camp fire. The rare
moment when we agree to die, it is
Orpheus, it is the quick thought stronger
than stone, stronger than tree or
scattered creatures, the song in its clearing
as one by one we stand and leave
in good order by the law of random numbers.

They have all gone to bed and left me here.
Singing old songs together in the evening.

And where does all this get us where do we go from here where are my glasses what are the practicalities of collective hope? Motives removed from history collect like insects in a glass bottle shake it and the bombs fall. They fall like rain on the mountain-side nobody knows why they are falling they think it is something natural like rain some order of the world. The world is entirely out of this committee humming over an elegant couple-dance. And there will be too, when the greed stops.

* *

When the greed stops
we shall all gain some peace
and a space in which to operate
the mechanisms that grow from the
first movement of thought, the goodwill
lodging on the lip, lacking a word, the ancient
honeyed madness. Hope sleeps there,
the quiet place, corners of matt stone on the dark hill
while the Burmese singer plucks at our sleep.

* *

If you want, the war can stop. If you want enough. All you have to do is want and it will, all of it. But only that, only all of it, not some favour, not some dream. Sing the slow long song and watch the forces part. Street, street, baleful street, paved with wishes, I don't set foot on you any more, my legs ache, I stay inside and contract round the point of harm.

* *

The founder of Situationism dies of red wine in a farmhouse deep in the French countryside. Once you see it, he says, you have won. What do you on earth do when you've won? Make silence speak.

* *

Worries in my hair like midges, buzzing and
getting lost among trees and fading to distance,
Mars, Venus, dusk on earthen spring.

The great fruiting vastness beyond these walls,
all the people living their lives and I cannot address
less than that, some favour or dream.

Only you, listen, are my opening eye,
piercing the lights. Venerable honeyed lips,
bitter wine. Earth's glories reclaimed.

* *

The area round the house is a mass of dry grasses with insects moving around. The hills beyond covered in small oak trees, east-west ridges extending from Greece to Spain. Far away to the left over the fields the village very little inhabited now, a few street lights at night. Lavender fields, harvested, strips of dark stubble and heaps of underbrush awaiting burning. A dormouse scratches in the roof. The Colorado beetle is said to have shown itself in the Beaujolais and there are *mites de nourriture* in the flour bin. We are careless and discordant with our alcohol and fat, and other powers.

* *

Help me up the stairs to bed
I have had enough
of my own skill, it
strangulates me. I think I am right to say
that there is hope in the world
if you look, in especially those parts
of the world where people shelter under
shadows it is there. The poets
dream of honour but hope
is self-propagating.

* *

How the wind outside rolls against the house, and in the skylight pale clouds move over, a blanket drawn across the sky. But that too moves on and then there is only that empty depth, with two points, two bright eyes staring down. They stare and stare but they can't see us in here. But still they stare.

* *

Mind going out into the world to seek its objects
speaking back. What then is this *grimoire* this
obstruction on the table? I close it and fetch the wine
which as Baudelaire said sings in the bottle
of the whole, of the redress. As the truth sings in the book.

* *

(after Bonnefoy)
Night with its greens and its blues and a bit of dark red curdling the bottom of the page. Quickly I write the word tear, then star. I write birth. I write shepherds and three wise men. I write the bulb has gone and it's dark.

* * *

So we can begin. Groping round in the dark
bumping into furniture. The "things of this world"
are here somewhere, biting back. The moon
rises. Singing together in the evening.

Floral wreaths attached to a lamp post.

Take me home, country roads.

The two stars, cats' eyes in the void
one of them moves, the other
suddenly goes out and I'm groping in the dark
for the things of the sky. The children
think I'm a funny old thing.

* *

(Carol)
Like the wren I sleep uneasy at the solstice.
Tiny bird, preferring darkness, heart
beats 450 /min. at rest, unlikely
to survive the winter.
Still under thorn Under shadow.

The robin brings alcohol and fat
the three wise men bring useless presents
the shepherds bring nothing but themselves
and the possibility of a future where
nor you nor we nor anybody
bound the world into its suffering.

* *

Wide open spaces of patience
gloss with light the faint opening wing.
I watch the caterpillars die in a ring.
It is not a tragedy. They were learning to sing.

* *

Darkness, not a human condition
but a condition of the earth, that renders us
isolated and uniquely empowered at
a turning point and if we are quick and careful
before the light returns in the silence when
people sleep because they think there is nothing to see
we can reverse the world's drift by a spasm
of thought carried across several mountains
like fire in a fennel stalk. And a bluish paleness
from the night horizons.

* *

Despair declines and a birth is anticipated,
the dark shadow covering the hill dissolves into the ground
and there is hope where hope cannot be, hard against the earth,
out in the fields of vengeance. Because a sequence has begun
which must continue, is bound to it, through the black light of
nameless states.

* *

Do but listen to the Bushmen music and the space is changed,
immediate completion on minimal resource
and nothing is hidden from us, nothing is coded,
evidence fills the space we inhabit in its
night show, blue seeking into brown and creating green
leaves scattered on the threshold, unconditional welcome.

* *

High window onto the narrow street, a few local lads
are larking around down there where the estate agent's window
shines. I'm separated from my library and if
any of my days offers the world an answer I
don't know which one.

High mind-bid for the present condition like
birdsong mounting to a spherical estate not
for sale where the beautiful pages shine on the
edge of a life like a Mexican harp band that
knows where it's going.

* *

Night corners, orange light on matt stone
in small stadia on the hillside whose edge
is lost into the sky, and some lit windows.

And there I sat, and there I stayed
and there I heard them sighing like
stars in the sky when the winter birds come over

And dark wings fold us into the earth
for night is our site and there we suit
our brows to the waiting clay.

The bigger the powers that combine to split the earth the stronger the local discourse that takes no notice of them. But mounts lanterns on the awning and books the musicians for next Friday and gets the big pots out of storage. They know exactly what is happening in the high offices and make sure that the music is level with the earth, in case of gunfire.

* *

In night corners small fires glow, travellers warm their limbs, there is food and drink and some tired dance movements are made. People cast out of their land, human flesh degraded against steel, gather in corners of vacant lots and face each other across a dark emptiness, a fulcrum of harm, a blueprint of corporate loyalty.

* *

Bushmen, the most persecuted people on earth, persecuted continuously for three hundred years and still persecuted, relentlessly and mercilessly persecuted as if they must at all costs be driven to nonentity and the world must be finally rid of the few, powerless and harmless, that are left. As if we cannot possibly have this tiny population crouched in the semi-desert eking a living and maintaining a form of wisdom almost entirely beyond us, that sends the mind out into the world to encounter the world's terms rather than taking the opportune thought-course that absorbs the surplus. And they know that God is vile and sense him out there in the darkness seeking their harm. They could teach us, few and scattered and night-cornered, of us, that we are, but we discard them.

Best alone at night with the secretive lamp I hear
the whisper of forest like a passing ship, more alone even
than in hospital and day after day the same discomfort,
everybody's, that nobody shares. Half elsewhere
I turn back to the night *His face is the blue shadow
of his hand* this ink life that takes me across the old cities dissolving
smoke into the air and veer into the future.

* *

Fifteen Ekelöf Incipits
(This page had to be removed due to copyright threats.)

* * *

The red blind is down and all I know beyond the window is a faint rumbling noise, with a fainter hiss attached to its edge. This is the turning wheel whose moment speaks of love. And we don't want this love. We shut it out of the house and return to a solitude with eyes in our hands, that are cast to the night.

* * *

Alone in quiet night will be my best pseudonym, absent from any centre. And I shan't know better than anybody else, why should I want to? My hair grey, my eyes brown.

* * *

Referred back to the lives of those who work,
in graveyard and ballroom across the land
from worm to star and back the entire dome
sounds in chorus for someone has again
placed a medal on a small earth feature
positioning an earthen future on the thin thread
of light the horizon's pain opening to a
wide meadow full of positive force.

* * *

The darkness that surrounds the heart, with a line of light in the far distance where the world enters, cautiously. Gentle murmurings of liver lungs and intestines, calming the heart, keeping the dream music going, singing *Heart of my heart...*

So the heart, flattered, won't notice the world as it comes slowly and cautiously through the door and won't kill it.

* * *

Ekelöf 1932
I shan't sleep tonight.
Forgive me if I write badly.
Forgive me if I write stupidly.
Death was ignored, and sat there
like some hapless employee.

The bands of night circle the house
the wind hisses on the gables
the circular graveyard
turns slowly in the night.
If I am wrong, forgive me.

Memory of a plume of thought
brushing down the hillside like snow
announcing the human victory
and purpose bursts out of enclave.
He gets up and opens the window.

* * *

These pieces are written quickly, with long periods between them during which they are not looked at or thought of, except that a beginning, an *incipit*, may come from nowhere late in the evening alone and quiet and it is rarely more than a disturbing sound, a scrape beyond a wall, a creak, a low bump, a cradle sound.

* * *

All I ever wanted, a hand touches a wooden table
And there is nothing to pay, looking at the hills
Through the window and hearing a faint cry from
The cradle, remembering a carved stone at Southwell

Of intricately entwined leafage: somebody was capable
Of setting aside the world's catalogue of ills
And I wanted a lot more than that, a cat's dream
in a quiet basket, of the great fix, the claw in harm.

The claw passes through air and retracts
At the delicate stone edge, the world stands
Alone not knowing what it wants,

An elite or an egalitarian structure. Call it home,
Let it settle round us and hope the wild fires don't
Reach it. There's nothing else either to want or own.

* * *

These hearts always at war,
Twenty years day and night.

O Earth you don't listen, you don't understand,
You don't speak when you see me dying.
O Earth you don't protect your children,
You don't lead them home from the killing fields
You just cry and cry.

Damn these years always at war.
Damn the liars who speak of community.

* * *

I am perched on the window-ledge waiting to get a connection. The faint crust of earth betokens itself in wisps of gendering, that is to say, shyly. I know that these whispers can break into gunfire when the contract is broken. The contract is in the very far ends of the tree tips against the sky making lens for star eyes. Making oculi for sincerity.

* * *

The greater the poverty the happier the children.
They sport on the boundaries of the killing fields, and
some don't last long. But are never bowed under the threat
of excellence. Our laments make them giggle.

And the insects and the art. The gunfire they greet
with mistrust, waiting to be told, and
may not wait long but escape from a world of threat
into their own excellence.

* * *

A church bell. The first bird signal: a note repeated anything from four to fifteen times in random order. It starts to rain, small circles on the river surface, there and gone.

O lullabye, my sweet little hopefuls, this is where you begin.

Notes to *Best at Night Alone*

'Street, street, banal / baleful street…' – Utca, utca, banat utca… Hungarian song.

'The wine sings in the bottle'. Baudelaire did indeed write this, as quoted by John James, who saw it emblazoned on the end wall of a co-operatif in Languedoc.

The several references to moths, insects and caterpillars refer to the French botanist and entomologist Pierre Henri Fabre, notably his most famous experiment, which consisted of capturing a band of processionary caterpillars, and placing them round the rim of a large urn in a continuous ring. Contrary to the belief that they had a natural leader, he observed that in that situation they continued marching until they died of exhaustion. Each caterpillar had no urge other than to follow the back-end of the one in front of it, and the 'leader' was lost.

Cuban Nights

People dancing in ones and twos, catching the rhythm
through the back wall of the concert hall among
the evening rum vendors, nowhere else to go and poverty
again displays its gay plumage, its crafted memory.

The dance is intellectual, the mind
balancing its routes, setting
paradigms of hope against lapse out of
sheer necessity, the leaf spinning from the tree.

The apotheosis of those who do badly,
sailing into city corners with one lamp burning.
If to do badly were the same
as to do harm, we'd know what to do.

But we live where we can and inhabit
our lives like a warm scent in the air pursued
through the streets towards guitar music and singing,
the voices edged with age, always saying goodbye.

And beyond forgetting is a social rightness remembered,
sitting in an old steel-frame chair in the yard
while the children run around and dance.
Sunflowers, bean plants with small red flowers.

Dreaming in La Habana

The dogs bark all night, there is dancing
in the dark street under the street lamps to the rhythm
that escapes at the back of the concert hall,
with small glasses of rum.

The state's promise trembles on the edge of capitulation
to large-scale injustice for the sake of nothing we really
need. But a warm ease settles on the street at night,
a rhythm, an island pride. What remains of the state's duty?

Protect, distribute evenly and be incorruptible, the dream of it.
Later the dancing stops and the rooftop cockerels prepare for their alarms.
Thin streets that know neither beggars nor homeless
slowly give access to small lines of light.

Sad Fates of the Songsters
for Peter Manson

Clarence Ashley
Short life of trouble pretty bird in tree looking down at me crystal hood clouded now.

Margaret Barry
Who can remember the names under the mantle of green and engraved on the halved coin?

Amadée Ardoin
It's all over I'm going home ouais ça me fait du mal diamond eye sea eye ever.

Lewis Black
Gavel cramp at the gravel camp "the politics of this is bleak".

Blind Blake
These dry bones shall rise again singing diddie wa diddie possibly neolithic somebody tell me what it means.

Dock Boggs
The greatest possible resistance good people.

Bob Campbell
Poetry as utopic space now working down old Starvation Farm.

Samko Dudic
Stuck up on a stage in New York trying to remember my grandfather's funeral.

George Gouldthorpe
Pity them what see him suffer all the way back to the workhouse.

Roscoe Holcomb
I am a man of the northern railways.

Peg Leg Howell
Skin game come too close everything I had done gone Geh unter, Welt.

Jim Jackson
We are dying out one by one we are dying out at every link I called his name.

Otis Harris
Good morning Mr Lowdown Mr Letdown I want to talk with you concerning this thing.

Uncle Dave Macon
Whatever it was became of me all over the town I used to be.

Fred McDowell
Baby don't you want to go where the acrylic light microwaves the worried mind.

Trió de Pánuco
En la tarde quando ponga you shadows are me shadows are always me.

Edith Pinder, Joseph Spence and Friends
Out on the rolling sea the oily truth took hold of me.

Riley Puckett
Growing too old to dream I tabulate the night wars.

Tallahassee Tight
And I don't feel good I don't feel bad poetry rubbish.

Henry Thomas
Poor helpless buffoons the wind among the reeds calling.

Geechie Wiley
Maybe the last kind word spoken on earth let's hope not.

* * *

for Ivor Gurney

Forgive those warriors brought up in council sheds
and college churchyards who grab the trophies
and kill the loser. Be the proud loser, walk
under the night arches towards a dawn thought,
that these warriors must be forgiven, and respected.

Respect is not enough, they demand allegiance –
"Music is forbidden. It is sinful." and the night walker
digs his grave in the Flemish plain as a slight
blue and peach line opens on the hill edge,
digs into that distance, and hears the dawn birds crackling.
Somebody passed this way 1923 smoking a Players
through the great green of meadows begging for peace
and got home at dawn to a fire in a small room
and a musical praxis that solves nothing outside
of its own moment, for which to live.

And on the other side of the continent the Universal Champions
the thick-set warriors, men and women, forge the ordnance,
close the shops, blast the currency, and screaming for right
destroy the little we have to be glad of. Screaming for love.

I don't remember ever wanting the world to change.
Walking in grey mornings to the school
and bright afternoons to the bread shop
I learned what had to be learned, bought what I was sent to buy
with what was to spare while the warriors hacked the language.
I heard their thumps and clangs across the town late at night
as I lay in bed, forgave them, and went to sleep.
Common as bread the song for all.

* * *

Long since the stars sank making love possible.
So get on with it, engage with the earth, get
out there and walk it in rain and pain, the
grasslands' brilliant costumes, the dark lights
gripped in the day's cracks, making love possible.

If love is possible. Heroes crack open the mountains
claiming the time in which we are cancelled. We need
a made thing that stands against this, a gate through
the hissing grass, the great belts of light on the uplands
building hope on thrush heads and their long tunes.

And the stars caught in clefts of rock,
white apartment blocks on the far hillside,
you out there, taking the weight, treading the pain,
pushing the air through your teeth to sing love
is indestructible, shield your eyes.

Vertigo

Moving out of the tree border onto the top grasslands.
This is the earth, and this is us here very close to it,
watching the great valley below, clinging to the ground,
small black ants on my arm, butterflies in pairs in the grass.
I'm working on a statement of political hatred. Black
flies gentle breeze clinging to the hillside bearing
a few birds down below. Shirt patched with sweat
drying to salt lines, chilled skin. Faint wood smoke
in the crowded breeze, cow bells among the trees
and an iridescent green spider. Seeking in this thronging
vocabulary to think a clear thought about human wrong
which does not disown us. Deceits practised within
necessity, deceits of the grassy bank. Small
shepherds' huts all over the slopes, secretive hiss
of wind through larches, endless forest and mountain
and clouded sky over all, over the oil plants and
railway sidings beside which people survive regimes and
rebellions with luck and custom. The earth written in black ink,
hidden under the fuel, the earth endlessly concealed.
So down into the black haze under the mountainside
the great void of images, the thought pit, fires glowing in it.
Down there we inhabit this darkness and harvest this blue wheat.
The limestone subsoil that smelts up saxifrage and self-heal.

Szászcsávás: The Older Stratum

Needing a pair of shoes and remembering everything.
The voice shaking but true, striding over the pain.

I'm going to where no one knows me. The strangers,
and the sky with its stars. Don't weep, little mother,
I'll buy you a red scarf with polka-dots.

At night there is nothing, silence of the earth,
impenetrable darkness of the eye, that cannot see
a human face turned up to it or tell the difference
between a turnip and the head of a child with nothing.

I have nothing, I earn nothing, but I have a good time.
I remember only one thing: an oak root under my foot.

And when they arrived, in the early morning,
the star was hidden. The beautiful shining star.

You should see this place in the spring.

Four Transylvanian Songs [1]

If you don't work
you won't hear the cuckoo

Or the water
or the wind whistling.

Do the work, saw the log, write the truth
and the cuckoo will sing in the tree.

Respect and love the old people
in a world sense.

All the work is good
that has good result

Sitting touching the cradle
in the winter.

* * *

My eyes laugh in your eyes.
My centre hurts for you.

I'm angry with your eyes
looking into mine.

I'm even angrier with your centre
teaching me love.

Whichever way the wind blows
it gets me.

* * *

---

[1] Reinvented from anonymous lyrics in various CD booklets.

My rose, think well of the beginning and the end,
with whom you will set the world before your eyes.
For it is not borrowed bread which can be given back,
neither is it unearned money which can be spent,
nor is it a hot pillow which you can turn over.
You have found your life's partner, rose,
winter blossom, fallen bud.

* * *

(Dawn song)
I ask unspeaking earth,
silent totality, for help,
to mend the heart
badly broken

And hurting. It is not the heart
but we say heart to describe the hurt.
The earth banging on my coffin lid
will silence all that

And I'll be a star in the sky
shining faintly above the forest,
and around midnight I'll poke around the houses
to see what my loves are up to.

Transylvanian Songs
after Johannes Bobrowski [2]

Father, the great raptor
flies into my chest and makes
his heraldry there.

Grandfather, the dogs bark.
Great grandfather, the mud of the road.

The fool, the tourist, runs down the village street
for his camera, disturbing the horses.
The widows sit like crows on the benches.

Their gaze passes through me, fool,
into the distance, to the edge of the forest
where the orphan bird sits. There the song
makes sense: *at the end of the road*
you will shake hands with the thrush
and the Collectives Officer and the man
from Boston with the GM seeds
all lusting for the black earth.

We walk in rings under the moon. The great
raptor signs our names in the sleep of trees.
Grandfather, across the pastures the river
pours through the stilled mill wheels.
Great grandfather, darkness fills the ground.

---

2 'Lettische Lieder' in *Sarmatische Zeit* (1961). *Werke, I*, 1987, p.57. Translated as 'Latvian Songs' by Ruth and Matthew Mead in *Shadow Lands* (1984). The italicised sentence is quoted from a professional funeral lament from Oltenia, Romania (not in Transylvania) and is part of a prescribed after-life journey.

The Children of Maramureş

A wooden bowl full of blue and red berries, fresh from
the bushes beside the roads, washed of petrol stains.
Take it: love with reason, their eyes say,
therefore hope, without reserve. Take the gift,
accept the reason, lever our hearts over the barricade
with an explanation.

The children stare wide eyed at the strangers
and smile for ever. The day moulded out
of light, the mutual seed springs open in time,
it costs nothing but persistence.
A linking gesture across the border holds the ring dance
open to the hearth, where the old ones sit.

Wisps of blue smoke rise from the houses
into the distance. The true moment moves among us,
everyone's work as it works, everyone's
fault as it fails, held in the song's return, a hope
balanced on a point of trust against fate's gerrymandering,
everyone's wish in your tear ever shining

And stabled there. Politicians and clouds
brush the fine heads of the children turned upwards;
a laugh, short and light, rolls down the land,
a reasoned hope by which they turn in the dance, hand on sleeve:
Welcome welcome, bird in the bush, fish in the flood,
futureless presence ringing the earth.

Ultimul Drum

To take again the long road leading
surely to the perfectibility of mankind
but with many trees and barking dogs
uncertain which world they are in.

We fend them off with curses in
colloquial Latin. How the branches gather
and ponder and piddle on our heads,
how the roadside doors stand ajar,

And we carry on regardless. Road,
journey, and perfectibility are mainly
a game we play leading sometimes
to murderous consequences.

We must learn our own consequences,
and as sure as the early white on the
blackthorn beside the road walk
over the land steadily singing
songs of equity to the bees, thrushes,
drunks who pass by looking for a city.
And in this city there is no one to blame.

Weddings of the Gypsy Flower Sellers

The world image spins in the abandoned theatre (O nubile shade etc.)
birthday ribbons pulled through scissors "Then somehow
my heart became a nightingale" opened its wings and flew
as blood flows, paths of haemoglobin through deserts of speech.

> *Devla, Devla*, what shall a poor gypsy do, but sing
> and tremble at the adversity heaped
> on a forked thing. O God who made me don't
> abandon me now but speak and I'll go.

> *Dela,* dance, so you can be seen, little taper
> give more light, little birch-wood taper.
> Ah *roma* we live well in night corners, our minds fly
> over the trees on beeswax wings 100 versts
> hour by hour *romale-le*, stealing big thoughts
> at night when nobody uses them.

> Where have you gone little gypsies *kaj jone romale*
> don't leave me now, for we shall live, not die
> and live well together. *Hey brother,*
> *have you seen any of our lot, with bears and monkeys?*
> Get into the car we'll find them.

The aesthetic supports the ethic and bears it further away
from God, who knows nothing and issues frantic edicts, forgetting
that He is the world and can't do anything but dance.

> *O Devla Devla*, what shall we do and where go, *cigányok*,
> to live somewhere, speak and wander (dance and sing)
> and hold the bright earth in its sky,
> empty theatre, resonant home.

Bukovina Song

Poverty stretched across frontiers fills
the resulting space with trills.

A life of repeated partings
stands behind the welcome and draws

Tears at the farewell. All our
loved ones were lost

Into unknown regions and well
may they persist for all we know

Sustained by consorts, trilling
like birds in the dawn.

Haydn at Csávás

The world heals us and casts us out, healed, into a black desert.
Every year at the new year fire we renew the terms of our
contract, the route to the centre, turn of the wheel, delight
in daily tasks while the new baby sleeps our sleep for us
entirely meshed in the chorus. Until next year, when

it again becomes time to know what you're saying.
The harmony includes cruelty and disdain, a bird lodges
briefly in the tree beside the graveyard and flies away
to the east. Haydn doesn't belong here and the gypsies
don't come to church. Someone's knocking at the door.

Something's knocking at the door, some force greater
than self sufficiency, longer than the forests and
wider than the army. It involves Haydn, out in the villages
listening to the gypsy bands and making notes, it means
the hymn, our last connective, ending and emptying.

The hymn ends with grace if the people we employ
get honest payment. Nobody in the wide west
believes this, the big numbers rattle in circular tombs.
But it is so, ultimately and yesterday and without end.
The gypsy band plays for singing and dancing

and every tune is our requiem, our bonfire in the snow.
The day of wrath approaches from the direction
of Austria, candle flames in the dark graveyard
as the watery star passes across the sky and
it is not enough to thrive, or to understand.

It is not enough to create. Look to the future
as a specific task to be completed before dawn
for the sake of humanity, the earth-bound music
that buds from the withered rosebush, called
back from the wild places, dark stone in hand.

From the black fates of Europe, the acres of despair just
round the corner, may wisdom protect us and lead us in
a linked circle for we have given thought and
worked hard. But have we stood on the ridge-top in
snow as the winter blaze dies down and viewed the harm?

No. But we have joined in the singing in the church,
Haydn in Hungarian from the days of the Empire
and felt the pull of intellection towards peace. If only
the gypsies too had been there the possible land
would have been a commonwealth.

To the Memory of Frank Cassidy

I can't play properly now. Never could, really.
Slow subdued Irish speech and immediately
broke into a *Bonnie Kate* that would raise every hair
of a bald man's head followed by *The Blackbird* at which
the soul lies face down on the green slopes of earth
hoping for political good into the dawn

Which comes bright or failed, levers itself onto the hill
wrapped in thin rain and those of us who are blackbirds
will whistle and sing to it, and like all good workers
pass on to unmarked graves for the sake of the good
that goes unacknowledged and builds piecemeal a future
with enough cracks in it to evade political determination.

And I did nothing else, and everything I did
was done by these barren shores where the grey rock
breaks at the sea's edge, milled into the dawn.
It was the only thing I could do, the rest was shift,
and I did it all for Bonnie Kate, who was lost to us by politics.
I watched her ship leaving, smoking gold leaf.

The Lark in the Clear Air

Is. I've never known what to say.
But is and is. Calling over the/ what's
that grass stuff called? I'm 70 this year
and something flutters in the sky that has
a meaning, and the meaning is
telegrams from the worked edge
saying (and I shan't let go of this)
that in order to live you have to die
which is banal but accurate and disguised
in song lifts the heart to a waltz with fate.

Good luck to you, new bird,
in the mean years to come.

Drowsy Maggie

Slouched by the grate as the fiddler plays on
like Mary Barton asleep against her father's knee
the casual elegance of a cloth twisted into her hair –
this is Maggie, drowsy, in her dialect fully informed.
Her image is permanent.

Her promise is true, representing good nature
as the image of grace in the human form as in
Piombino or indeed, if you like, the pop version,
Botticelli. Bodily, and female, form, diagonal
against a tomb. And drowsy, thick in ceremony,
her preference is for now.

Safe from harm at the heart of the dance
through the night until it is enough and tiredness
redeems us from fantasy, sadly enough to return
at dawn to the day's demands, the first crows,
the first lorries setting out. Come with me, she says,
across centuries, and drowsily, but her offer
is specific, her concern falls on the child.

King's Cross to S.O.A.S.

Euston Road

Out into pouring rain. News vendors in red boxes. *They will cut off your head and run away with it so that you cannot think* and cannot deploy the knowledge gained in courts of equity life-long. Never stop thinking: the dangers ahead, the inward turn of the market, what to do with an inadequate umbrella, run. To a subway. Emerge. Dive for a shop doorway. The dream on offer is birth, turning from death's clear portal. They lurk in red meat alcoves, shouting war, naming names. *The only names you need to know are those of the powers that obstruct a good fate.* Cower, at the rain, at the hard journey anticipated, into the Street of the Many

Argyle Street

Hotels, naming without meaning. *World, world, we owe you nothing but you press us down.* At least I have defeated the traffic scam. *There is a spell, world, against your weight, and the bright sparks that clog our feet.* I have forgotten this spell. Someone, world, stole my mouth and I shan't find it among the refurbished hotels, where shreds of hope are spun in the small hours. World with your gliomas and your bibles, damn you world. *May the fire burn you, bitter world, may the earth smother you.* This spell I learned in a field in Romania, probably it is obsolete. Sometimes the best response is to burst into tears, and see through the mist what we are. Not doing that, but something lesser, I turn into a hotel entrance to

Derbyshire House

shelter from the deluge and complaints of society. It is not a hotel, it is one of those blocks with a covered entrance. A man clutching a motorbike in the alcove, waiting for the rain to stop. He has nothing to say. He has a message to deliver. *Everything you see could suddenly disappear in a stroke of vengeance leaving dust and rubble and parts of people like red rags*

Whidborne Street

on the road. Only a world concept can provoke that. The rain lessens, the messenger drives into it and I carry on down Argyle Street, out of the hotel zone into the council flats zone. I don't think I have the password for this but nobody's noticed me yet. *You who heap plastic tricycles and defunct TVs on your balconies, respect my silence as I pass by in the rain.* I say nothing and I don't know your name, nor the tension in your living-room nor the fire behind the heart. Don't shake your enormous shorts at me I have The Book of the Dead in my pocket and I recognise the wallpapered grave. So far so good, the doors stay shut. *We are bound back to back, we never see each other, we never speak* turning the corner past

Cromer Street

the laundromat where a little old Asian man in a white robe runs through the rain head bowed, pink flower patterns on his shoulders. *Walk. Song. Thesis. Inscription. Make up your mind what you intend to be.* Passion's monument, older and deeper into solitude where people carry plastic bags in a hurry under cloud. A small split in the sky, a blue flag in the wind. I need a ferryman to take me across my eye, over to the east, the breaks of pastoral colours (sky, leaf) over ground stone. The boat is in pieces and I can't name the parts, the oars are words *They have reduced what is great to what is little. They have created war and internment.* The pedestrian lights change and the river stops to let me across. My eye has

Judd Street

a floater, I didn't need a ferry. And continue through the smallness, with the tall buildings on the right (on the way back they will be on the left) shadowing progress. The shadow in the desert, that enlarges the small traveller's longing for home. The air clings, the water runs along the sides of the roadway and down grids. This is a diagonal journey across a N-S grid, left right left right, go east go south bit by bit street by street until we arrive. The labyrinth has no centre but the true voice which is not so hard to find. The big building is a hostel. *They have created war… What are their names? I don't know their names. It was a long time ago and they are all dead.* It was yesterday and the widows are still shrieking. *My speech went down the grid* but I have reached the very heart of my pupil. Another right turn, polished red brick of apartment block. It's a short street, but its name continues ahead, into death and destruction. Like a spark at the end of the street, caught in the target, core of the retina, an ordinary morning. "The senses report to the heart, which forms thought and sends it to the mouth. Opening the mouth re-enacts the conflict between Horus and Seth." Walls polished by blood, body parts flying through the air. *Cut the hole for my mouth, I have something to say* we have brought war on ourselves, and daily fear, on the very edge of our enlightenment, which stands but a few yards SE of here: Coram Fields, Handel Street, Brunswick. Orphanage, health centre, public gardens. A global pact. But still the eye is drawn towards crisis, a flash and bang at the end of the street. We are blasted OUT. They are sucked IN. Avert the eye and turn another corner, to the left, avoid the crux or thought remains for ever unformed, numbed under blame. At every corner I become a different creature: Now I'm some kind of tall crocodile in the shopping zone. *Gods in caves, eating the dead.* The dead of Tavistock Square and the dead of seven wars. And who will believe us when we say there is nothing to fear from the distant villages on the edge of the desert? The people who wanted to kill Dougherty. *Somebody has cut off my head and is eating it in a retail outlet.* Day and world bound together, back to back, eyes that never meet. To enter every shop in Marchmont Street one by one and buy

Tavistock Place

Marchmont Street

Russell Square

back the body parts, for reassembly, to reconstruct a people out of their debts. And what is this people? *It is not me, it is not you, it is not Islam and it is not "us".* So hurry. And keep eating, eat as you walk, eat up the fear, words are food, grab a vocal sandwich and sing, consume and be consumed. Sooner or later the outcome has to be settled, war or peace, fragments or wholes, everlasting despair or vast hope free from distractions, resentment, impotent rage. There's plenty of time. Gather the parts together as you pass Brunswick Square, recently translated from shopping to corporate spectacle. *The creatures that live in the pupil of the eye* are called into assembly, and stand in a row looking at a glass-fronted housing development maturing into the sky. A city made for the people. The people here and the people there. Regency clearances preserved for the commonalty while business interest scowls in concrete sheds round the back. A fountain at the centre, and unconditional welcome. Also a nasty report in the distance up Woburn Place. Destruction of sub-standard dwellings, destruction of persons by random violence: a state, a world state, is at work, spreading its double wings. Where is the person that we need, *der / Die Todeslust der Völker aufhält /* who restrains the death wish of the people? *Expect no heroes, no singularity. A patchwork of body parts.* There's some kind of hope just round the corner. *I have turned eight corners and passed through eight states as eight creatures* and now I am in an open space between night and day with a fountain at the centre. It's not far now, round the last corner. I shall arrive separately as each of nine mummified ibises to listen to the music of the eastern lute. It's starting to rain again. I asked a load of questions and they weren't answered. The music that approaches (round the corner) is the fall and rebirth of the city. It says,

S.O.A.S.

I wish I were a swallow, then I could sit on the top of the Gherkin among the uncountable rods and watch the city centre squirming and fighting across its channels and struggling to make sense of its thousands of streets along which contradictory wishes crawl... How to measure the pricing of our ease, and not link our fate to a dying oligarchy of oilmen. A bird with one wing dipped in blood and an illegible message written on the other beginning "Within the bounds of hope…" Round the corner and up the steps. Before me the island of the horizon dwellers, *the floodplain at harvest*. I hear the wing beats from the basement. The open mouth, the unlocked doors, of the shops, of earth and sky, the message rising from the peaceful centre of contemplation, a point without volume, free of hunger, a painted flower *"Within the boundary of the people"* I eat the enemies.

The Road...

The road to Baghdad, is it straight? Do they
kneel beside it to their own passions, ink-
wells of light, the rose that becomes a route?

Only the wounded pass through the gate showing
their red passports, only the killed arrive home
and take their mothers' coffee.

The stained floor of the desert, vultures wheeling
over the tank routes, forgotten tunes in the
far hills. Death steps over the river on stone syllables.

Sky full of stars, body parts flung out of transport systems
or suburban markets, dissolving into the greater
and closer light, moon on silent prophet's tomb.

Is this journey legal? Is it permitted? All that's left
of Palestine, a few small red flowers close
to the ground, a seething patience.

Kneel among them and beg for such patience
while the dove sings in the cedar, the song
of Yes, there will be pain, yes,

There will be horror at the dark traverse.
The coffee simmers on the heater,
its perfume fills the room.

The Road (remix)

How long, Babylon, how much more
blood soaking into sand, glitter-
ing failure on the floor?

A goat bleating under an olive tree
beside a ruined wall at the end
of a dry track, soldier,

This is the home you fought for,
grey stones tumbled on the ground
and a wooden flute serenading death.

The black eagle flies from cairn to cairn
with red messages: we shall make
our final space in sung words.

And in the vast green plains and hills of
eastern Europe the Jewish population
completely eradicated, not a stone on a stone

Not a board nailed to an upright. A wreath
of rose heads and bone for what remains.
Take it in patience, listen to the pain

In the dove's throat, water
pouring from the well, beating
of wings in the air.

The Road (carol)

To Bethlehem, is it really not very far? Do the shepherds
come to the road's edge to beg for dollars?
Do the hawks' star-shot eyes keep watch from above?
And when you get there, is there a hospital?

Note.
*The first three lines of 'The Road...' are an adapted translation of four phrases from
the poems on pages 111 and 112 of Adonis,* Le Livre (al-Kitâb) *traduit de l'arabe de
Houria Abdelouahed, Paris 2007.*

Shadowy Waters

A boat still on dark water,
an old man with nothing left to do,
connections severed, moving
closer to the fire in winter
and in the gaps of a cloudy mind
passing hope forward across darkness.
Hope of what unable to say exactly
but loud with mental song.

The shadow of the hill
falls across the river at evening,
a small bug walks across the closed laptop.
A disillusioned and perfectly contented
old man uncertain about destiny
but solemnly observing the living thing like
a small rowing boat crossing the shine
and full of incipient melody.

A song of final justice
unheard in the day, at night engraved
on valley and river and the air
that's always leaving, struggling
with shoelaces, letting the soup burn,
shaking head in self despite, shuffling from
room to room, of the few rooms there are,
muttering at the windows Why
have they left me alone here? The trees
respond across the river, the leaves dither.

Hope lies in practical mutuality.
The light plays on shadowy waters
this way at day this way at night, the cup
of cocoa goes cold on the kitchen top

the wheels continue to turn, the song
louder and louder, fuller and
better throated across the silence.
Everyone is invited and expected
to sing, and louder sing, sing
outright: a hope survives
by being passed on, and translated.

The wooded hillside is completely invisible.
The packet of cigarettes must be somebody else's.
What happened to the bug did it reach a journey's end?
From the far side of the valley the song of reconciliation
can easily be heard. At the end of the road
stands the conclusion to a different story
and a rivulet catching the dawn.

Shining Cliff

In December 2006 my daughter celebrated her 30th birthday in an isolated hostel in Shining Cliff Wood, near Ambergate, Derbyshire, among twenty of her friends.

———————

Forfeit world and win
the shred of earth that spells true
that wills itself through common need

Keep it for ever if you can. When you are 80
meet here again and take the same oath
in each others' eyes.

The robin hesitating on the gate,
the blackbird peering into the grass.

———————

Crossing the small wooded valley
knowing the world's instability, learning
the colour of its fade, to keep a record

For ever if you can, meeting
and passing signs to the future
long after any of your birthdays.

A different robin on the gate,
blackbird on the young elder.

———————

Meet across the world's divides
and there is your shining,
where it has always been

Through the night closure (cunning world)
and the future when you will move slowly
supported on frames

With birds to cheer your way then as
now calling under brittle leaves.

———————

Hope engendered in company
sorrow's picture staring down
the long song against despair

Secure your beautiful white hair
we shall not always linger here, scooping
fluff from the machines. Listen,

The thrush at its limit, the totally
unreasonable wren, piping through the gates of death.

———————

The long high song echoing
over the trees down the slope
the leaves flicker a world picture

A tempered wish, a tied purpose
slices the air, our failing
falling ecstasy, our trade.

The caged goldfinch, a memory of Baghdad,
robin and blackbird suddenly flown.

———————

The ring in the air, the green mottled light
moving on the side of your face, you will
have to insist on this validation

For fifty years through all the exits and ignorance
star and leaf in tension through the sky
as the mist descends, and

The ring is not for love now, the ring
is for war. You know this and continue,
arm over the magpie's shoulder.

———————

Birches and small oaks. Fear and anger
stirring in the wind, which is not strong,
swaying like warblers on reeds, we make our progress

In slow careful steps, over and through
the barriers the world creates towards
horizons of thought, purple patches on leaves

And off you go, on your own as we all were,
sorrow band across the forehead, opening the gates,
the birds flock over the stones.

———————

Bright surety here where it always was,
flying on unsure wings
to perch high on the world's lack.

We forget it, fumbling
with connectors at the edge
of our spaces as the days roll over.

Starlings and blackbirds
high in the trees, presiding there
where the president failed.

———————

Down in the valley below high in the clouds the old tension
is stretched that snaps into love and hatred, red leaf,
put these cares on your portfolio.

We edge between our failures
some of our failures are vast enough to blanket the world
and hope survives as a heart-light calculated on the dark earth
a point gathering others, small fires dotted on the plain.

Keep them burning into the next century,
you old drunks.

———————

The pristine burn of thought that
rends up from the stones
what must be done

The earth must be recognised
The dead must arise and the washing up must be done but first of all
the earth must be recognised

And when recognised released.
Tell it to the astounded pigeon. That bangs
into flight.

———————

December, patches of bracken stalks
brown leaves clinging to some of the trees
and strewn in the pale grass, thousands
of chestnuts rotting on the ground.

The A6, slightly visible, slightly audible
down the end of the valley through the trees
your route home to southern business.
Remember this north before its bitterness.

Hairclips, Cuban rap, analysis
And a farewell to the song thrush.

———————

In five months' time flowers will start to emerge
on the ground and in the trees
but none of us will be here then

We'll be somewhere else
pursuing our centres
to the world's core and closure

With passion to reach the world's
gravity. For they exist,
the little ones with nothing to eat.

Bright eye, yellow beak.

*How then should I your true love know
from another one?*

A voice, a message, a promise,
a wrong to be righted, a future
moving in the forest at night
towards a conclusion, and an end to oppression.

May he reach you from the ends of the earth,
humming-bird caught in his hair.

* * *

27/12/2004, 11 p.m. Kemptown, top floor, a strong wind. The potted plants on the balcony vibrating in front of the white wall. Solid cloud sweeping across the moon.

Offer this to the distant ones, the perfect, the children's children: They need it, this fault, this being right here. The fan heater makes a fluttering noise. Flights of elsewhere that sustain us, wired into now. Was it one of you that hung up the paper fish?

28/12/2004, 11 p.m. Kemptown, top floor, no wind. The big glass panel and the white wall beyond seen through an image of the room. Low cloud layer erases the lights on the hill.

What can you do with this, merciless ones, the powers to be? You don't need it, leave it alone. Dawn at Guantánamo, turn it off. You don't hear the wave break, structuralists. The wave breaks anyway, across the earth. One of the survivors constructs a paper hope, red green and yellow, with two enormous eyes.

Essex Skies

1
A failure, but it is the same for everyone in the end,
in the dark, under the lights. Driving back from
the wedding between the dark fields, the night layers
carefully hand aeroplanes down to Stansted,
and somewhere over the fields is a small embanked lake
with one elm, under which the controller
of weddings and stars sits crouched, tapping messages
to the enormous circular horizon. *Think what you're doing.*
And all that wealth in the sky, the sparkling
aeroplanes gliding down like swans to Stansted
to deliver cargoes of people back to their worries,
their weddings, their new babies. The dark field corners
are open to the great circle of mind, but waves of fear
shake the tree canopies. The earth turning brings
sky to the heart of its circle, across which
the indolent aeroplanes flashing and droning move
like waitresses from one side to the other of our
wedding feast, our immense resilience
and inevitable failure: big words
that shake the trees in the night, soundlessly,
black webs on black depth, interrupted by stars
and aeroplanes, following their rulers
and controllers, directing all that wealth
away from homes, into black holes.

2
The skies here are never less than total, and to live
under such spatial wealth must enclose you
in particulars: night fears, golf scores,
trouble with gypsies. The weddings call in
clans of hundreds, all offering their own fates
over which the principal celebrant is the baby, two weeks,

a superb performance and doesn't believe a word.
Career anecdotes, sex jokes, regulation and subsidy,
the baby has it all worked out and receives the applause
with graciousness. Nothing else unites this society.

And miles away, right out of earshot,
the travelling fortunes encircle a pivot, keeping
rigorously to flight paths, coiling towards rest
and someone sits under the elm
in the dark beside the still water
singing *sotto voce*, controlling nothing
but her own heartbeat, inhabiting the rare
release of calm which unites this society.

Whistling Sands

The waves rolling to the shore and breaking.
Seeing this through many eyes, the waves
crowding to the beach and turning over, watched
by the generations. Our attention turns and wanders,
preoccupations block transmission: what we do,
the results we have, elsewhere. The land stretching away
behind us, full of snares and recompenses, the angels'.
eyes in the cemetery, stone spheres seeing to eternity.

The baby's eyes seek proximity, the sheltering arm,
and any unfamiliarity can be referred to questions of dinner,
but returns again and again to the funny thing, whatever it is,
making this noise and repeating itself and spreading
across the sand. The old man's eye is uneasy,
glimpses wandering shades and suspects a darkness
advancing into the corner of his vision, in the distance,
and worries, with little hope now of shifting the structure.

The mechanism by which shared senses come together,
and, hearing the salt hit the sand, form an alliance,
which carried through language into act could move
against harm, like forming a household, a mutual trust.
The wild waves weave and the whole land
faces this edge in the arms of a connected script…
But the child is frightened, and the old man is tired.

Whistle across the sands and there at the far side
of the great sweep of bay is the black ghost itself,
stepping out of the concrete retail shed and coming
towards you, the invited ghost, the relayed failure.
And the baby sees it, and points to it, and laughs.

Lancashire Graveyards

Gritstone slabs invaded by
black lichen and forgotten names.
Rain in the wind, the tops in cloud.

Is labour also buried here, singing
in the ground *the day will come?*
We no longer have the means

Of conducting a life in such surety.
But we can still dance. Proudly behind
the brickwork our boots clang all night.

And the more we dance
the more we think, of a society
not run on mutual deceit. Many

Have led such a thought through their lives
but later died and the thinking
had to begin all over. And it does,

It truly does, generation after
generation in ever deeper colours
pushing push-chairs up steep hills and

Writing theses on participation…
the real thinking continues in the practice of future,
the art of precisely here

And how to maintain hope while the world
leans into its empire of failure.
Which leaves us free to die at last.

Bury us here, where labour is buried, under the dark sod
and set up inscriptions on gritstone slabs
in memory of our great persistence and optimism.

Chapters of Age
Stone landscapes of Inishmore and Burren, May 2010

Chapters of age: increasing anxiety,
Histories beyond credence.
Massive stone forts in mist.

Ruins of small monastic settlements.
Stone distances beyond thought.
Dull pain to right of middle back.

Use of walking stick to lessen this pain,
Inclined to the side of the road.
Singing and laughter behind stone walls.

Loss of secure equilibrium in darkness
With tension headache.
The massive lintel.

•

In Carna they sang as nowhere else
And I did sing, at least once I did.
Nobody held my hand.

"I kissed my love by the factory wall"
Did I?
Liability to mental paralysis when challenged.

And sing still and louder sing,
Psalmic impulsions rolling over the moor
Seeking an imperfect cadence.

•

A man lives in a kind of box in the garden.
Where is the musician or architect
Who built me this weary smile?

The blue and white teacloth,
Symbol of a domestic contract. Outside,
All the world is grey.

This worry in the evening
That the young of earth might wreck everything
But all they do is fall over

Singing "Dirty old town". Outside
The windows and five fields further on
The stone tracts become statutory.

•

Thatched cottage capitulating to damp,
The chair outside the door
Where he used to sit

Facing south across the *chevaux-de-frise*
Remembering blood on snow, Lord,
Keep us from mystery and impotent rage.

Saw everything from there, the rich
And the poor, the cloud descending,
The cattle driven over the cliff.

•

Thousands of gentians (spring, 5-petal)
And mountain avens
In the cracks of limestone pavements.

A line between shadow and light
Full of bone and flint
Full of flint and bone.

Lines across the earth, head
Looks at foot, foot steps across
Gaps in stone where gentians grow.

God, I used to have such a pure foot,
You couldn't see a single vein on it.
How our forms rush to the gate.

How matter obstruct us
And yet forms
The delicate street at night

And the endless stone deserts
At which the heart grows weary
And the mind longs.

•

Bleak godforsaken peninsula becomes
Bleak godforsaken transport development.
Earthly tides come and go.

A quarter mile walk to a locked gents.
The coast too is all rock and gap
And here comes the inspector hopping.

"What are all those fuzzy looking things out there?"
Trees, clouds, stones, floaters,
Little bright-eyes calling me.

•

These lonely towers falling to ruin.
The rook flies straight in the window
Causing eructations.

Law school in a stone ring. "Old age is either
Wholly centralised or the centre atrophies."
Centrifugal dehydration process.

Megalithic tombs surmounting the thin fields
That run off into the distance, harbouring
Old men who ran away with babies.

"Over a thousand years later a newly-born baby
Was buried in front of the portal".
Loss of short-term memory.

Finding the way to the bathroom
In the middle of the night half asleep,
Strange shadow, shed door ajar again.

•

Baby curled up very small in the centre.
Two men doing a fiddle combat.
Unbearable histories,

Famine and persecution,
Fighters disguised as priests or violinists
On the night path over the hill

With nothing said, only the wind in the hazel bushes
That are eating up the open land, tossing
Back and forth over the graves of heroes

Who died for a free Ireland
Now
Mortgaged to international finance,

That secret chapel in the woods
And the wide routes thereto across the open pastures
And poor little Jimmy Murphy under the deep green mossy bank.

•

And many another, as plentiful as the stars
And the stones underfoot, of which at least two will be raised
And carefully placed at the limits of our science.

Dig my grave both wide and deep, a marble stone
At my head and feet, and to my chest there comes
A turtle dove, to tell the world I died for love.

Tell me something else, tell me the source and extent
Of this silence, not in the grave but in the homes and
Parliaments of the world, heart of stone.

"This awful silence that emanates from me, standing there
Trying to remember what real people would say
In the circumstances". Head stone foot stone cumulus.

Head stone foot stone cumulus, the day
Is ended and lost, nobody said anything to relieve misfortune.
The day is destroyed.

Unbaptised children set in separate graveyards
Mere bits of walled-off moor with neither head nor
Foot stones but massive cumulus.

Head guides foot the route home.
All I asked was a legal answer,
A ring under cumulus.

•

What then is the lesson of the stone tractates, what
Is the tune they sing back to us after all our naming?
"A Labouring Man" and his fear.

The questions flying at us every day –
What is the plant with dark green leaves and
Tiny white flowers? What is the answer to fear?

For there are answers to fear,
Common or garden,
That singing up the coast.

Notes to *Chapters of Age*

"Nobody held my hand". In the social singing of ornamental song in Irish, for which Carna in Connemara was specially well known, it was the custom to give the singer support through the difficult performance by holding hands with him or her during the song.

"chevaux de frise" (Frisian horses). In this case, big elongated stones set in the ground in a mass in front of the fort, to hinder invasion on horseback.

"The cattle driven over the cliff". This took place on Inishmore in 1881 as part of a protest against evictions and land-grabbing.

Entire sentences are quoted from:
W.B. Yeats, Tarjei Vesaas, (*The Birds* and *The Boat in the Evening*), William Carlos Williams, Georg Simmel, the on-site information board at Poulnabrone, and verses of three British songs, one of which I didn't know was by Ewan MacColl; I heard it performed by a semi-derelict trio in a hotel bar in Clonakilty.

Swavesey Lakes

Thought I'd have a last wander
in the flat land, visit the bench ends.

Pig in the poke, tern at work,
guided bus-way, these forms

pluck at my heart
but I shall go.

Exactly between measured worlds
face to face across the distances

You remind me, fox and goose,
of long-term promises.

XIX

Greek Passages

there must have been children sleeping
in sweet abandonment
as the unknown sailed into the harbour
and the world stopped

Kelvin Corcoran

Ten Preludes, Exo Mani 2002

There was no journey. The moment we opened our eyes we were there: the colours across the bay, the red on the blue Trinakrian Sea, its turning islands, and all thought of betterment in the world… Bringing trouble, that lives here like a stone. Bringing upright posture, anxiety, and longed-for repose. That live here like the flowers of the mountain.

•

At dawn, a white light on the top of a mountain. Things start to move: an old woman side-flank on a donkey, at dawn, wobbling up the mountain, picking over the stones. A Mercedes glides past, the light there in her eye ever shining… Slowness of the dawn beetle, western promise, worth goat-dung.

•

And at evening the sky falcon stands over the bay, sun sinking into measure. The lights go on in the houses. A man gets out of a boat onto the stones of the shore, walks over to the bar and is recognised. A jovial shout goes up embracing everyone. A treaty is signed in the moment, and brought on into the dance. Slim as pencils, the leaves throw themselves at the music.

•

Thinking simple thoughts, like a dawn bird in my niche I set forth, stepping lightly, walking the shoreline, testing the stability of simple things, words, stones, against each other, the light radiating between sea and mountainside, the air hot as blood. The very living blood that bears our histories.

•

Who was it, sailed from this harbour, sailed out together, Kelvin tell me, from this small harbour that time, deep in the power. We threw all our money into the sea. And what became of that thing they call love, what powers massed, what quiet graves, what carried that emblem to the sides of the earth? Sea surface tensed out, ultramarine against the white walls, the wind ready, the boat edging out at the gap, everything we ever owned flung at infinity.

•

The sea noise ringing in our ears, the return a cadence of the departure or the song thus broken. Always at that opening to the whitechapelled sea the spirit enters its turbulence, and little owls on the electricity wires.

•

Something almost forgotten, making possible a dazzling sanity. A buzzard swoops over an abandoned monastery garden in the hills, like a jet passing. 'Whoosh!'. Keeping an eye on the fig tree. Gods came this way and scored the earth with our amalgamated desires, each for all, and the stars struggling all day to get out of the sea.

•

Caves in the coastal cliffs, pirate storage or homes of acolytes, now bricked up. Tortoises plodding around in the undergrowth below. The geology down the coast echoes the treatises of light, waves of soft rock halting against the void. Swallow at the door, sun's red eye in the bay, compass leaves descending.

•

And such light I've never seen such light, all round us land and sea negotiating over our blood, casting translucent banners across hard earth. Thin grey leaves fluttering, thunder in the hills, a new wind across the harbour, the small boat setting out... The old women knitting in the alcove, keeping an eye on the mating rituals, threading the world into their harmony. The world watches the small boat moving out across the wind, prow set for the world's end, for a year and a day. Small chirruping cries, echoed along the coastal cliffs.

•

Sweetly then, the whole thing complete and sailing away, singing *Noë noë noë...* Sings and shouts: new, new born. Bound for a world of trouble. Welcome home, little turnip, welcome to the old song.

Argolid 2003

I

Pulling the net onto the shore, the goods to market, and market fears, swallow so high. And market loves, the goods brought home across the bottomless Lake of Lerna, great void in sense where monsters thrive, the Hydra on the skyline shaking her heads. Now drained and producing purple aubergines.

•

Our sustenance dragged across our fear, purposeless gloom in half light. Long fields of grey stalks pulled by the wind, our profit hauled onto the land up the long valley and into the hills. Turn and look back, strong hot wind in the face with some water in it, the olive trees thrashing. Our wealth, weighing, working, wearing us, on, to the empty monastery.

•

Elleniko, the watch tower, keeping an eye on the sea. A fleet of wooden ships approaches up the bay on the wind, bringing trouble. Fifty maidens breathing abhorrence, hotly pursued by fifty princes breathing longing – an enormous administrative problem. Floating towns as tall as the lower mountains anchored against St Mark's and dwarfing it. A privileged position, and where to go next. Monetarist evangelism, dialectical negativism, scientific fundamentalism, consumes its own path, where are the binoculars there was a silent bird.

•

Silent that looks at us sideways and shifts away behind the leaves. No reason to be scared, little beauty, ring-dove, deeper into the leaves. Another wave hits the stones, grey pitching into rose O don't you see yon lonesome dove sittin' on yon ivy tree? He's mourning for his true love, and so shall we.

•

Advancing towards us up the bay, Phoenician traders. The king's daughters walk down to the shore, to see the foreign goods. Trouble: suicide, putrefaction, bulldozers, war, waving her heads over the wildered plain. *Trouble so long, been troubled so long trouble don't worry my mind...* Dark milky clouds settle on the bay, night comes from behind the mountains. We rest in perilous ease at blood temperature. Revenge, my sweet poison.

•

Wind, waves, trade, our money sits staring at us. White concrete villas along the shore, with big open verandas trailing vine leaves, fish for sale at the boats. Again the white threshold, the old fears echoing in the distance, trouble hovering, and sheep bells in the hills. The light of our souls downcast onto the stones of the shore. *Money, what have you done?*

•

Sheep bells in the hills tuned to the shepherd's flute (they were 'very particular' about this). I am ill, I lie on the bed, bad news comes in: another Palestinian wedding party shelled, another history denied. Take up that harmony, between particulars, to remember the slowness of the light rising in memory.

•

In memory of justice, the length of the night. An animal runs past the window, probably a marten, earlier there was gunfire – a wedding, as in Palestine, they fire guns in the air. Here it frightens the wildlife. Death striding up the stone steps, the dark boat on the pale shore, the creak on the office carpet.

•

They died, as we all do, it came up the bay at them like a new song.

•

Wake into fallen dark, the labyrinth cut into the open. White egrets, and the great white heron on the dark shore where they dump hard-core for the new discos. Palaces, megastores, always more than we need, shake the earth and the shy bird takes wing. Wake into the question: what if nothing results? Would our biology keep us going? No, the mind seeking itself strikes the shore, a stone turns, a tone returns.

•

A tone saying: Never mind, death had to come sooner or later. Larkspur, wild gladiolus, and the orchid Ophrys bearing signs of lamentation, the dark letter on the gay petal. And the squad at the watch tower signal another arrival, some new monstrosity drifting up the bay. I have a bad cold, it was sent as an aid to thought and observation. Cyclamen, bright flags nodding among the dry stones. Seeking foreign partner.

•

The good ship sails and a gradual understanding comes upon us of transmission broken at fear, across the globe. Lady of the Lake, her terrible heads, her fishy tail calling back the dead in the new darkness. Flee this axis, go as far as you can before turning, three times round went she.

•

But you will turn, in the end, and look back across the silent waters, the roaring gap deep and wide, perfect justice on the other side. Listen. Small bells.

II

Dear, we are in this small white house on the stony hillside, millipedes curled up on the walls like question marks, the great bay below and somebody shouts in the night, language seeming to grow out of the rock like autumn cyclamen. 'A power, a concentration, a figure, a voice.'

•

A sound in the night, the dark uninhabited space of song. A cycladic figure, on its back, suddenly has eyes, and opens them. Tell me what you see. The ceiling of the museum. Why am I lying here in the night so far from home? Outside the world there is no comfort.

•

Helen of the war, dig the grave here *in far countree*. The church clock of Elleniko chimes on the half hour all day and all night. After midnight the next three chimes are identical, single stroke. Helen, this world lay before you, was it worth a single thought? Her eyes thought so.

•

A great wave comes up the bay in the night carrying sharpened coins. It breaks and dissolves against a stone chapel in the hills, wooden iconostasis tuned to Radio Tarifa. 'You can't love what you don't know.' Tracing the map of England, in small love, her eyes fought so.

•

Dear, I am so far away, I am nobody, out in nowhere, millipedes curled up on the white walls like coiled springs, mulberry tree at the front door. A ringing in the night, what is that? Phases of delight and alarm coil round my heart when I catch that music, tuned to the distant hurt, the small voice.

•

Vulgar men our impoverished vocabulary our power handed to nobodies, pretences of men, unknowables. The lights of Nafplio across the bay from the shit-house window. Divine interpreter of my song.

•

O me it's O my, what gone become of me, I used to fly high like a turtle dove, now all down town just hangin' aroun'... Uncle's song, dead relatives gathering round the house in the night. *Last time I saw my maw and paw they were in my dream and I was shouting at them You got no right, to come back, from what became of you.*

•

Old dance-songs that sweep up their words from the floor. The old style of Cretan lyra with sympathetic strings running under the board, and pellet bells attached to the bow. The coin- and bell-hung dresses in the folk museum at Nafplio. Every move you make is a guidance, and a pulsion of the exchange. The extraordinary silence in the Dhofrion Gorge, from Élonas, above the vegetable fields of Leonídhi. A great fall of space, down past the trees in clefts of rock a single thought falls into the earth. Truth rises into meaning. A nun trots past holding a basin of hot water.

•

The white rock eyrie, and all that space off the end of the line shouting itself to nothing, in time to the sea. Echoing the plea. Take its hand, Susie Lee.

•

A quiet Sunday with slight rain, the old man plays his flute in his abandoned house down the fields. Can you hear me, advanced people? I know I am very far away beyond the clouds. I'm telling you about Mr Vanghélis, down the fields, the stone wall builder, the man with the sharpened senses, whose every action is a completed action, fulfilling its arc. I'm not asking anything for this. The winged archer perches on my brow.

•

A mobile phone rings in the middle of the night. Sudden bursts of wind like little tornadoes passing. I don't make a narrative, I await an arrival, singing. I'm getting to know this place: three steps down turning half right into the kitchen, in the night, every window showing coastal lights. Hello, yes, what? 'Christ is risen'…?

•

The narrow shore behind Lerna, barely room to walk between the sea and the tall fences of the orange groves. Cloudy day on the stones. And suffering shall cease, and we all return to a pre-Aurignacian repletion, end all this advance, torment. There is no path, it ends squeezed between land and sea. A dark town across the bay. Clumps of giant fennel, used in ancient times for carrying fire, the pith inflammable and long burning. We trust it and it ends and we turn back, one by one it ends. Roy Fisher hears me, up in the northern hills, and turns to pat the dog that died.

•

Old steam locomotives rusting in the sidings at Mili among eucalyptus trees, close to the sea. Their couplings fall off, their doors are open. A small village with three bars, where youth pauses. An overwhelming frustration and anger, a world emotion, lives in the cracks in the floor, making it difficult to dance.

•

There we wept, by the rivers, by the new software, exactly where youth seeks change, by the electric fence, by the spring flowing into the sea, by the open arm, there.

III

We eat outside under the lamp as it gets dark, in the company of moths. The lights of the bay gather at this end, as if pointing the way towards Mycenae. Lay down there, and rest, exhausted by profit taking, close your eye.

•

All the big lies assembled at Mycenae, all the rights to live at the expense of others. They took the old man's samovar, his one pleasure, in lieu of taxes, since he had nothing. For we hate the poor, and think they should pay for our dinners. Our credit with razor lips sings this song: *Lay you down and die.* And the big stories came to Mycenae and wiped themselves against the stone walls.

•

Tales of snake spirits, that are repeated out of each other and don't know which they are. They sit in the glass cases of the museum like Cumberland sausages waiting for the millennium, for a narrative. But four thousand years is nothing, common people commit such murders every day, the nuthatch on the stone wall lost in a wine of, a possible fullness. Streaked across the eye, secured for the day.

•

Kefalari. The water bursts out at the foot of the hill which shall wash away these stories. Churches, and a lollipop kiosk, claim the place. Coachloads arrive wanting to buy something, something redemptive, though it might not last. Up in the windy hills the rain marginalises us, serving every cell of the landscape.

•

The King of Asine has gone, and Seferis with him. The citadel, a boss of rock above the sea, the caravan park, and the massed hotels along the coast. King, poet: a vertical thrust through all that horizontal continuity and steady cash. A clearing, a void, a cry across commerce, remembering honour. A citadel, with about enough grass among its stones to graze a donkey for a week as the sea diamonds shoot overhead. Come, little donkey, I'll hire you for a year and a day, and you shall bear patiently a collection of CDs of rembetiko, demotika and Byzantine chant in two wooden boxes along the coast road and across the vegetable fields 15km to a semi-ruined stone house in from Iría, which when we get there proves to have no electricity. But we know the tunes by heart, and sit in former time like little waves against cyclopean walls. Ten thousand years, drinking of the wine. Old poets, remembering the oceanic tones of a just peace.

•

Justice that survives in the tales while the actuality lies ten feet down a shaft grave. There was no justice. Tiryns, a fortress of privilege guarding the end of the bay and every advantage structure to be had. Again the split brain advances, at someone's cost. The King was so frightened he leapt into a large storage jar. Excavations under the summit palace, left partly open, reveal a Bronze Age circular structure divided into segments. The guide was maybe drunk, didn't have much English and kept saying, "It is the marigold, you know, that little flower, it is the marigold."

•

We have our guides. Poetry guides, culture guides, war guides. They clear the path and take the fee. They expel the reactions and determine the causes. They know what is important. Greece, they tell us, was where farming entered Europe. Western men, they explain, want to rape eastern girls. A bit of resistance, they claim, is good for you. The keys of the piano are actually so stiff they can hardy be depressed at all and Greece entered Europe in 1923 singing *Yiá sou Lámbrou with your kanoún O play that thing I've got heartache and pain and I'm going to die, och, amán amán.*

•

Asia arrives constantly, by one way or another, and all the mindless killers we send out can't stop this flow, of desire. I lay my head on the salt sea bed, and wake into white sheets on my nostrils, the edge of light. O take breath, open your eyes, they are all busy out there in the fields, Count Tolstoy in his smock.

•

The mind is a cold and lonely place, its doors locked. Outside in the moving air is where things happen. The vast stone mountains of Greece, with fertile coastal strips and some high plateaux insufficient to support more than a few citadels run by killing machines, heroes of expansion and development. The orange butterflies speckled black or brown, that vanished with the first rain.

•

We are out of favour, we are not in the know. We read books with titles like 'What, Then, Must We Do?' and 'Who is to Blame?' We kick stones in the road, the dirt road that winds up into the hills, to the empty villages, the houses locked or decayed, an erasure across the forehead, the movement of clouds in the distance. The great redeemer, floating in the mind sad and cold, saying, 'A monumental trust lives in the heart.' But there is an immediacy, a smoking chimney, somebody looks up from the news. The singing is unstoppable. A gecko runs across the wall-o.

•

I lie in bed dreaming the street plan, corners of dark northern towns, complex of small back streets I can't quite remember. My mother held my hand at the street edge long ago, and we had our thin riches there too, the future sailed up the bay as the potential, it seemed, of the entire land held in the local hand. I dream this. Sound outside, swishing of trees in gusts of wind, the red earth under the sky's black cloak. That I should come so far from such streets, rejoicing in the same fear.

•

It was Troy's turn, the surplus needed it. We destroyed your house, helped ourselves to all the goods, cattle, women, though we got very little of it home. And what did arrive at Mykines sang of total loss so full and sharp, we stood confounded while our governors hanged themselves in pantiehose shouting *Freedom and Democracy!*

•

Old socialists, I think we were trying to arrange for a bit of *space* around humanity, to breathe in, to venture some trust, multiplying our senses of what we are... We are forgotten shoes in a shed creaking irritating questions, about living off the labour of others, which everybody thinks is just great. We are reduced to a single moment, a shout of denial, a syllable in the night. Then we are finished.

•

Though my story is hardly begun. The white flower falls to the ground, the jay screeches across the fields, now freshly green in November. For this is Asia, and always has been. Here we live what we are as a delicate garden, small blooms at the edge of the desert, invaded by ultramarine and the rosy pink cloud unfolding at the gates of dawn.

•

A reason for coming here. And dreaming in the night, of a steadfast resistance, and the joy and fear of belonging. The shout outside, its moment, as it encompasses us, taking us up into the entire landscape of mutuality, shouted out onto the mountainside. Thus the double wings of the small brown moth on my arm, fluttering open in the breeze.

•

The Argive Heraion, the first place last. Vast arena of hills all round in low sunlight and the wind threshing the olive trees. A German tourist in shorts who walked from Mykines, the patient guardian in his hut watching television, everything shaved down to a film on the earth. Power's monumental lock on sense, a smear of stone on a rise of ground. Immense possibilities of breath, and, secured by distance from market fluctuations, passionately affirmative.

Argolid 2004

I

Again this house on a Greek hillside. Autumn. It is passion, not madness, the voices speaking through us, isn't it, Kelvin? The madness, you remember, Barry, the revenge, tried to swallow the world and swallowed yourself. I think I know this place, I put out my hand in the dark for the door frame, I cut out my heart in the paper it might be serious. I welcome myself back. I step out of the back door at night in my pyjamas, looking out over 20km of sea and mountain marked by small lights or none. Some kind of insane moth flutters at my right ear. Learning the language.

•

Great curve of bay, great curve of disco bars, depot yards further back with heaps of old tourism clutter, separated by a perimeter fence and a bunch of reeds from the remains of the Lake of Lerna. Still water, choked, smoke rising beyond the westward horizon, and a bell ringing. An ancestral immunity to malaria (many-headed beast) among fishers and tenders of small water-mills, not shared with passing geographers and exiled dramatists... Last juice of Mycenae trickling down from the hills, oil snake on the water. What form of world leads us out of this guilt, what demography carries the soul westward? 'But if the entire Manifest of the world is absorbed into gold, the world will be destroyed.' The disco bars are magnificent architectural fantasies in honour of the young heart bags of cash and great balls of fire.

•

Over the vegetable fields behind Iréa and up into the hills. Rise a few hundred feet and everything changes: dark conifers against white rock. To the "Egg" Monastery at the end of a dirt track hanging over a small valley. No one at home. *The knowledge that knows nothing, the empty room where brightness is born.* Creeping through the narrow white corridors and cells, thick with grey dust and fallen plaster. At the centre a dark casket, a muscle that reflects the small lights, grips the world's fear and keeps silence. Lunch by the harbour at Vivari, watching kingfishers.

•

Pelei. Low white houses scattered on humps of bare earth, some of them closed up, some of them falling down. Among them a new tank, a bright white cube with a blue pipe attached. White hopes, some of them fallen. 1913, rows of faces at a colonial boys' school in South Africa. Some of them can speak Xhosa but don't let it be known. Buried hopes germinate. To know the language, to learn the sayings: *Everything is for those who have none of it.*

•

Coming down that little road to the sea near Mili, that calm, level, vast pool of light before us, horizonless, merged into the sky. Coming down that little road and later walking the dark shore near the abandoned factory. A few waders in the shallows, perhaps a spoonbill. How the money came and slopped around shouting 'New!' and was gone. Where did it go? Debris scattered on the shore, and the bright white new apartment blocks, standing in the waste land like refrigerators, like sealed money-boxes. Truth gathers together the lines of the land, the forms of, tales of, melodies, of that little, final, road. A heron standing knee-deep in the light, carefully studying it.

•

(Midea) Hilltop citadels, defended positions for the exploitation of areas of production on lower ground. Foreign stations, exacting 'tribute' on pain of punishment or erasure. And accumulating a surplus, of cash, of days, becoming 'civilised', exercising 'culture'. Expert horsemanship, expert cruelty, expert appetite. Art, another new block. And never gaining anything, living a frustrated anger that burns along the coast and guides kings to their wreck.

•

Charming small Roman portrait busts in the museum at Astros. Wisps of hair behind the ears. A large tortoise crossing the main road near Xiropigádo, objects to being helped, hisses. Points of confluence at which doors open, points tying memory to the route. Wisps of hair in marble like sea fossils. Small furrows in white glaze. It is not nature that needs guarding, it is us.

•

The rock thrush calling from the cliff. Lines of water curl round arms and shoulders. The great hulk came floating up the bay, proclaiming itself in wild lights and amplified machine sounds, hotly pursued by 200 managers. 'We bring freedom and democracy.' We fled to the hills and found employment, poor but direct, to return when trade had again become possible. They never knew that it was they who were going to be developed, to have their images straightened out, right here. Señor, ya estamos solos mi corazón y el mar – alone, my heart and the sea. Plural of 'alone'.

•

Gulf of Korinth
(1) Perachóra, the double sanctuary, the small ancient harbour emerging from scrub land, pink stone foundations in a nook of the coastline, hermit crabs under the pier, remains of a curved stoa overlooking the sea. To sit and talk in the cool of morning and evening: philosophers, those who discuss, and surmise, and let it pass. Ever open door, a place where people can take refuge, knowing that the sea traffic on the horizon will pass by. Here Medea killed her children. What there might be clinging to the edges of the route, the great plain around Thebes now cotton fields, fluff in the margins of the road like snow, Asian stories ringing across the day. What might start up from the darkness. Dhístomo and a hilltop mausoleum. June 10th 1944: 232 males aged 2 to 90. Classed as rural-asiatic disposables. A wall of glass-fronted wooden boxes. Baby skull like a hatched egg. As the light dims, a bleak cross-roads among hill slopes, turning onto the road to Aráhova. Not another car in sight. Here Oedipus killed his father. Shadows throng on the earth.

•

(2) At Delphi the oracle spoke clearly and rationally, perhaps in verse, and directly to the inquirer, giving advice on matters of protocol and procedure, the likely course for the best results. Or pure echo function: ratification of plans already decided upon. No evidence for afflatus, mania, inebriation, fumes, any kind of wildness (the instance in Plutarch was reported precisely because it was exceptional). Nor any extraordinary utterances or equivocal predictions, no ambiguity, no sphinx responses – these 'of folkloric origin', or historicised myths. The stranger who leapt up from the side of the road. And thousands of people each day from all over the world, aware to a greater or lesser extent where they are, or what they see: more stones, more nuthatches, snakes concealed in tales of gold. The Cephalian Spring closed, gate locked, fenced off – there have been rock falls, and we wouldn't want anyone to be hurt, would we. Anyone in the world.

•

(2a) The discussion on the Syphnian Frieze: what must be said, passionately and immediately, for the future depends on it. Bodies signalling like letters on a page, the arm strikes a line between the organs of perception, back and forth. Like a line of poetry channelled to the soul and back. Everything we have, entrusted to a straight line, a direction, anywhere in the world. Until the crisis is past, if it ever will.

•

(3) A ferry over dark, blue, grey, sea – Egyio, Diakófto, and a slow drive up into the hills... Dear Rough Guide, You will be interested to hear that the two hotels next door to each other at Zakhloroú, of which you recommend the one called Romantzo, are now both called Romantzo... Zakhloroú, 8th February 1944: about 20 men. A small moss-grown memorial in the middle of a small public lawn. Kalávryta, half past two, 13th December 1943: 1,258 males over the age of 13. The church clock stopped.

•

(4) The mountain railway not running today, the cloud base coming down and lifting again and again, among the pines and rock slopes. Another monastery, 17th century crucifixes with minutely detailed wood carving, speaking of immense skill. What kind of wood? The speech which springs directly from the earth's width, which creates its own usage to meet the possibility, to know what forces obtain, what is to be done. The speech that actually speaks, in words, pitches, arms, numbers, things, in minutely carved olive-wood. A road-side stall selling honey at a remote corner in the hills, in the mist. Try it, he says, taste it. A malt-like streaked honey with an addictive aroma. It is from those trees over there, he says, maybe spruce. What is to be done? Ancient Sykion. At last. Acres of foundation ruins among brown grass, on the slope from a low ridge. The clear picture, the better articulation, the linear spread. Lord it is lonesome among poor remnants of success, struggling to recognise the world.

II

Lying there in the darkness, what do you see? Darkness, and traces of two windows to left and right, attained by starlight and the street lamps far across the valley. And in that strange light behind my eyes, I see a street map of districts of north-west England: Stockport, Didsbury, Marple, Aigburth, Macclesfield, flickering through sleep, with their persons. I see the streets I hear the persons. Following the streets one by one. Following the old streets out of the world.

•

Readers, customers, friends and supporters, I'm trying to drive you all out of this paragraph. I need it for myself. As a dark space with two vague presences resembling windows. There to welcome the dead, to trace their journeys, marking the shallow sides of the path in the sandy earth. 'Withdraw, and separate.' And together we'll lament the frailty of the classics. And when the time comes, stand up and say, Well, I'll be going now. Shake hands, walk outside, and jump onto a bicycle.

•

Another night map, basement flats in London in the 1950s, where promises are made which last the rest of a life, whose fracture spreads from life to life… 1920s, the young Ezra with his malevolence: 'not entirely satisfactory' which lasted a lifetime, his technique, crafted to hurt like a fine blade, beauty as incision. But the promises which you are born into and cannot step outside of, then 'beauty is admissible, and the love that creates it', the benevolence, is this possible? 'In beauty is deceit' (but not malevolence). *Why should I climb the look out?* Wandering the shore at Lerna again, thin band of stones nibbled by the sea, wire fences. A bounteous spring flowing straight into the sea. Deep, clear water, among trees.

•

Autumn, the welcome cold. It rains, the fields begin to show green. In the dance the hands forming letters, like the letters on flowers, cursive, Arabic letters inscribed in the facial features, where a Sufi will read messages from God. 'When I saw the new Roman inscriptions I was full of apprehension. The letters had taken the forms of buildings: they were temples, markets, houses, gateways, mills, shops, columns… in lines on the stone page.' How to begin, from the slightness we know we are, and the promise we inherit, and work towards truth, unarmed. But we did, and a sweet forgetting ruled, dancing with signs for hands like the signs on flower heads, winter hands in hand over the strata, singing us back to where we began. All the guns of providence were ablaze.

•

Arkadia
(1) in Arcadia, in… Dear Rough Guide, You will be distressed to learn that the Hotel Trikolonion at Stemnitsa, described (p.261) as family-run, very pleasant and hospitable, and reasonable in price, has, alas, fallen into the hands of the people with too much money. It was bought about a year ago by an outfit called Country Club Luxury Hotels and has been completely done over. Plate glass doors, stench of new leather, smart young person at counter… Cheapest available room in October 130 euros! A disaster. So then in whose Arcadia? Whose justice?

•

(2) 'To understand survival logic, poverty is essential.' The upturned palm, *that* Arcadia. Monastéri Podrómou stuck to a cliff-face like a swallow's nest. We would like to stay the night here, it is possible, but the monk in charge will not speak to me, I am ignored and hang around the place like a ghost nobody believes in, entering the shrouded cave-church, hung with gold, turned inwards to its dark muscular centre. Whose peace? Whose reward? The dark heart at the centre.

•

(3) The dark mind, the dark chemicals. Listening for the greatest possible distance. The approach of, 'not a deity, but a substance, to be inhabited'. Whose work, whose truth?

•

(4) Withdraw and separate. The bar in Zátouna. Also general store, café, barber, hardware, agricultural implements, pictures, music… Where Theodorakis lay low for three years. Gorge 500m deep with monasteries and hermitages stuck to its sides, hill towns higher up where it spreads out, the remains of a working mediaeval economy scattered all over it, all depending on water coming down from springs. Grain mills, fulling tubs, tanneries, wine vats, silk mills, all connected by mule tracks. Small stone-edged wheat fields on comparatively level stretches at the top. Village communism, independence. Withdrawn and separated. Resistance. The pictures on the wall. 'My father the bouzouki player.'

•

(5) …over the Arkadian mountains, passing Karkaloú, possible site of ancient Th[e]isoa with a sanctuary to Zeus [Pausanias]. A little plateau approaching the summit of the pass, farm buildings among orchard trees, red ribbons on the corners of the house. The answering, the brightened heart, a refuge because a resource and a resilience, a burgeoning, a dazzling sanity. Trees on the turn, bees on the urn, the flying birds on the top corners of the larnakes (clay coffins) in the museum at Thiva, amateur heart tracing the hopes of death. Pick it up by the corners and fly away with it, the poor being, the forgotten name. Turn out to sea with it, and off for the islands. The white crowns floating on the springs.

•

And all our ghosts will assemble along the sides of the route, shining through the night, leading us home. We have it all, we have it all to heart in its bits and pieces, look, there, the plurality shining in the night seeking questions for its answers.

•

Coming again to the Argive Heraion, where gain and loss, night and day, question and answer, are all flattened. The hard ground thick with little purple flowers on bare stems, bees busy among them, bee-loud ground, among small trees and foundation stones. Aromatic herbs heavy in the air, from such thin cover, the earth unconcealed. The joining powers diminish, the fat things fade. To float a stone slab on the dry terraces.

III

Living under an unjust war, which can only create more wars. And to speak of 'democracy' and keep secrets from your people. Governance serves its own, makes up international law as it goes along, removes obstacles to plunder. Parsimony becomes aggressive. People are frightened. *Cloudy weather, the sun refuse to shine. Some old day, your troubles be like mine, Where on earth you go.* Fingernail on wire. Dead voices, responding. Denying everything I say.

•

We held our opposition for so long, so defiantly, up in the hills until it seemed that what we opposed had scattered itself into the land and melted into the landscape and it was time to return and claim the vacant home. And this was our victory, in the sellotape and sausages and plumbing and wiring and the writing of 'Everyday Life' our nameless country. Ring of hammer on metal, spectral music.

•

I put on a CD of Byzantine church song, it says 'Christ is risen'. But risen as what, it doesn't say. A justice, a redemption, an umbrella, an aerial? The representation in stone of wind-blown silk, or wisps of hair, impossible for a thousand years, and the secular complexity devolving on hope, the lyric of everyday, our actual spatial engagement, obscured, for a thousand years? A possibility kept alive in ephemeral heresies and desert monasteries. A stake in the world, a dry stick thrust into the sandy soil on the edge of a migration route, and twisted and twirled into depth.

•

Pull all these things together, pull them onto the single image, the stone in the road, that small flower. Withdrew the dedication to Napoleon and tore out the title-page.

•

A point at which reward of any kind is abandoned. 1850s, exiles from all over Europe in London, weeping failed revolutions. I suddenly remembered the small monastery on the main road between Florence and Fiesole where you could ring a bell to see a Botticelli crucifixion. We were shown in by an old monk of quiet, genial disposition who coped well with our poor Italian. He showed us the fresco, and the vegetable garden in a cloister, and said, 'There are twelve monks here, of whom nine are dying.' *How do we see our way through this darkness?* Closing both eyes, like opening a book, and seeing. And what do you see? People.

•

People of whom nothing remains. Peasants, builders, workers, suppliers, teachers, who kept the thing going while the governors partied, and whose songs were real songs, lyric, not vast chains of proprietorship, catalogues of brutality and reasons for entitlement to free dinners, but movements of grace on the offered instant, which survive as the flowers in the vase survive from vase to vase, year to year, flower to flower, yellow red and purple clustered in the sun.

•

Beauty comes and goes and obeys the whip-end, turns by the moon pale and full, turning to a new tune. The coats of cattle like scattered leaves across the slopes, orchids, rusty dolls on stalks. Does not beauty then, the hard and distinct differentiation which it is, does it not then necessitate a certain aggression or at least a separation? Warming the home heart by turning a back on the outsider, temporarily, is it, in the moment? I don't know. The thin kine picking a sustenance on dry plains, with coats like emperors' robes.

•

Athens
(1) Ring dove in the park, I throw a crisp at it, it doesn't want it. This is true democracy.

•

(2) The Pnyx: a democracy, a concave auditorium, inverse of theatre The Attic grave stelae at the Keramicos: the floating baby, the final handshake, the downcasting, wisps of hair raised in the breeze The gates of the city, where there is always a fountain. Bring it all to the one image, where we are. We are at a backpacker hostel with a help-yourself hot water urn for instant coffee in the morning. But the messages in the air which encompass all this detail and draw the species together – we breathe them in, like poetry. Remember, they say, the tombstones, the fountains, right of asylum. Remember the words we don't use any more. 'A democracy to silver the land.'

•

(3) Dear Rough Guide, Some of the eating places you recommend in Plaka are little more than dens of food bandits. One you don't mention is Kapnikaréa, tucked away in a corner of the square of the same name. They don't give the stuff away but it's good food at reasonable prices for the area, casual, friendly, and seems to have impromptu live bouzouki music from about 2 p.m. People doing things well. If you can't find it in poetry look for it somewhere else.

•

Last bus to Argos. The day sinking away, small lights emerging in the hillsides, among the olive trees. A solemn theatre of lights, moving and stationary, across the still perfectly visible surface of the earth. A town centre at some distance, clusters of luminous blue and yellow flickering through trees. Distance itself, welcoming itself to the heart from somewhere, nobody knows where, from Asia. Flames leaping from an old oil drum in the corner of a factory yard, consuming the day's residue.

•

Trouble in mind Awaiting a return (of ? socialism, peace, honour, justice. Words we don't use. Freedom.) Living in anxiety. 'If the people are unhappy, the dead will return and try again.' Ghost nation, your delicate air, world hidden in world, concordance of ear and eye. One word shouted in the night, whispered along the arm, restores the nation of sense, word out of word. The bay below, cloud on the sea at dawn, the hills emerging like islands, the sea hidden in the sea.

•

Bright sunlight, sharpening the edges of the house, the blazing secret of it, the day. A reason for coming here. And gathering messages from petals on the stony hillsides and the feathers of birds in flight, and small moths hesitating on grass stalks. The hopes and fears of peoples, cast on the sea, shattered into particles of light

•

And bounding the inhabited zone in a musical tone, from some contraption or other, radio, flute, goat bell, disco… The song, a simple thing, but which has to keep moving, uphill, the pull back from gravitation as from speed and the lone ranger stalks the plains. You know this, wherever you are, you hear the faint tone, the onomatopoeic bird-name signalling the entrance to the silence of ever. The apples shining on the far away tree.

•

Up there looking down on the Argive Heraion, which is almost nothing. Stone lines, a medlar tree, edge of fallen wall, in the late haze. A slightness fermenting at peace, richer than negation or gain. A dream-breaking stranger in the mind for ever after. 'We will outshine the sun'.

Ten Postludes
Exo Mani 2005

Arriving at dawn in the foothills of Taigétos, the dark spaces becoming grey, sense unfolding from the eastward slopes, a little misty, beginning to breathe. A golden jackal crosses the road. The recurrent beginning of more than a day. And if in this newness the lost brother returns, the hormonal bandit is forgiven. Down into the waking streets, slow beetle of dawn, the light filling. Peace is promised by the very earth: an end to your long duties.

•

Dancing in from the sea in a sun column, human gratification. The martins dipping over the harbour, their intricately structured lives, darting to and from mud nests under the balcony, acts which adorn their own philosophy, their shrill call. We are bent to our inhering promise as the song is raised above the waves, to venture forth, to trust the stranger, currently asleep in the bar, who will one day re-establish the heart's true, stone-set, perimeter. There is also a small bull grazing salt on the stone shore. Europe enters Asia with lowered eyes, clutching a begging bowl. Rice or forgiveness, whatever you can spare.

•

(a) White-throated sea, discursive light, pale red wine holding a gleam in the glass. Dionysiac calm.

(b) The little owls that live in holes in the walls of the tower, busy all night and most of the day.

(c) Intermittent bursts of warm wind all night shaking the dry leaves like waves breaking. Lying in darkness in the small stone house, listening, slowly submitting, waiting.

(d) Dionysiac silence and stillness, Cretan thoughts, that any length of time fully furnished runs with the moon-slick towards the encompassing arm, all its facets conjoined.

•

Kranaï, now called Marathonísi, 'Isle of Fennel', opposite, on the shore, the Sanctuary of Aphrodite Migonitis, 'of the lovers' embrace'. The fire carried over the mountains in a small pouch or a piece of fennel stalk. Here Helen and Paris ratified their love, in an arch-shaped discourse, if you believe it, if you wish. Up in the hills, fortress villages, stone cubes clustered on ridge ends, door locked or gone. The constant wind beyond the thick wall at night. Safety and love pursued to a point where you do not wish any longer, but know, the little circuits of blood will never cease their journeying.

•

Arching over all that epic tension, the little owls go about their businesses. The two falcons screaming over the cliffs towards Trachila, courting or fighting in great parabolas. And those lovers, who sailed out from the white harbour, secure in their domestic purpose, tending their day, towards a new home under the sun's eye. The dry grasses scrape in the night breeze with messages of slightness and absence, and I am more than ever bound to it, the death letter, *grinnin in your face*. And it will, you know it will, the boat moving out from the harbour taking us both with it. The little owls know it too, shouting love through the dark stone.

•

Deep Mani
(1) To Cape Ténaron, one of the ends of the earth. Where is the city, we say, where are the ruins, the mosaic, the temple? I can't see anything but stony hillsides falling to the sea. Where is the entrance to Hades? All ends of the earth are entrances to Hades.

(2) Forsaken land, prison land, fortress villages. To get away from the sun, its optimism and welcome, hate it, hide from it in stone cells with tiny windows: an aristocracy. An unlocked door in one of the towers of Vathia, an iron bed a wooden chair and a lot of grey dust, someone's office, someone's tomb. O you can shake it you can break it you can stick it on the wall the truth is always ever wider and brighter than it was.

(3) Retreat to hotel on sea front, windows flung open (Yerolimín). Sun's red eye in the bay. Evening gathers, the rocks cast whiteness into the air. Well-being, handled so much better by poverty than by wealth, through mutual aid and then it is moral: red snapper in lemon sauce.

(4) Sitting silently in the churchyard at Haronda, stone bench in west front. White walls, forming across the yard a house or raised room in which someone perhaps lives. There is an electricity box on the wall, and a light at the top of the steps, but at present no person to be found, some small bird raising hell in the bushes across the road. No person, no answer. For as long as we live. We travel so far, again and again, and we wait where nothing will arrive, and in that pause is a book, a learned book, putting itself together, a mosaic. Conversing with the dead at another entrance to Hades, continuous with the sky.

•

Such fair darkness, such deeply infused light. Time, halt awhile your pressing. Deep blue almost black of the slender rock-thrush standing on a rock on the edge of the sea. The mind dances on words on the edge of nothing to the delight of the blind and the lame, who join the dance, and see the blue rock-thrush, on the edge of the sea.

•

Out across the flowery fields, white flowers and some blue, hanging on thin stems, the cover already dried yellow in late spring, bees and wasps hard at work all day. The equitable, evident, persistent, fair floweriness of the fields, until we approach a 'property'. O, how the dogs to bark!

•

Helen scattered everywhere, setting that foot on the shore: Troy, Egypt, Pephnos, Yíthion, islands… In the deep light of early evening blood is on the move, there are meetings under the lamp-post, on the corner of the street, a certain little lady… The light that holds us, lady light, burning in the night, attracting moths, missiles, dry old souls fluttering at the window. Until that final, safe, island, in the Black Sea, where the record is maintained. And lyric redeems narrative, and hand in hand on the edge of the sand… The small boat entering the harbour, turning the engine off, drifting to the quayside, carrying home, by the light of the moon.

•

The dream of awakedness, a little shell against death's advance. Not being here, being somewhere else, but knowing what is here. Thunder up in the hills, blue-tinted white flowers in the brown fields, sharpened under moisture. The boat comes in the catch is unloaded the man goes home to sleep, as dawn unburdens the coast. Take us there, where side by side the swimming souls delight together in renewed trust. We live there and always shall, one after another, the truth shell, that holding thing, against death's rush.

Greek Passages: Notes

The island in the Black Sea: Leuke, the White Island, in the estuary of the Donau, where "Passing sailors could hear Achilles and Helen at night, singing the story of their lives in the verses of Homer." Peter Levi, notes to his translation of Pausanias (1979) summarizing Philostratus.

The story referred to in the third piece and dispersed throughout is the plot of Aeschylus' *The Suppliants*.

Cycladic figures were deposited in tombs lying on their backs, possibly representing the dead and were originally painted with facial and bodily features.

Radio Tarifa is a Spanish musical group working in an eclectic style based on the congruence of pan-Mediterranean traditions.

Mykines is Greek for Mycenae and the name of the modern village near to it.

The 1940s dates and quantities of persons (executed) in the Gulf of Corinth section, refer of course to the activities of the German occupying forces. The number I give for Kalávrita is one of six different counts I have found, varying from 511 to 1,436.

Books quoted from substantially, or leaned on heavily.

Pausanias, *The Guide to Greece*, translated by Peter Levi. Revised edition, 1979.

Aeschylus, *The Suppliants*.

David H. Turner, *Return to Eden, a journey through the promised landscape of Amagalyuagba*, 1989.

Joseph Fontenrose, *The Delphic Oracle*, 1978.

There are several quotations from the songs sung by Frank Stokes and Uncle Dave Macon and from one sung by Roza Eskenazi.

XX

Due North

Morning and afternoon are clasped together
And North and South are an intrinsic couple
And sun and rain a plural, like two lovers
That walk away as one in the greenest body.

Wallace Stevens, Notes towards a Supreme Fiction

I

Housman's Question

XXXII

From far, from eve and morning
And yon twelve-winded sky,
The stuff of life to knit me
Blew hither: here am I.

Now—for a breath I tarry
Nor yet disperse apart—
Take my hand quick and tell me,
What have you in your heart.

Speak now, and I will answer;
How shall I help you, say;
Ere to the wind's twelve quarters
I take my endless way.

From far – human groups moving

over the great grasslands with the herds,

    sucking the milk of gazelles, sleeping

curled under the fleece / gleam of eyes through black hair

    vast green and red lands without division,

    footsteps measured in millennia.

and morning: raising the head, learning wisdom

in a form of desire, a distance to be gained, learning to wait,

    absence of question-marks, Orphic stasis.

Moving and staying, bearing the location with us
    advance built into the structure of settlement. Not "travel" –
    there were needs, and displacements – economy collapses pack up
                                                and go
        but to somewhere and together
        in the same heart-space, the encompassing world arcs.
        To the high pastures with the beasts every year.

from eve – outpacing the desert
trekking in a great curve across the African savannah
towards the northern swamps and forests
the great diadem that divides the sky
into days and days into hours, captured
        in a circular stone hut with entrance facing SE,
        arrive and attend while the sky ticks on.

                            * * *

Here / First memory of the call to distance,
the 27 arches of the viaduct striding across the town –
    what children are taught: cleanliness, modesty, application, alphabet
        retaining the pivot, the customary right
        we are not beggars, we are neighbours' children
                We live here

and this is our decade and this is our language:

    words fulfilling themselves between people,

        in the air, reaching across expanding distance, free to all, stuff of life

    free of ideological baggage.

From/ cotton mills, smoke drifting over railway sidings, canal boats,

learning to speak from, slow increase of, understanding in daily return journeys

mill operatives, office clerks, tenant farmers

        Bunches of red and yellow flowers

sempiternal succession, interrupted

by disdain and conscription.

Lands thick in scarlet panoply, streams of blood and water mingling.

        Little tiny child, what shall we do
        to keep this hour and arrival intact,
        while skies of slaughter blow
        the twelve ships to harbour
        and all the bells of earth

and morning/ spruce standing in snow, in lines, eight

then fifteen, wood smoke drifting across the fields

    dividing thought   between love and duty

    and by the winds of earth to a compass rose

twelve quarters of sky—I remember

        the sound in the air, of wood on stone, the sea breaking,

the stone rings, gates of the dead land beckoning on the horizon

steam locomotives in the night, tracing northern fates.

Am here! Unfractured, chorale.

    North wind comes knocking on my door
bed of clay / chiming throng — chime on,
    silver bells! healing in the wing that moves
out and in, healing in the lungs: these are real
    midwinter acts, enjoined under wicker arches
(love and joy be to you) (we are not
daily beggars) (you know us, we live here)
    but we don't belong here
    we come from far away.

Macarena, the paint sniffer: "I don't belong   *[an obscure allusion*
in this country, I come from somewhere else.
My parents are waiting for me there, my sister
is at school, she is doing very well…" Beyond the forest
beyond worry about belonging, the terrain opens
to the sky, a pale blue death certificate sheltering
her trust.   *[but probably she died*

Now for a breath — this caravanserai, lakeside inn on the edge of the world
where we learn the tables of time and change: you can
stay here for ever in the decorated moment, wide and deep,
temporary shelter that will not let go of you / gradual
and piecemeal shift to husbandry and cultivation, so slow you couldn't
say it happened. It / *blew hither* / updraughts on the edge of day
    remoulding the compass rose, competition
    for control over storage. War.

        * * *

Afterwards we pitied the fallen
and sought their homes, to comfort their mothers
a loving cup against the malice of a carved line
while she sat there and knitted…

    migrating geese in the sky
    coffins in the backs of horse carts
    coming over the heath in a line
    all the names forgotten now
    the wind on the river

ruffling, *stuff of life—*

with a backpack of names
    draining like an hour-glass onto the road
migrating geese in the sky
    ancestral bone polished brown we take it wherever we go.

Tell me – how from the vast emptiness of the million words
the short phrase strikes the bone between the eyes,
tell me how the world is altered, *so little*
tell me as little as possible, tell me *falsetto*
    tell me all night –

What have you in your heart
        – coal smoke, long-term hope
      folded against the cold,

        the grass growing on the weirs,

        the entwined briars in the graveyard.

There are catalogues and histories in my heart

    and timetables, running through the night.

From death, returning *not alone*

with no baggage, with workers' power

under cover

    to reach

the shaking-loose of minds

in quiet urban corners with yellow street-light through the trees outside

to/from/far from *a western brookland* kept sealed

    Pound, treading the back roads of Languedoc
    dizzy with love and malice, muttering the genealogies
    of Italian landowners and professional soldiers
    working out codes of command in papered-over
    cracks between legend and science

tarry, disperse, the time has come, the power of the thinkers

    burns in the raging forehead

of the desert soldier, the Pakistani newsagent in his

    ransacked shop

desperation forged into a ringlet—

Take my hand / Tell me

        looking around, what do you see?
(we lost everything)

        In the circle dance, the hora,
        the child's hand reaches for mine
        to be steadied, to be brought forward
        into more and more of where and when, into
        a safety, while beauty is stronger than freedom.

                Who wants to end in a croak pit,
                telling the world it is finished?

Then sustain it, *tell me*

    what you have, lost or left

    in a language beautifully linked

that you could tell the links one by one

like the links in a silver chain, a silver

    tested and coined, fixed in the moon's side,

        over the end of the world

and we'll get there, reach

    the flowered arbor, the chambered tomb

        crawl into it and read the stone

with difficulty (about honour).   Then answer

Where are you from?

    – war and bondage
    gross disparity of incomes
    everything is a commercial for something else

and I would turn and answer
among the springing thyme,
Oh, peal upon our wedding,
and we will hear the chime

    and sing the song

    of parting, to be a soldier

    far across the sea *I had a dream the other night*

    dividing the token across time that will

    endorse our rejoined cognition

before it is too late, quickly,

my hand

                                 lies on my chest

    and everything is still.

        The child at the door
        asks for nothing more.
        The city at her hand
        voids the echo. We
        dance together in
        the slight grin of knowing
        each other's fear.

Ere to the/ return of piano with spread chords

four quarters in settings by

Vaughan Williams / Bartók / Janáček

nationalists, working down to the local where it opens out –

sčasování – holding the fading tone at stations of perception

overlapping language units, a temporary home

as the Empire dissolves (in blood) and the palaces are for sale.

The wind across the plains divides itself
    four, then eight
    forms in compassionate conflict
for there is more to music than marches and waltzes, more
to history than the Austro-Hungarian empire
          At its demise
  all the love flew out
    in bouquets of discord to found new
professions, rushing in with offers of help.
Some of it saw for the first time the lives of the people.
Some of it reached here, knowing nothing
of the genealogies of Italian land-owners, learning
the price paid on the fields of Lombardy
for the slightest deviation from the feudal code long
after feudal honour was disowned.

> "This is Lucio. He is only a baby now,   *L'Albero*
> but you will help him [to live] and later   *degli*
> he will help you," she holds him   *Zoccoli*
> and he looks up to her eyes   (a
> rests his forehead against her cheek for a moment   film)
> and looks up again.

At the Ospedale in Florence, little trains of orphans
guided by nuns through the cloisters
    in a sense we all came from there
        endlessly, *endless way*
where *from* I don't know –

Tenant farmers above Halifax,
world of clarts and slopstone
and the rain singing in the yard.

II
A Lost Patrimony

Far from "art". Crannogs and beehive huts / herding
horses to the docks at Belfast, priests in black gowns
walking the pavements   Tenant farmers
in the hills around Halifax –
    walking mummies in dungarees and flat caps
    life of slopstone and clarts, the curlew
whistling failure over the top fields and obviously,
souldom gained and lost, thoughts that bite, dreams told to willows
by haunted streams
        (the muses in a ring about Apollo's altar sing)
and the pipes played The Flowers of the Forest.

To market in real time, the northern towns in their hey-day
five easy miles from cowshed to choral society the road decked
with warning songs: the danger of breaking the contracts and
cracking everyone's future (make me a bed fit for dyin')
    and the sea in the far distance beyond the hills
    calling its account.

Full hearted governance, free library, honey-coloured
perpendicular stone, mutual aid societies, wool market,

"chapels for almost every class of dissenter"

strict codes of punishment for breaking contracts

       The poets I worked with and learned from and
       loved and feared recede one by one
       into somebody else's career, like birds into a mist.

       Pound wanted the warrior classics back,
       the quest for the perfect leader,
       these 'effeminate' times, he sez,
       the blooding stroke is held back (as
       if). A child's hand for a time
       seeks his in the twilight, and retires
       (Cf. later on Mayakovsky)

roll of mist clinging to the stream up the valley side

conditions for social success in poverty

    lost and found stations across Europe

From near

      where everybody was welcome, what

  happened then, I went

all the way to Transylvania looking for whatever it was

The trees and streams were not pictures, the houses

not marble, the daily bread-making in the yard not by Alma-Tadema

birch-wood pillars carved with sky lozenges, horse carts,

    leaves shaking in the wind, clinging to bare branches

    by Corot, fragile places, "tonal values" at the day's edges

    graveyards full of iron crosses

> Beyond the faint border the money lords were waiting
> to advance.

Advance Liverpool to Halifax, Halifax to Stockport,
Liverpool to Manchester, cotton mills, speculators in wait
> *far and near* never to return *and low and louder*
> *the calls of earth* dispersed up the valleys in Pennine wind
> the advance that picked us up in a claw and dropped us where it chose
remembering a western brookland

> And another child is born,
> somnolent in white lace
> and always welcome (what
> is a sky without a star in it?) 1830s urban
> infant mortality rate 50% (what is a sky
> without a soul in it?) soul tugging at
> soul under a black sky.

And there we were, serving new industries
cotton and print mills, brick cottage rows in
cobble and dirt streets without so much as
a tap and the great sky held, the great arch
of experience stretched over the parklands and we
gained our own, the long songs and stories
were ours for the telling and our sad fates
woven across the night nobody, nobody
stood any higher than us in the meaning of the world
whatever mess we made of it our heads were alive

with our dialect and the end we saw coming

clearly over the town we lived in.

And we didn't use banks and we didn't tick boxes

but stood at the quayside as the ship pulled out singing

don't ne'er deceive me with that break (X) in the voice

            "acrost the ocean" the song that

knows the entire wound, and the price of the state

Shallow Brown, you're going to leave me.

Manchester, the great currents sweeping through the city

individual and group senses brought to a third term, marching to music,

canal warehouses, red-black, wooden office floors the wind

combing the city streets, of international hope/despair

pub meetings to discuss Marx and *Falling*

in love again / Never wanted to (What's a poor girl to do?)

but agree   and cling to the principles   "in your heart" (dis-

persed apart by war and paranoia)   an impoverished vocabulary

but vision straight as a die, for the new industry

was real and trustworthy and bore us on its back

until the demographic crises broke over us, or at least

| Yorkshire | We were not etymologically determined |
| Lancashire | We meant what we said |

    and the lark in the clear air.

There is a turning point: the past becomes a hope,
the future a loss
                depopulation of islands
those who enrich themselves at the expense of the people
bird bone on the shore, black star in the heart of the mountain
but localised aesthetics persist, cultural
and political boundaries not coterminous, Sardinian *tenore*
        filling the gap between bone and brain with harmony
        full-throated echoes of well-forgotten courts.

King Oliver played to us and if there were flaws in his playing
we didn't notice them, or put it down to his teeth
    the flowers that bedecked the stage and the burning
    lakeside lights, these things knitted us together in the art of staying,

stations built of overlapping chords, where we
laid our heads on the hard wooden benches and
dreamed our own cathedrals, man woman and child.

The old men still there, in a row on the stone bench
round the palazzo, watching the tourists, sharing the wine,
    to be willing to talk, to learn from anybody (Mandelstam)
amplifying a procedure, a work between stations

work of day night weeks years on end
    to be something, something more
        than bits of paper blown in the wind, more than words,
            to be bound together like
                words in a sonnet, to enact a solution
instead of replicating violence. Anything's better
than skulking deep in some university
casting spells and hating the world.

III
The Generations. The Dispersals. Funereal Duties

Not a shining, not a performance – an *endless way*
    not a crisis
  but a labour, getting on with/out,
  the 'muddling through' which creates the territory
  field by field stone by stone and a labyrinth of paths through
  daily stupidity, asinine persistence, willing a response.
    Brilliance can only deceive.

The world becomes evident
    and language pricks up its ears,
    the world's known potential
tugging at the heart /*how shall I help*
like an Indonesian shadow puppet the light arriving
through apertures in the human frame
painted on the inside / pain
spelling Job's patience year by year
well enough known in the northern hills –
lives of clouts and slapsticks
    clinging to earth, true
    to the lapwing's call in the pre-dawn
        with a fence wire to hold on to,
        sense and trust.

Of sense, of trust *of life that made me*
and makes me again every dawn a lighter thing
> *the lightfoot boys the roselip girls*
> sleeping
> under the stream

as the year points to the stars chattering
in the morning sky with a lark's clarity, the stars fading away.
How shall the blind see but through others' eyes?

Seeing direct into the eyes, not noticing the skin colour
dancing together in the playground
> *Pizza Pizza Daddy-O!* / the muses in a ring (etc.)
> *O admirabile commercium,*

that what died speaks in the eyes, that
the great revolving thing in the sky
breaks through the soil as a flower
> a solitary dandelion
> on its way to waste

that we took and blew, into the eyes of the warriors,
calling time, and saw through the mist to the heart
and the ashes under Uricon.

> As I came into this world far from
> any centre, *pratensis* "of the fields" so I
> moved out, seeking a hand in darkness as
> a child against the wandering fires in the night fields
> learning to breathe in the world's fullness
> a single truth, that held a dying hand, far from any centre.

Admirable, that the falling tone twists into a farewell
    truly meant, that the earth
presses against our breath half-closing the throat
    into a tune carried across
distance to make a language that means
    what it says, and the otters laugh.
Well may they, at our boondoggling
eagerness.

        Tell sorrow to the stones
        that are smooth as wax, and silent

                    The sky, and the dark trees
                    rustling, listening for
                    words on the wind
                    across a child's ear cupped
                    by a child's hand
                    listening for
                    returning footsteps
                    through the rain

and "the old wisdom of the romantic tradition"
    that in whatever fields of failure wandering
        offers collective support at stations of transition
        and consolation for tragedy.

The hard-hearted and their "necessary decisions"
    knocking on the door in the night

don't leave me here alone   make my bed

soft / near / under the sky, the hearthcloud and

seek beyond the earth's divisions, healing

the wound, close to the ground, hearing

    lute music

(lute music includes common sense)

    rain, thunder, passing trains. Elektra's

autism.

The world which is always the same (*here I tarry*)

the past which is reliable (*in your heart*)

will agree to war sooner than revolution (*all to die, all of them*)

                      Children sleeping hand on ear
                      while soldiers die behind
                      the partition, slow fear creeping
                      alongside the cot
                      and away behind the hill
                      and waiting there for ever

Keep close to me and calm

the wind in the trees will do you no harm

consolation for a life of dread

as death is warmed to.

Perhaps we do not warm to death,

don't go gentle perhaps we shout

between two forms of fantasy

the collective and the solitary

perhaps we burn them up

"The reason the mortality rate was so high was not because
of plagues and famine, but because when they got ill
they took to their beds and hoped to die" and avoid
the horrors of longevity and becoming a burden to others.
    star-defeated sighs
turned into corners, concealed from *sky and plain*
awaiting dispersal *four quarters*

    A two-storey chambered tomb, each "floor"
    entered from the opposite side,
    sun rise/set, summer/winter
    the door always open   the rain in the yard

That liquid touch on the fingerboard, the small bones at work,
three-finger *portamento* technique and one-finger trill on the violin
    star warmed tenure, sliding away, believing nothing
two steps left one step right
    under the kestrel's path we moved
out and back, seasonally or daily,
    going to Marks & Spencer's for a shirt
well beyond the northern limit of the nightingale.

    Sea-girt, the northern isles, the green slopes
    relenting to the shore, thin stone shoreline
    under constant wind across the bay
    (Orkney) that blows through the tombs and stone calendars

over the concrete bunkers and gun emplacements

and wafts us out of our indulgences

to the waking place, the narrow cot, the birthing light

        not far from the duties. Or Elektra's

        sentence.

IV
Strangers Arriving. Soldiers Returning

Smoke standing over the houses in the valley below
we tempered ourselves into an ecstasy of forgetting
and farmed ourselves into the next generation
and rolled down the hillsides to the town
to set up shops, and ache with servility when the man
calls in to take away the profit. Consolation starts to slide
    into counsel, tragedy into accident.

And where there was a local consolidation is now
a subsidised farce. Our old romances return
freshly laundered on the backs of migrant workers
from former colonies and recent war zones.

        Child on tiptoe
        show me how
        in your earth-bound space
        the elasticity of matter
        becomes an asset. Take
        she says, my arm, through
        this noisy defile, to the end
        of the first sett: curtesy and
        bow to the arrivants.

They arrive in thousands all seeking

the same peace. Turkey, Romania, Pakistan,

China, Bulgaria, Jamaica, songs of hoopoes and

nightingales, messenger birds sent out after

lost children. And we knew the songs

as we knew the departures, we looked into the eyes and saw

feudal dues, we saw conscription, bleeding the land dry.

We saw Ireland again, green and fertile river vales

fenced off, the people condemned to grow oats on stones.

And still they come, Croatia, Moldavia, Poland, Ukraine,

and return, *disperse apart* to an agrarian society

exhausted of its violence, again maternal.

Take me with you, returning stranger, make me

a bed fit to die on, read me The Diary Of One Who Disappeared

                        Potkal jsem mladou cigánku…

                        Once I met a young gypsy girl…

her dark hair…   Take me with you.

Take me into a war

where the compass point searches for the heart

and a continent gathers around a companionship of respite.

            39-45 was for my father and most
            of the men of his generation the only excursion
            the only visit to the art gallery the only theatre ticket
            in their lives.

> Child, be still, tilt
> your head onto
> my shoulder and
> bite your thumb until
> all the absence is localised
> and the cloudy sphere takes you
> into its fancy folds. Listen
> to the soldiers singing.
> Child on stilts, look
> down on me, pity the pain
> of my radical thesis.

We returned, and sat on the hillside

looking out over the town, trying to blow

the smell of corpses out of our nostrils, and sang

> How are they solitary now who were together?
>
> And how has the centre become a province?
>
> How is it that what is ours is sold to us
>
> and every public word is an unkeepable promise concealing
>
> threats and curses? Pulling the wool over our eyes. Let us sleep now.

Or lie awake in stone houses listening

to the wind and the night birds and the more we

think of the war the more birds there seem to be in the air

a feathered strafe riding down the wind…

> Bushes and birds, barbed wire and bullets
>
> "The bird whose song kills" (Cocteau, 1917)

    Little, *dainty fine bird*
seeing night and winter approaching
    with broken vocables, the heart
        flies out singing
           away over the hills towards the sea.
Nymph, transparent carapace, transported in
a movement of air that hardly touches
    the autumnal plant residues.
            We stood still
            looking at the sky
It's going to snow.

I know, the north wind knocks on my door in the night
and no more information is needed, no further input
Go now, *disperse apart*
            the Big Sleep begins.

There is too much poetry, it infiltrates alien discourses.
The financial news is given out in metaphors and stage accents,
and only the initiated know what's happening
        We were lured into the war with metaphors,
           with metaphors as premises

and lie on our backs in the night in a remote rurality
listening to imaginary birds, remembering a future,
the past released into labour and purpose

green leaf turning in the hearted
space, the earthen response.

Waves break on the far shore, rooks replicate
the night messages, *tremolo* my father's spirit at the door

rose of the winds
                         that formed me
revolves in the trees
                         wakes me up

    Out of my depth is where I stand,
    where I've always been, silently
    breaking metaphors apart until
        their sides shine like flint
            the edge of a thrush's voice

en la tarde in the evening, when I consider
the termination of my life the owls call, meaning no harm,
and the northern winds rattle the windows.
A shrinking recess in the dark surface of place
holds such authenticity as is left. This stinking Eden (clarts etc.).

And wake in the morning to find the birds have formed a co-operative
and the children have all remembered their fathers' names.

Child on bike
it's all right
I'm still here
holding on
don't worry
you won't fall, go
faster.

The city distant on the plain, indistinct

in the day's haze, pale domes and dark chimneys

the houses of the poor clustered around, leaning

inwards to the place of consultation.

V
Locospotters

...and the people who promote this madness are always calculatingly sane, and build reputations and careers on the madness, while the people who are mad hate it, and destroy themselves, because they know they are mad.

While we were away God tricked us!
    Promised me a silk shirt, gave me bronchitis.
It's hard to find a new love, to kiss in the dark
        a pink rose hangs on the barbed wire
        a lonely rose on the edge of my territory
    and to brush bodies together
        as if by accident

Like leaving school, a sudden cold field,
Yes/no questions: *what are you going to be?* (c1956)
Dread approaches cross-country
but the blue sky opens through the cloud (as if by accident)
    and we take the long way home
    the path on the edge of the town, to/from
        one purpose / hope / love / one kiss in the night
    "my sweetheart is a soldier boy"
        quietly
the bells of the town fade
        les sonorités opposés mingle (as if by accident)

      A precise liquid touch on the keyboard
   small cloven hoofs on the packed stones
         and the soldiers Cocteau knew, who didn't care if they died
     O the fair faces in the bonnie broom.

Walking long streets of house rows
deep and clear autumn sunlight between cloud masses
all the fair faces in the rooms and their abandoned destinations
      with no hope of repair
betrayed workers, paid up and forgotten,
their language vilified, the plain speech we offer the world in
all honesty described as "a source of evil" by
     priest academics chanting etymological curses
while the world bears its own evidence on rays of sunlight
        all along the rows of dancers.

Indeed we know we are nothing, our language is lies
   my sighs, my broken words, the sink of my passion
into inarticulacy, the everyday which is where we live
in which we are trapped
    Gentle shepherd, rain on the window
      It is an honour.

To be faithful to what we are (we are no doubt "mad")
     we are no doubt evil

being ordinary, bearing the pain of this honour from
generation to generation, getting on with the work.

Gentle fold in the hillside where we sit and sing
of the world's lapses – gentle maiden, a kiss in the dark
        and a future stretching beyond our white lies
        and the white heather plucked for luck
for a charm against philosophers
who are paid to uncover reality. We are not mad. Reality
is not hidden. We prove it, with our hands, at work, perfectly clean.
A bitter wind in the night, cold and damp infiltrates
the house through the walls
    hope through dreams of fear.

        Lie still, children of war
        in your stone beds under
        the dark adjective. The woman
        with the guitar will sing to you
        of places whose names you know
        and the strangers who sent you here
        across the toiling seas. *Keep close…*

Through the labyrinths of the northern railways
madness (somebody's) pursues us, holding
notebooks and catalogues, inhaling
coal smoke in the shunting yards of Gorton and
Stalybridge and up to Hyde were the child murderers lived
whose madness so drew the "curious" they had to construct
roadside kerbs along the entire Glossop road

over the moors, to stop us ghouling around,

driven by the casual and cynical madness of the press.

*In Cuba they don't report murders in the press, why
should they? what does anyone ever learn from them?*

Cultivation of anxiety and resentment as national temperament.

We pull the wool over our own eyes, against the blast.

      Always as if searching, for what to be,

          on station platforms, in Kinder gullies

on railway bridges in Heaton Norris in wild

          costumes of the soul with small notebooks

on the footbridge over the London line at Cheadle Heath swamped

in goals, insane children collecting numbers

          a mania from somewhere that pushed us

          into a war, into anti-semitism, into lists of things.

The lists have all blown away. Between these lines one by one

reactions to the death of Anna Mendelssohn come in by e-mail

who lived in poetry, in the foolishness of poetry

carrying everywhere a room full of artistic vertigo

from Stockport to Anarchy and Surrealism

as if there's wasn't enough madness in Stockport

as we poked around the railway sidings seeking a qualification

and the edges of overgrown parkland.

Doing badly, all of us, doing very badly
ineducable, unemployable, talentless, aimless
        streets of Manchester hands in pockets
      the wind blows Spring into our faces
hanging on, to some remnant of pride, shaking
others' guilt off our backs, dumping the baggage
and walking on in the rain w/ a certain skip in the step

                    Wind catches the stream
                    in a cusp of ground
                    the grass trembles, water
                    pours down rock and plumes back,
                    pride in the wind, gone out/with.
                    The children leap from stone to stone.

Whistling ghosts in the night, calling us back
from Surrealism to the Stockport of death, the great
brick viaduct still striding across the town in 27
arches like letters of the alphabet spelling p o é s i e our
lives bent to the workbenches while they
pranced around in masks in Zurich but from there
        at least a certain lightness in the step a syntactical
        novelty grinning at the cold, might keep
        a few toes warm in the northern winter.

And our hands always perfectly clean. Work cleansed them.
We dug and there were lights in the soil
        distance/proximity focused on cold
crystals of commonalty. We were told

> we were alone and refused to believe it, the wisdom
consolidated in rock shelters told us not to – not to listen
as group rights were eroded in favour of individual "freedom" which
> we laughed at down pub
and eventually the entire public world dismantled.

I like this town   "I want to be remembered
I like its nervousness
I like being excluded   as a blue cloud
I want to be forgotten
and melt back into company   in a white sky"

Known and substantial things safeguarded
> day subsiding to the west, one light in the valley
> > one mind awake
> > > one white house on the shore
To reach the shining port of our melancholy
> that levers us into a new world
> > through a darkness with an arch over the entrance
> > > reading "Work Makes You Tired".

> SO THE FINAL DESCENT into madness and death
> is down a Pennine hillside, leaping small streams hung
> with elder and hawthorn chest pain image pain stumbling
> over tufted meadows down cinder tracks, vetch,
> ragged robin, cow-parsley, dandelion, speeding

between hedgerows into the edges of the town the

garden fences the meeting places the towers, then

to slow and stagger panting and fall silently

across the threshold of the public library in all the gladness

and relief

of total incomprehension.

which is not error, and not stupidity, and not exclusion. But courage facing the impossibility of the world. A kind of insanity.

VI
Water Songs. Schubert/Goethe. Mayakovsky the Russian Scarecrow

In sleep "we" is restored to the choral "I"
and the singing can start
the great chant of humanity suddenly unafraid
under contract, rights offset to duties

Song of Myself / the boat on the water / the water on the window
expanding from unison through all the suburbs
    to the cemetery beyond the town edge, choked with growth
in which (uncomprehending) we build our singing platforms
and lie waiting

The spirit over the water
    drawing the heart into modulation
        water pawing the ground
           We come with the water
           we go with the wind,
           liquidated, floated,
           ripples on the stream

    Angel of the morning / ne me quitte pas

What after all have we got? *ain't got no money…* (fame, power etc.)
a few sticks of furniture too many books and our selves, our fibre,
no choice. We don't want choice we want reliance.

Tired child after school, pokes the fire.

* * * * *

All' mein Wirken, all' mein Leben
All my working, all my life
All my doing, all my finishing
    devolves on you
attentive ear, shielded breast.

    Ruddy clouds over the town cemetery

    spring grass on the small mound, old blood

    in the soil weaving purple into the flowers

    that *blew hither,* herald of new flesh,

        from ghost lands, a flicker on the screen

Quiet winter evening	Wilderness at daybreak
planets conjoined	wild rose in the heather
sitting at the window	possibility of peace in the world
sinking into dream	mist in cloughs
dreaming defiance	insurgent sleep
and reparation	hope for the deprived
	lamp in doorway all night

red wine spilled on snow canopy, clouds calling over,

politics guarding the edges of the land

ethical spring at the centre, work to be done

"to have peace among us is the work of intelligence."

* * * *

Mignon (the little one) (Nursery Songs)

Wild rose among the heather
snow and sunlight on the windowsill,
brush the snow, remembering
kisses in the dark, at pre-
cisely midnight, birds in cover,
completion of tasks.

                        Day brushes night
                        up the hill, streams
                        pour down the valley
                        noisy, jabbering ideas
                        I feel dizzy.
                        I fall towards your fate

            Fill the ring, keep your word,
            let me seem what I am
            my white dress made me old
            the earth stayed young, the beautiful earth
            unhampered by my power

                        "Silver tones" and the world opens its curtain
                        revealing the cold skies of ending.

"I am not from here,
I'm going back where I come from."
—Macarena, the paint-sniffer:
an *obscure allusion* to a Romanian documentary film
about homeless children in Bucharest, but probably she died.
Probably she went back where she came from.

Back there the soft glow in the fruit trees, calls to market,
and under the canopy my father will ask me,
"What have they done to you, poor child?"
What have we? We have squandered generations.

       A glance, *ein Blick*, a flash from eye to eye
       a kiss, barely brushing the lips but a token, a some-
       thing said for ever while the heart reaches
       to the houses at the end of the road
       where a small girl opens an atlas.

       where a small girl opens an atlas
       or a dictionary, for a word,
       hope, life-scoop
       while we sleep.

       * * * * *

Confusions and Contradictions of the Russian Scarecrow

        Events, lives, spinning into light or dark through dream
The grammar of our quest a squaring
of this spin, lakeside cabin in snow
                An earthly sufficiency against harm
ethically secured against shamans
and their lice   *It's not a shaman* – **IT'S ME,**
           "inspired sewage disposal expert of the earth"
                        IT IS I, I, I...
            Mayakovsky, professional public self,
            finger on the trigger. Hated children.
                <u>Song of Myself</u> (and my lice)
        (the lice taught us more than the shamans ever did)
                     sung (outright) unafraid
O noisy not-self, ventriloquist's doll, glass eyes
and wooden jaw, immensely bossy schoolteacher
                    Don't worry or be afraid
                         it's only me
          undispersed substance, firm on the ground.

Spirit voices that rule the world from the word-prison
– disobey them, be a person for a change, be a person in charge
        carrying a bucket to the shed or a curry from the takeaway
"Language infected by commerce" (without commerce we die)
              be an I (we) of purpose in the world

gladly lost under starred domes
                        but positioned on the ground when the call comes
heart act linguistic and naturalised
                                      unashamed global hooligan
until throat closes, not the end
but persisting, sounding the caverns
            Music reaching across forgotten courtyards with moon songs
keeping us together   in the night
warm night   night of pollen.

A quiet glass at day's end, on the factual earth
and a slow cart into the hills. How to keep old vehicles
on the road, tools salvaged from the war, sweet-smelling
flowers on the window-ledge in old bean cans and no despair,
no concessions to global guilt and its artist-priests.

Dying, she turned towards me and gave a last, sweet,
pout. "I gave my life to poetry." At the funeral
we got through nine bottles. Miles of damp fields.

VII
Lateral Spread and Forward March.
Erwartung. Préludes.

    Teenagers in a garden shed working their way through
    Novello's Harmony Primer Book One (undated)
    on electric guitars

        "All you need is love"
        (The Beatles, William Burroughs, Patience Strong)

    40 years on the dole
    and we laugh at your pulpit, we tread
    your words into the ground

        A generation of war babies that missed out
        on social continuity, fear and mistrust
        seem to dog our steps, trying to tell us
        what we could have been.

But there are no experts on us, no undermining,

we stand "I" on the ground we undermine. Nothing

devolves on us, we move out, nobody

carols our colour, it washes off. Our way

of shining is across the land.

        We are from Vienna, when you speak
        we know what you really mean. When

> *you dream we know what you want.*
> *We are from London, when you sing*
> *we write it down*
>   *and claim the copyright.*
> *We are from Prussia, when you try to think*
> *through the whole structure and out*
> *we add you to the shopping basket.*

Held to our promises as we took the risk of being explicit

the houses our words build, to know

the whole traverse of sight through the geology

darkening as a great curve across the hemisphere

the terminals and the nodes, spanning a life. The fall

> of my true love's hair
> rosy fair, and two brown eyes
> blinking across the nation –
> my understanding, my home and halt.

> Opening and closing wings
> senza vibrato (love-torn flight)
> and the descent of moons
> in amateur kitchens.

> Nation-building exhortations:
> hear them and rush to the border

We got out. We walked, out of what we were

into another group, and out the other side of that,

sometimes cloudy, sometimes clear,

stepping lightly, stepping west, stepping

over the earth following the sun
like Felix we kept on walking, noticing
a musical trace in the air, one moment Serbian
the next cabaret / the man stepped down from his hut
to the ferry, a few black shapes in the night with lamps and against
the sliding water they asked us what songs we'd brought with us.
We sang them across the river, someone wrote it down
and we asked the way, to the next labour market, or the next war
and were told to follow our noses but when we get there
we may have to wait, under the lamp post, by the barracks gate,
for a kiss in the night, or a ticket to Warsaw.
Perfectly freely, we partook, innocently, solemn and apart,
saying little, learning the tongue, spurning privilege
    and on into the forest, sometimes crying.

In the forest the owl woman, recognised from the old song,
trapped in her obscurity. Dark boughs, endless
anxiety, children waiting for a return
a restitution, to humanity, its bright red band
its tensed, cantilevered chords. In the forest flooded trenches,
dead leaves under foot. The vocabulary changes, world
is dark, and unhealthy. Refrigerate after opening.
Modernity, we are lost in it, strips of dim light
through the branches, splintered music.

Working a way. Stench in the nose. Pressing on.
On and through and out. From village to fake village
and on to more villages. Trudging on in the moonlight and down
towards the house lights across the plain, untiring mobility
getting trapped or not, getting trapped in enclosures,
haunted houses, science, toy shrines… We walk, we go on,
into universities, think-tanks, to be taught duplicity:
tour the world rubbishing the body that pays you,
and out the other side, avenues of trees across the city, thrown
into language cells, clawing at the window, begging for clear air.
In the company always of a delay, an endearment,
standing still on the edge of the marshes watching the old jew
in the faded kaftan walking painfully the sandy track "I bear
your distance and expectation on my shoulders".

Delays. Laments.

Evenings in Granada. Gardens in the Rain. With what can we confront these things? *Moon Viewing on the Terraces.* Do we have to? Couldn't we just get an exit pass from the whole critical strategy, or leave it to those who are paid for it? *The Girl with the Flaxen Hair.* Learning to wait, recognising things that have to be waited for *About the woodlands / To see the cherry hung with snow.* The delays that are integral to development or the whole thing falls into inhumanity. *Blush Roses in a Glass*. Without commerce we die. Someone pays. We get by *Sounds and Scents Revolve in the Evening Air.* Sustaining pedal held (Janáček) and the whole heterophonic spectrum slowly subsides en masse *The Moon Sets on the Ruined Temple*. Swings and roundabouts. The pull back of Bessie Smith, or Kathleen Ferrier / back *from where, from* the Century of Nation-building, the Century of Massacres. Back from advance. "Thanks for loving me". *I really could have danced all night.*

Becoming unstoppable we spread out, indiscernible
because dispersed through all the professions, solicitors,
social workers, engineers, beggars, holding ourselves back.
The whistle-blowers, the people who keep an eye on the tactics
who fast forward the news, who don't aspire to office – delayed,
still hanging around between forest and marsh watching birds or insects
watching the evicted family's cart disappearing into the hills
knowing that one day it won't happen any more, if we have
anything to do with it. We'll evict ourselves when we need to.
So infiltrated through the entire structure
until it is all ours – City Lights. Passion Music. Affluence.
Good dog, follow alongside. Affluence with a quaver in the voice,
an old question, *Can I help?*

VIII
Nicholas Ludford. Derek Bailey.
Restlessness and Serenity.

and leaps across full ditches.

Wandering all over Europe very much at home
talking singing from shore to shore
gathering the daylight, long straight forest edges
like black cliffs, paths out of the backs of
suburban housing estates across abandoned
coal mine sites, miles of telegraph posts and electricity pylons
      some with kestrels' or storks' nests on them.

The lines bend to the ground at points of regret *For all I rue*
and I rue and I rue   (she turns her face towards)

Migrant workers, Jewish artists who fled central Europe
longing for home, old or new, remembering the particulars,
      the forms and colours of molehills in the family meadow
      The lonely desert-man sees the tents of the happy tribes
          "Man with brother Man to meet,
          And as a brother kindly greet" words
          past nations / public words
          distant hopes / whispered in the night,
          far from the ken of the broadcasters.

"Horo Mhairi dhu, turn ye to me" (in the dance)

(in the dialect) an almost silent message threaded

from shore to shore by mountain and valley

corner shops and multi-storey car-parks, a sustained

assurance that silences the amplifiers.

> Everywhere embarrassed and humiliated
> everywhere alien
> where in the world can I moor my heart
>
> but in the long moors of the north,
> heather and brown peat under which
> the murdered children lie

Turn, speak to me if you can, whisper in earth tones

remind me of the optimism of the infant

and how it will grow, if not arrested,

into an extended speech, a moral vocabulary

to defend the civic concept, the width of society

crowded with dialects freed from comedy.

He walks in covered in splashes of cow-dung and says, "You seem, Mrs W., to reprimand Wordsworth for not writing in a thick Cumberland dialect…"

He walks in covered in smears of axle-grease and says, "You seem to think, Mr A., that the northernness from which you gain your fame and fortune, is a bit of a joke…"

First riposte to Judith Butler
> The "I" in the mode of knowing, knows
> its own vulnerability, and thus others'.

Second riposte to Judith Butler
It would seem that all the persons that constitute me, some
here, others mourned, unknown, not even the name,
lost sight of in the northern tracts, it seems they all
consolidate into the simple, unique thing: speech visage and name,
"I", the only one of these things finally capable of thought and act.

The strongest among us feels the pangs of failure

when the latest human lapse

flashes onto the screen, far beyond thought

and the great performer loses his place in the script.

We are that faltering tribe, crouched in the sand,

waiting for the bombers to pass over.

Rising into narrative "I" is again "we", the lament

takes up again the living-spaces of the territory

caught up in guitar tones and 6v polyphony the song

grows into history. We follow it we trace it

on the curve of the motorway arm the red procession

we follow wherever it goes

For we are permanent.

We have permanent smiles and permanent frowns.

The shining in the night, in the glass towers, is also us,

the force that jumps the white fuse, the precept.

When the tension is too much we complain

in night whispers, arm across arm

Our past works buried in sand, a glazed brick waiting
for an archaeologist, too late – scrubbed clean and
lovingly contemplated, on show to the nations
but we have gone our ways into the lost trails.
      Tower of Blue Horses (too late)
      "the generation that squandered its poets" too late now
oh it's too late now, Radnóti sinks into the mud, Jobbik
(they could get 20%) speaks openly of imprisoning the gypsies.
Should have thought of this earlier. If the left
had deigned to participate in practical politics some
time in the last 60 years we might still have
a socialism worth voting for.

The big songs thought of this and wrapped it up. The largest sense
of person walked and talked it across the earth long before, and something
constructed from an entire life at that point was set on the ground
to include hope in a realism at a moral pace, an insistence,
a sufficient apple in the old red hand, but it never happened.
The big song turned inwards on itself.

The small song whispered itself over the Atlantic Ocean
with the emigrants, bounced back as clear as a bell
and become unstoppable / Mansoul glides over the water
    the little song balances itself on a light tread, antitheses and repetitions
    a chime at the turning of anybody's life

>   The grandfather's song, singing
>   the greatest possible particularity
>   into the greatest possible unity
>   immanent tones of the world
>   constantly returning home
>   where the small hands reach.

There are only long-term answers.

    The lament is full-throated.

    The linnet is falling thought

        from across the world

        landing on the ground

        shouting

            O Spring, come!

            Open! Grow! Twitter!

and then adiós.

    Amor, muerte: I

shall elicit a lot of caring

        from your mental lips

en tus brazos me durmiera

        y la vida no quitarte

body or soul

        yo soy un hombre correcto / sincero

        and have things to be made known

    For the siren

    finally convinced me

    que es muy bonita

    and there will be a long peace

        on the earth's sutures

the fluttering butterflies

the rusting battleships

in the harbour.

IX

The great tidal wave of negative and interventionist thought that swept across Europe from the east following the collapse of the Austro-Hungarian Empire. The scramble for nationhood at full cost. The scramble for new intellectual professionalisms especially by claiming to have located concealed strata of the mind or of language or of something else which can be reached and manipulated only by experts, offering explanation and thus redemption through sectional management.

All the fragments that cling to our coats

parochialists wherever we go, picking up what the wind slides to our feet:

tracts, wine labels, pressed flowers

      looking up to the sky hieroglyphs

forgotten signs clinging to our foreheads

      bee stings on our arms

"heading for the future with no baggage"

      we gently descend to the valley of unharm

            asking, prompting, offering help (how can I)

      (ere I part) (into dust) (no hurry)

That my years may endure through generations

      for a harmony grips us

      a tuning of the heart

      remembering a majesty

      native to all tribes of earth

      documenting a true history

"the constant dignity of ethnic music" (Bailey)

pieces of moth wing on the lapel,
the little body returned to calcium.

Such the fantasies of collectivised northern farmers on a day trip.
The bus takes a tight bend badly near Penistone and everyone
suddenly remembers, groups of people
trailing through the forests carrying pieces of bone.

Listening to things that house the dead –
sea-shells trees stones washing-up brushes bronze heads
falling water, grass in wind, distant traffic
Shostakovich's String Quartet Number 8
      songs that house silence
      staring fate in the eye

And in the progress a weariness, a renunciation –
      Now the poet drops his pen
      And moves around like other men
i.e. **thinks**, as anybody thinks
      hard thought burdened with proof
      slow thought of the witnesses
standing silent at their doors and outside the bars and tobacco shops
as the soldiers pass by. The courage to speak would be folly.
The courage to think is something, a targeting of hope
and turn back to the gramophone, and the boiling kettle.

    Listen, the music bends us out of crisis
    into sea fevers, fireflies on the verandas of Pyrenean inns
    circling the suspended lanterns (1957 El Serrat)
    playing us back round to the present,
    to the final relief of a broken for ever lap-top,
    and then know
            Apocalypse too is lullaby.

The kingfisher, a blue streak along the river
is not a model of the world (I am not the soul-doctor to a sick civilisation)
every event has a potential trail of language waiting to be fetched out of it
leading towards a new form and its apertures into truth so much more
                                              fulsome
in the longer circuits, followed wide round from night to night
by the smoke on the horizon the ferment behind the hill and watch how
the small bird like an arrow flashes past a spark a disturbance
to the colour template an act of imagination but in every way normal.
Words are empty and deceptive noises until they receive this insignia.

These jewels of thought stick to our heavy coats, half way round the world
arriving at dawn to knock gently on your door when
you are suspended between two worlds to make sure
you choose this one, it wants your vote. The stars in the sky
become invisible in the blue sweep of light, angled onto work.

Awoke at dawn with his head on the table (Pasternak)
in a position of farewell already a day old, to move back into
the streets and stations, to set ambition into reverse

        Tenuously
        in the darkness
        fingers gently crooked
        to knock on your door
        but you sleep on
        fortunate individual
        and softly
        I go away
        noticing the rousing of birds.

    I walk home at dawn
    tears running down my cheeks
    dampening my shirt collar
    another dream unmoored
    sinking back into darkness
    and the new baby in a brown babygrow
    a serious proposition lying there ahead of me
    not waiting patiently for anything.

What clings to us (ashes and diamonds)
also falls off us
    into the mud
laying strata into coal measures
    fool's gold and stencils of fern.
The rain stops, I take my coat off
    and hang it on a bush for an hour to steam dry –
and resume, endless trail, unstoppable, invisible, powered
by just thought (not "theory") aimed at betterment

and we say nothing, ready to move out at a moment's notice
when the national circus headlines us,
onto the road again
      to witness more wet fir trees
            and derelict factories.

We return, we come round again (like a rondo)
return home, if we ever left it, pick up the letters from the doormat
smile at the thought of the bureaucrats (not "bourgeois") trying
to encrypt our false names miles and miles away, to capture our sleep,
our lost marriages and unborn children indeed all our sorrows coded
into sales pitches.

...and consequent collapse of serious ethical thought into the aesthetic.

How we survived collectivisation, by not being around at the time.
How we need help. What *kind* of help we need,
our fight with death. How the magpies chatter in the holly tree.

How tides of malthought
clogged the channels of guidance and the clerks
betrayed on a daily basis.

How the wind shook the Essex bushes
and the pilot cruising down towards Stansted
took some care with the wobble.

How we evaded the experts on our condition
by not having enough money to pay them
and the roses thrust through the wheat.

How my people speak in crevices
like hilltop gentians. And we…
Who or what are we? I don't know.
The silence and subservience of a work force with
nowhere to turn. The obstinacy of owing nothing
and paying no attention to the ideologues.

    Driving the long road at night in the rain
    rains so hard I can hardly see the road. Looking
    for something. Highway 13. Looking for a family,
    a contract, a greengage tree heavy with fruit,
    a lost child, rain comes down so hard windscreen
    can't take the rain, driving through the night, rain
    beating on the car's roof. Moving out, heading
    for another city, another cheap outskirts, looking for a job.
    Rain, rain, never stop. And I remember
    walking the thin path through the meadow grass
    to visit my sweetheart's house, darkness of
    fate descending slowly on me, taking steps
    in the right direction and the sky sang out
    and all its population.

X

Ife Heads. Gamelan. Vesaas. Night Letters.

Carrying silence in a side pocket through morning thoroughfares
how it pulses, holding trust like an old watch on a chain,
woken into oppression resentment and anxiety
after hateful dreams, working populations of Europe.

Silence folded against the flank as the sky is folded
tight behind the morning fogs and closed shops
and there is no refuge to be had across the great
housing estates, sleeping citizens of eternity.

The long awaited silence, light through paper
dissolving the shadows filling the absences and
every step taken is an act of wish every
thought a prize, hovering names of loved ones.

Gentle pulsing of *tremolo* technique in a pavan
for viol, by Daniel Farrant (†1651) a blood-flow sense,
smoothing the furrows of habit and picking up
roadside attachments, emerging families of the far plains.

A failure, a silence, close to the heart,
a writing on the silence saying "too late"
as if we had a nation with us, as if we could *speak!*
Poets of the closed cupboard, this is my Rubaiyat.

In prehistory each unit (group/person) had one melody or tone-row
which was sung continually, maintaining contact
through forests and across rivers, coordinated to food source.
Harmony was then the meeting with the other.

An external articulation. Gamelan in Irama Dados, speed
ratio, 4:1, there is always a slow referent, a sustenance
alongside, clearly, over there through the trees.
And the moon rises and freezes the world. Bronze chimes.

Bronze heads wrapped in red textiles, buried in dry earth.
Walk on. Speak to yourself. Walk through a war if you can,
everything you remember lost and broken behind you, humming
a simple tune you can't stop repeating, immortal invisible.

Bronze head, lips slightly parted, staring straight ahead
a soundless singing. This is where we stop, at the ancestral chapel
the parental double grave. Be quiet, say nothing, follow the argument
of the music, monothematic, drawing together, "a marriage of true minds".

A chorus of 15 bronze heads singing in the museum at night
the music working to its close, "The Philosopher" the brain song,
earth-toned lines, earth-bound demands, this
is all there is going to be, where the sun never shines.

Singing across all the anxieties that return during the night,
between dark and light, sleep and waking, truth and invention
bearing the infant in mind, the bronze heads breathing song:
pastoral song panic song choral preludes measures of fate.

Not enough breath to disturb a candle flame, circular breathing, songs
of storm birds and steam railways, syllabic patterns, shepherds' comfort,
sentences of trust, chorale preludes *Let us live to make them free*
Unlock'd her silent throat.

IT IS THE MIDDLE OF THE
FUCKING NIGHT. I CAN'T
SLEEP & I HAVE NO WHISKEY
LEFT

[Track 9 "*Nohy, a woman of Andigoza village, singing 'Mba ferigneso' (have mercy on me) over and over again as she weaves a liana mat...*"]

Unnoticed people.

Are we not extraordinary?

We are the only extraordinary thing.

I am the housewife of the universe

I shall defeat death and harm, fascism and tyranny with a sink plunger.

        Anxiety melts down as leaves fall from a tree

        Lines in the sky / We carried a silence across Europe

        and now we listen to it.

"This terrible silence that emanates from me

standing there trying to remember what real people

would say under the circumstances."

        An inaudible singing through bronze lips.

        când m-o făcut mama-n lume

        when my mother brought me into this world

        she intended that I should speak

        and what did we do? we sat round and nodded.

        We did nothing to prevent misfortune and misery.

        The day was destroyed. There was no day.

                (The Boat in the Evening)

        Say something. Say precepts.

1. The virtuous mean is a kind of extreme.

2. Our ideas must be brought into harmony with human acts.

3. Above the tree line there are sky blue butterflies.

I waited for the 'change' but it did not come. Perhaps he lost his way here. Poor me, now I shall be alone in hell for the rest of my life.
I shall leave this place

Shepherd's inscription on a rock surface previously used in prehistory, Mont Bego, high valleys of the Maritime Alps. Wind-swept rock arenas, immense solitude.
and I shall hate it for ever.

Then at the lakeside inn at the end of the earth

the accordionist, who sings and dances

in all the lost languages, late into the night

when no other light remains in the valley,

the people in dim bars in the evening sitting

silently or with a quiet murmuring, the day fallen

and scattered like puddles in waste land, the day

lost and forgotten, strips of light pulsating on the water.

The mind astray, becalmed, without habitation –

I gaze with longing / with supplication

at the backs of towns.

Aristotelian precepts carved on lintels.

With at all times the choice open for better or worse. A sense of reality includes the difficulty of the choice but takes it. Our halos are mouse-traps.

Our auras are open invitations. The stream runs beside the road.
The police helicopter worrying overhead. Our common weal.

The church bell's after-tone, the mountain sides darkened.
My path be it ethical or aesthetic, one or the other,
my whole life <u>clear</u>. Clear as the evening sky.

Come, you great art, you facture. Do something useful.
Take the old fellow upstairs a brandy and help him get to sleep.
Speak out. Speak for. Reconstitute the missing day.

XI

The Ascent of Kinder Scout

Wrapped in luminous cloud, pushed by the wind, we walk up out of Hayfield in the steps of the glorious trespass, April 1932. The cloud is not a metaphor, the art is terrestrial. Eventually our heads will clear it. Stamping the ground, stamping mystery and privilege into the soil, we walk up into our work, hauled on our breath. The foundation of the state is not violence but education. Thought is free on the wind-steps. Rills under grass arches. It can only be a completely open field.

A stone path up the ridge end, ghosts fleeing in the wind, calling, most of them scout leaders and members of Class 2B 1952, most of them long dead, half-remembered and gone. Echoes fading across the fell side. The original calls were reciprocal, to a purpose, keep away from the edge, maintain contact in the mist. They blow away into the silence and dignity of the objects of earth. We can't see where we're going and there is no secret knowledge – what, then, do the ghosts want?

We call ourselves to our own purpose, a reason for being here, the pains to be taken. Memory thins, but the calls of 1932 linger longest around us, calls to unite, calls on record, and cannot be forgotten. Cairns set on horizons, the village long vanished but the tumulus stands, sentinel at the gritstone border. That name I was, blown away in cloud as this life must flit with the winged seed driven under the stone, calling in vain for respite. No central European despair can blight this act of trust.

Stone upon stone. How beautiful upon the mountain were the voices, that announced the end of war, feasts in the streets and honey in the cup, the rose opens, all in the arms of the modern state, which makes everything possible, and makes strangers of us all. Kassandra in the language of birds, the language of inscape, saying Don't despair. A flock of passerines that stays together in the mist by mutual signalling shoots over my head on the brow of the hill. "We shall return," they say.

Making no claims. No amount of erudition or vision raises anyone a centimetre over the heads of the people. Work your passage, earn your living, bound on the same boat as anyone. Break the lifeline down to the pain and desire that everyone knows. There is nowhere else. There is nowhere else to be or speak. The earth enters you back into its folds unsatisfied, there is no other song; there is only September, when the falling year offers us everything there is, and teaches us to measure the distance.

We thought we were so grand as to join heaven and earth. But all we did was wallpaper over the crack between myth and science and lose our homes. The farmer's wife sang a truer song, told a sweeter story, of hope and despair hand in hand walking back into society. Company on the mountain, pulled upwards, out of a pit, a hand on a stone gatepost and a chill wind. "We belong together and we know what we are." In the very teeth of the mist we know. Goodbye, Johnnie.

    Goodbye Johnnie   the arms of the sea take you
    migrant lover and we turn sadly home
    to our own futures, the day that opens slowly
    when the spotlight is turned off, Johnny Shilling & Pence.

    You run off into your success, Jean-Louis,
    your mysterious lure
        and we turn sadly home
    to doze in the turning of the new dance
    beside the stream, under the oak, prelude to the long song.

        You mount into the sky and turn to dust
        as a punishment for betraying the people

    Transcendent sense, we last saw you
    in the arms of the darkness as war
    closed over Europe
        your star turned green
      a failure of sociality and
    the crying night birds will wait for you for ever

> *gypsy singer, the song*
> *feeds on your mouth.*

And the ship moves out of harbour, leaving us here
– *on the quay, holding the baby* – behind us
all the pathos of the modern state,
telephone wires stretched across the land,
a common tongue, which makes everything possible
and sinks us into the hands of corruption and disdain
and disperses families across Europe, searching
for each other between life and death.
Was ever such promise betrayed?

> At the end of mythos & cosmos the world politely
> shrinks into our arms and is held in our principles,
> vast stretches of history fading away in mist and dust over
> > the plains
> no more epic, no more expensive dinners, the strength
> of hope in the new baby's round dark eyes and the diadem,
> that circles in the sky, in our slow northern understanding
> > repeatedly.
> Goodbye Johnnie, big-boy, daddy-o, goodnight Irene.

We step up onto the shoulder, the cloud disperses, the land retreats before us, walking backwards into private estates. The butterfly patterns of the fields, fluttering into the distance, all that money sinking into dark undertree pockets, all that erudition frittered away in fancy-talk. Smoothly the hills bend down and curve onto the plain.

Following the edge, facing south-east, fresh blue sky, and that fearful moan from far away – "I don't know where my parents are buried. I have no place to be." They are buried in Europe, in where it happened, in history. Not in language. My parents are buried in an operatic chorus, a photograph album, a seaside comedy.

Scattered ashes, and a name in a book. End of a long journey, into the world's nonsense and brokenness, and back home, to occupy a quiet space among fruit trees and wooden frames protected from snow storms and ideological programmes in provincial ignorance and limited vocabulary. Oblivion in a cemetery of claims.

The wool is locked over our eyes, the classics methodically trivialised in public channels. Look in the public mirror and you'll see a little toy with big eyes. This is your baby-doll soul, acting out your civic rights. My parents died into this, in the long brick terraces of the Manufacturing Districts. I fled, and hovered trembling in the hills.

And built myself a parenthesis. In it I now reach Kinder Downfall, the pool catching the sun half way down the slope below, the line of water tossed in the wind in an arena of broken strata. And walk on ever barer ground to pause at the summit trig. point, denuded even of peat, a grey desert of gravel and scattered boulders.

From west and from east they came, the Manchester and Stockport men up from Hayfield, the Sheffield men from Edale and met on the summit. And shook hands and ate their packed lunches while gamekeepers' staffs banged on their shoulders like the jazz-band ball, swatted off like flies. Waved and set off back, knowing something new.

I've known these denuded sites for fifty years. We came here to find out what there was, at the end of a climb asking to be walked, at the end of a history under erasure. There was peat and grey outcrops in mist, unidentified birds and a mediaeval boundary stone, there was a pivot of decision about what you want to inhabit.

Wind-carved monoliths, a waterfall blown back on itself in the westerlies. Here we say goodbye to the pit of eternity which destroyed the classical world and by purposed seeing attempt to regain the earth, the high moors bearing a mediaeval boundary stone, the state's ensign, calling in all our lives as the wind scoops holes in the grit.

Be called in, whatever we can muster of that calm which opens the human condition to inspection, wrap it round the statue, twirl it round a stem. The steady heterophony of a working city swelling between day and night like wing beats, tuned to the double flute. Crouched in a cleft of the uplands, seed and soot shooting past on the wind.

There's a kind of line, of light, a thought line, which cuts through false histories and comes towards us from the devastated zones. When it gets to the British hills it twirls round a stem, if it can find one. Gravel, boulders, and dark banks of exposed peat. And always the experience wrapped in the line is that of the work force.

Somewhere behind me, towards Manchester, is a patrimony unclaimed. Ahead is a saddleback ridge with a tumulus at its end. Our passionate speech is of the love that defies principalities, and we shall at last find rest where our speech was forged, link by link: famine-stricken families in cellars of the urban labyrinth, nursing the dying child.

So the top of the mountain is where the wild self ceases to exist, dissolves into a yearning for sociality, and a stated purpose dedicated to its safeguarding. Then the stars are cast down to float on the surface of the stream and a hawk swoops over the saddleback ridge. Locked at last into earth we begin the descent.

A network of bright lines falls over experience, like a field system, breaking the grip of totality as the wave breaks on the shore or the air on the mountain side. In and across these polygons we attach principles and mitigate conflict. It is painful walking downhill on stones with exhausted calves but script will bear us to the end.

The principles are in any old book. They never fail. The pain is in passing through and beyond the boundaries of our homes, and all our fond attachments, a pain that shines clear as low sun on white flocks, indeed shines exactly there at near distance and I shall send you a telegram when I get there, about the weather.

Do you know this land? Its field corners and its fruit trees, its corner cafés and police stations. Something will fruit here, that we have deserved, some consolation for the dying child, the barrier against return. The air wafts gently over the sharp stones and in the agreement on worth the "beautiful earth" is born, *die schöne Erde*.

Do you know this valley? The cold water in the cleft, under the hawthorn, its white dress. To breathe freely and (therefore) think without constraint of reaction. For the ear is not closed and the eyelashes are not blinkers and there is more, always there is more, here, in readiness, a more which turns back to comfort the dying child.

Or the footpath, and the stone steps down to the road? Escaped from the ghost-ridden summits the prospect burgeons into deeply lit segments, for we know no more than we believe, the town walls caught in late sunlight, streaked with script, but with wires under the metalling. We are our own result, inscribed on the map of lives.

It could all be wiped out at any moment by a falling aeroplane or a Tory axe, this town and all its chat. So it is also necessary to be able to get out, to maintain a summit line in secret, to be still up there in image, spinning on the crest under the moon. Forest! Forest! Moors and mountains! Electronic networks! be there to protect the forsaken.

And the glorious trespass of April 1932 also walked back down from the mountain, into the vales of reward and imprisonment, the dark divided vales. Touching the edges of settlement a joyous relief meets a slight ache, questions only met by result. A white stone path reaches down dark fields towards the pub as if longing for reconciliation.

The path goes beside the river towards dinner, under trees, continual chattering on the stones, house windows lighting up, and cuts through the sports fields. Say no sententious thing in this locality as tense as any with claims and despondency. Take the weight. Black pudding, the night rears above.

Blood pudding, history passes through the whole structure, the dining room, the camp site, the antique shops, the post office. Some of it takes the bypass and is merely an irritating noise in the night. On the horizon Kinder Scout is a shadow lost in the black sky, an enormous gravestone in memory of the welfare state.

But the courageous venture also descended the hill, shook hands with friends and rejoined families and the air was full of regional accents as the rooks over the graveyard complained in chirps and coughs of the wind shaking their homes, as many homes were to be shaken over the next few weeks, but the promise was established.

And will never be lost. Tramping over the hills for health and exercise was the least of it. The promise was in the combination, and a kind of elegance in the dance that led over the dark shoulders of the landscape, completed and resolved in the village square, couple dances under strung lanterns, to laments of infidelity and injustice.

Then disperse in the dark forest, in groups of two or three quietly in the night along the estate wall, hiding from the money, safe from a cultureless future in guarded compounds, cold and tired but on our way home from an achieved purpose that no amount of punishment can erase. Then there's just me and a story long ago concluded.

All I did was walk up the hill and back, had dinner and returned to the campsite, where rabbits do somersaults on the short grass all night long and taking off the walking boots is harder work than anything else I did today. "What did you do today, Peter?" laughs a bob-tailed bunny and jumps ten inches vertically.

I said goodbye to an old friend whose time had come. Johnny the railman, Johnny the magician, Johnny preacher-man, Johnny no more. I loved him dearly but when I reached the summit he wasn't there, he'd crept under a tombstone and all the world-saving jumble was offered to the nearest charity shop. Language failed him.

As it fails us all, and we tighten the cord on the tent flap asking sleep come shine along. The rooks sing to themselves in their twiggy cradles up above as the night wind comes sweeping across the valley to stir up a whole gamut of noises from different trees, elms roaring and firs hissing. Sleep will protect us from language's deceits

And offer us linguistic coinage, with which to pay the world for all the rooks rabbits and dinners it has provided to help keep us going and then we speak to it direct, whether it is deaf or stone we tell it what it's worth. We see it disappearing from sight and call it back, we kneel to the moon holding the baby. Persistence, optimism, grace.

XII
Angel Meadow

I.

The future sucks in the victims of a demographic disaster
through canyons of brick warehouses, the future
congeals, consolidates. Power inhabits a darkness
with patches of light –
    Open libraries: Portico 1806, Free Public 1852, John Rylands 1900
    A belief in human equity: reform, education, philanthropy up against
    up against a constant refusal to act, Tory spite, corporate disdain,
                                              coterie verse,
    creating darkness out of coloured threads.

We wait, we live but poorly, we toil, we don't have long (we don't belong here)
Neither did we eat any man's bread for nought
but wrought with labour and travail, night and day
then walked into the dark forest.

Angel Meadow, mass graves paved with tombstones
the workhouse cemetery under the forecourt of Victoria Station
destitute Irish fleeing the famine, those who survived the crossing,
Ashkenazi Jews fleeing central European pogroms.

The Rookeries at Ancoats, the dark continent
> *"immoral, degrading and dangerous"*

The struggle: focussing and reparation
against constant resistance from above and below
and we are labelled "incapable of thought" as indeed we now are
who escaped rural destitution to die of typhoid or cholera in a darkness.

> The streets I used to know, the brick towers
> damp pavements under gas lamps
> the old violinist taking the bus home after
> a concert at the Free Trade Hall, where I probably heard
> Kathleen Ferrier singing *Das Lied von der Erde*
> and certainly the premier of Vaughan Williams' 8th.
> But free trade was secretised, and Manchester
> soon ceased to be the future. Less secret
> was a murderous tramp to the east in the 1840s
> and another was called cholera, people dying into
> the success and obsolescence of the entire structure.

The wrecked town centres east of Manchester, Oldham, Blackburn, Rochdale,
the waste lands west of Salford (Liverpool line)
remains of canal systems, wharves and pools grassed over,
empty lots thick in willow-herb and buddleia. The
minimal landscape of Ancoats, nothing left but churches, mills
and pubs, all disused, red-brick piles scattered across the plain.
The long-term cost of child slave labour in factories in the eastern hills.

> The rivers, when they went over
> weirs produced large quantities
> of a brown-cream froth lumps of which
> were blown off in a strong wind and
> sailed over the meadows and along the streets.

Here and there among modern estates a length of old wall, brick
or sandstone, the corner of a walled garden, with a chimney,
new lines crossing on the map. In the hills lumps of

dressed stone lying around everywhere from
demolished mills. Street names of the northern quarter:
Dantzic, Hanover, Copperas, Sanitary, Silk.

    The River Irk strolling into the town from the east
    bringing sweet water from the moors until the future
    turned it into sewage and animal waste from the tanneries
    alongside Angel Pavement, stinking, barely able to move
    and disappears under the station.

I remember, seen from the raised tracks out of London Road Station, miles
of dark brick rows, east and west, a black church riding them like a galleon.
All these streets have disappeared, and their songs with them,
poor, derivative songs, bellowed out on coach trips.

    Insane children writing numbers in notebooks
    inhaling coal smoke by the sidings at Gorton
    the stench from the Astoria suet factory in
    the streets of Openshaw. 1952. Named from a meadow.

        Moon city, pulling the waters, parting the land.
        Pleasure clubs among factories, painted black
        Standing on dry bones.

Deathly courtyards of the labyrinth

tap on the door and walk in

    In cellar bars they sing the awakening of the world

    gently from sleep, a gradual voicing

Angel Meadow: the face at the window (Kertész)

How shall we sing our song in a strange land? (Passionately!)

> Infant mortality among the Manchester 'Low Irish' 1830s: 50%, among the Kalahari Bushmen 1970s: 50%

A persistence, that this dark and fearful barrier will be passed through.
We live the world's tribulation in our small corners.
> We have one goal, one hope: to survive.

Who treads the path at night?
Whose is the face at the window?
Who comes in the form of a black dove
and flies into the future?

> *One day we'll get out of this darkness*
> *and sail from island to island.*

II.

Circumdederunt me gemitus mortis. / Dolores inferni circumdederunt me.
(I am but a poor factory girl) in silent night, while shadows
flicker at the window, she walks up and down by the river,
living the darkness, to be born here, to search for honour
in the rubbish skips, and *all the teares mine eyes have ever wept*
her image in the night, shawled figure waiting for life
watching the dark river that falls under the railway
for although I'm a poor girl I think it no shame
her speech, the notes of the night-bird: a future,
here.

Noticing, green moss on the corners
of eroded brickwork above the black river

As it gets dark and the stars. And an old woman
singing an Irish lament somewhere in the labyrinth.

Our benefactors are elsewhere, studying for the future,
locked in their classes. A faint luminescence.

A faint wail. The Banshee followed us to Manchester
and half the globe, working overtime, for death is our default strategy.

The old woman reigns in the sky, with her
sciatica she burns through the night.

My wedding trust is to her memory.
In animabus nostris adfirebamus panem nobis.

•

I am nothing and shall write a letter
with tears in my eyes. Dear Sir,

How am I to resolve the contradictions? Parts of the brain
close down and the music touches the heart. But to rescue us

We need the mind entire. The mind the place the night the river
the stars the black bird and the wine. We cannot afford wine

Or toffee, or mother's milk. All flesh is as grass but
we can't afford grass. Yours faithfully.

Without a sound the river Irk creeps past,
a faint roll from the underground waterfall.

I am here beside a polluted river at night trying
to regenerate the present tense.

History is a song. I'll have it sung at my wedding
if it takes all day.

•

Now that sky earth and air are silent
and the mammals and birds gathered in to sleep
night conducts its starry bus across the sky
and the water lies below without a ripple I stand here
I look, think, burn, weep and the destroying angel
stands in front of me, the goddess who locks us
into this darkness, as we find ourselves so we must be.
Hope and despair from one source, one hand reaches
towards me from a black cloak, the angel of
Angel Meadow that shall pull me out of this sink
or toss me into the death traps we call home, our
promise to love and our infant mortality rate, our lives
renewed and cancelled ten times a day.

•

Proud to be born this "I" meaning poor
that shall poorer get in the brick corridors,
with trapdoors. The domestic *is* the sacred, the rational
facilitates the imagination
                      by extending thought
and opening the trapdoors to reveal the secret shrines
of our masters, small horror toys, men with wolves' heads,
mummified hawks, priestesses holding snakes, the double axe
also contracts of bailiffs employed by mortgage companies to evict tenants
and reports proposing the demolition of insanitary dwellings
marked "refer to long-term planning" in blue ink.
Catalogues of failures I scatter the leaves on the river.
For heaven's sake give me a clue, a red thread, a vein in the stone.
Listen to the Oracle's thin growl:

> "I am a poor old woman tricked by poets
> into being a goddess.
>
> Your questions and problems are bits of thistledown
> blown across the killing fields.
>
> When the flowers return you may not be around.
> Get out of my way."

So I, the dark flower of these ruins
will end up an angry old woman,
my marriage cancelled for reasons of security
i.e., the arrest and execution of my lover but not before
a future is engendered.

Notes

This work was written between December 2009 and July 2012 in Cambridge, with some additions and adjustments made during 2013 in Hebden Bridge, especially to section XII. I'm grateful to Melanie Warnes for the title.

The eleventh section was published as a booklet entitled The Ascent of Kinder Scout by Longbarrow Press in 2014; thanks to Brian Lewis. That edition was enhanced by the reproduction of two paintings by Paul Evans.

The quotations from Housman were all fixed in my memory by songs of Ralph Vaughan Williams and George Butterworth.

I. Macarena... refers to the documentary film *Children Underground* by Edit Belzburg, 2001, about homeless children in Bucharest. It is referred to again in part VI.

sčasováni. A term only ever properly understood by Janáček.

L'Albero degli Zoccoli, by Ermanno Olmi, 1978. The scene is one of handing over an orphan baby to its adoptive parents in a convent.

II. *acrost* for "across", as heard in a singing of *Shallow Brown* by Joe Heaney.

III.

Pizza Pizza... Playground dance song of mock coupling.

Uricon   Housman's word for Viroconium.

"the old wisdom of the romantic tradition..." and following lines: adapted from Ernest Gellner, *Language and Solitude* (1998).

"The reason the mortality rate..." Graham Robb, *The Discovery of France* (2007)

Two-storey chambered tomb. There is one on Rousay, Orkney

IV. Cocteau: *Discours du Grand Sommeil* (1916-1918) (also in V)

V. Anna Mendelssohn, a writer and artist who lived in Cambridge and died in 2009. Like me, she came originally from Stockport. See end of VI

VI "to have peace among us..."   Joseph Hill.

VIII "The lonely desert-man..." Title of a wordless song by Percy Grainger. "Man with brother Man to meet..." Burns, "On the seas and far away".

Mrs W. Not Mrs Wordsworth.

Tower of Blue Horses. Painting by Franz Marc, 1913, which was "lost" by the Nazis in 1937.

Jobbik. Far-right Hungarian political party.

IX. "Now the poet drops his pen..." Edward Shanks / Ivor Gurney

X. *Irama Dados* A pace or tempo in gamelan.

"It is the middle..." quoted from *Night Letters*, a book of the gouaches and messages to his wife done by the artist Roger Hilton in the last two years of his life when bedridden and insomniac.

XI.

The Kinder Trespass of April 1932 was a protest by about 400 people against the permanent closure of large areas of the wild uplands of Derbyshire for the exclusive use of grouse-shooting parties which took place on about 12 days in the year. See http://www.kindertrespass.com/ Different accounts of the trespass exist which disagree about its route. Mine, in which the main group walks up from Hayfield to gain the summit of Kinder and there meets a group of Sheffield trespassers who have walked up from Edale, seems not now to be the most respected one.

"I don't know where my parents are buried..." Paul Celan

XII

Angel Meadow was a notorious slum and focus of concern to reformers in Manchester in the mid-19th Century, inhabited mainly by immigrant Irish who had fled the famine. The first, separate, edition of *Due North* (2015) has as appendix a prose description of the area as it is now.

"Neither did we eat..." One of the inscriptions on the frame of Ford Madox Brown's painting *Work* (in Manchester City Art Gallery), quoting the *Second Epistle of Paul to the Thessalonians*, 3.8.

"Proud to be born..." quoted from Alice Notley's poem, 'Lady Poverty'.

XXI

Poems

Hebden Bridge 2013-2017

Milia

1
An olive-wood fire and the local
pre-phylloxera survival red against
the cold wind outside. And that's enough
of being, as if it were so grand.

Night folds its corners down
the terraced hillsides and
walks upright on the
wandering streams, but

No sound, of stream or wind, reaches here
or almost, and the fire darkens. Breathe words
across my ear, breathe a fear, second by
second, fear of war and world, be explicit.

For a resistance to grow here, far
from world but close to mind, how
close it lies, to hear its breath
against the inner ear,

A breath to question fear.
Then the streams flow on
and the air follow,
down the valley towards the world.

2
Thought that distils
against my ear a tear
for the time and
a fixed belief in peace. Our hopes

Are sunk in the total and lie
calm under tumult. Our dead
recede behind the night clouds.
Remind me of what I once knew,

Breathe the truth back faintly across
my ear in this walled shelter and hear
the plants shake, the earth tumble. There
is one real peace, much further out.

* * *

I'm out at night on the stone road, the bridge
over the river. I wander, I err, I slide,
defiant, jubilant, sober on the dark and
lonesome road I psalmodise. I hit the true note
as often as possible. All the things we know, how they
cluster round us in the dark and open to show
a fair world, fairer than is said of it.

5:39 from Lyme Street

The flat lands between Liverpool and Manchester
stretching into sunset,
people of short stature reading about stars.

After Rochdale the street lights rise into the sky
and we, side by side through the darkness
we stayed together, in our woolly hats.

We get out at a 19th Century station,
50 yards of wooded darkness
and the rustling river steers us home.
Our lives are coastal sand.

Food Bank

Let me still in dim industrial ruins
between the river and the railway
harp on about hunger, the world's
wrack and the world's abundance.

Up there on the downy slopes let us make a site
of mutual aid, a campsite, and the fat sizzle
and the water boil. The voice in the woods
says I hear you, I will come.

I'll walk under the railway arch, persist and
forget, find something to conjoin the sentences,
mend the lesion, serve the tea in tin mugs
and return next day mouthing Langland.

How the fields fold and lean into each other
in descending steps, forming a temporary home
where we dispose of the crusts and marmite
within sight of the world's abundance.

Of which denied a crumb, we give and go until
all are gone and I alone left standing here
in the world's wrack that falls across
the downy green slopes down to the valley ruins.

Let me still, faithless word, make my bid.
Let us again, faithful void, raise the spirits of the air
and tune legitimate pleas to the singing in the wire.
Cold spring, unsheltered ones, come and dine.

* * *

I shall fail in a mill town
governed by Oberon,
snow edging the upper fields
green carpets out to dry
pierced by black rocks.
Will you be able to hear me in the after,
in the ever, ever, after, will there be
a score to follow?

* * *

Stumbling down the moors we
love, the full of, the crossing,
over the upper pastures, pushing
through dead branches in darkness
crossing the river by the stone bridge
I was late, I missed the opening chorus
and sat sniffing on the town hall steps.
Fortune my foe now get me home.

* * *

Round the last corner the late sun
smites the hill slopes tumble
out of the horizon a white horse
takes the full slant of light a
wordlessness of babies resounds
across the world and the show
must go on, it must go on.

Ferryports

(i) Bardsey

You walk above in the light
on soft ground, creatures of thought,
glow off the sea and the distance
to be reached. Haze on the fields
spreading upwards.

We live through the days, climbing
the stairs to the bed-loft each night
and lying there, waiting for news
from the sky. On the morning window-ledge
sunlight passes through a seagull's wing.

Days and nights of wind and bird sound
the sea pushing its lines towards the land
a hundred and twenty-one seals in the bay
and out of all this a speaking to a purpose
out of this a reciprocal chant.

Saints buried under the track, streaks
of limestone in the grass. Who went
unrecorded, their messages followed up
somewhere else, far away, Doncaster
or Freetown, in acts of heartedness.

Strange birds fill the night with cackling
and squeaking over our thin roof. We lie
in the loft trying not to sleep until the sky
is quiet again, dream components
drifting towards the island.

The birds are Manx shearwater and they
know their tunes by heart all over the night.
The form of thought that they represent

mentions global fidelity and the ever
rising price of groceries.

Massed voices from the sea, statements about the world
in scribbled notes blown out of the hand, lost in the wind
found again in a book or a bone flute. Decked
in red and white bands the unmanned lighthouse
attracts migrating birds to their deaths at night.

To know the details, of sea currents, cloud
formations, whereabouts of the hut circles on the hill.
And sit on the bench against the harbour shed
in late sunshine watching the lobster boat coming in,
without candy floss, without writers in residence.

Stay and get older day by day as the
mind quickens to the task and acts
of judgement become acts of justice.
How does this happen? By what principle,
as delicately toned as a blackbird's egg.

Salt corroded iron ring in a stone stump,
bright red. Cist burials in the shoreline bank.
Catch my breath before it blows away. Trust
the principle. Leave the door unlocked at night,
only the sea breeze will visit. Be sure to vote.

Alert at night in the loft, free of the eyes' commands,
breathing like sleeping babes, thoughts always open,
always clear, thoughts you bring with you,
language that pursues you and here
come those crazy birds again.

Sunset comes straight in the door.
We don't hear the news but we know
how it goes: crackle and squeak
to drown the noise of massacres
and reduce hope to a facsimile.

There is no voice. There is no sense of.
The sea's eyes are closed under the soles
of your thought, year after year inching the self
towards a question to be asked about what stands.
Wind. Birdsong. Death Stones.

That's no answer. There is no answer.
There is no silence. Listen to the mad
cacophony of the shearwater, making
species calls to their young all night,
is it you are you still there?

When day comes, listen. Listen
to the grass. Listen to the gravestones.
There is a whispering around the island
that does no harm, clearest
at night, when the mind takes its part

And clear in the day when it rains.
Look it up in a dictionary, write
to the newspapers, tell us the facts,
getting older, moving slowly,
comfort lying further out.

This word and that and some others
and I sense an approaching proposition
creeping here under cover of night,
but everything I think is interrupted
by two thousand rubber ducks in the sky.

Creatures of thought, raging in the night sky
stamping your syllables into the soil
from which emerge baby birds that fly away
over thousands of miles of ocean bearing hopes
that have always been the same.

(ii) Mull in the Rain

* * *

Forestry tracks through spruce clearance in the rain.
Villages reduced to grassed-over humps.
I'm parked in a corner of a white bay
against a black rock, with an orange umbrella
humming songs from the bars of central Europe. Not long,
not so far away, one war zone being much like another.

Rain and spray, sand pools ruffled, one figure
far up the shore gathering something.
Villages reduced to humps, suburbs to rubble.

* * *

Fresh squid and a glass of demi-sec for lunch.
That was far away and long ago.
I shall set my back against the open sea
and row to the island.
I leaned my back against an oak
and bore two fine children.
I rest my back against a black rock
and watch the wind chasing despair across the shore
and into the forest, as it did,
far away and long ago,
when the work was good.

* * *

Getting darker. Stand and walk. Sorley MacLean
found he couldn't live on Mull because
you can never get away from the clearances.
The humps of Kildavie in the rain, traces
of stonework in the sides of earthen platforms.
The mill site by the stream. Ghost houses.
If it's cold be cold. The clearances:
"imposition of an alien law". I frown again
at the insoluble archaeology.

* * *

We find the car and return to the house.
Warmth from the Arga, windows over Ulva,
 remembering Dun Ara and the sea darkening.
And it was not in the steel towers,
it was not in your Mahoganny. It was here,
in the hills and shores the rough glens
and fishing villages that the law was lost.
Dun Ara, a flat-topped coastal rock stack
with a walled area on top
"about the size of a modern kitchen".
And from this modern kitchen
ruled the entire province.

* * *

By outboard ferry to the island of the dead
and all the things we do or don't want:
information display, restaurant, cold rain.
We take the track along the south coast,
remains of the villages and wild sea.
But the people are not at home.
They have been cleared away, cleared out of mind.

Bay full of small islets, spirits fleeing in grey haze.
What shall we leave behind, what empty shells
full of meaning? A hurt from Britain's past assails me,
I don't know why we don't act or speak to the harm,
why we are so bound up in our edges.

The people who know the dead and speak to them regularly
have lost their tongues. Notice their roofless houses, hear
their roofless mouths saying O and A to the desperate histories.
Return home over the sea, followed by those ominous birds
asking the world to think harder, feel further.

* * *

In the noise of the sea I seem to hear
McArthur's Piping School on Ulva, I seem to hear
a funeral service aboard a small boat,
the assured heterophony of smallholders
a hundred years ago, in which the secrets
of our hearts are laid bare to the sky
wrapped in cloud. It is the choral voice,
uncoordinated, carrying across the sound in
first light, everyone so elegant, everyone
holding true for the duration. There is the voice,
the song calling everyone together, there is the hope,
there is the love in the voice, and there is the hand
flattening the villages.

* * *

The voice and the hand
are under the same aegis, the same
dispersal. I walk out slowly with
bent back as far as Eas Fors,
the waterfall. Gaelic and Norse
calling together. *Songsters
of the sky, wake and assemble —
be ever constant – the land free and at peace,
the Universal Tongue tunes this world.* The voices
not quite together, over a great rushing noise.
Hiding behind a tree from the wind burst.
Every day is Saint Cecilia's Day.

(iii) La Gomera

A wooden room near the summit of an extinct volcano, looking down almost vertically on the villages far below. Reading the Mail and saying, This is not where I live, I don't live in any of this, this theatre of cruelty where nobody believes a word and the markets operate on fear and despair.

An island, a calm of mind, at the heart of society at the heart of the clutter and threat and false humanisation, a working pause. A hawk moth caterpillar on the doorstep. The donkey brays in the next field at night with all its strength and we live only here. We live nowhere else. On all sides the remains of a working agricultural system, the slopes striped in disused terraces, empty cisterns, water channels running from the summit laurel forests down to the coast. We live in the ruins of a public speech.

And what accrues from all these riches? A cloying of the spirit and for the victims a vast displacement, imprisonment in a desert. In a pause from anxiety we look around at where we live, a scatter of housing on the coastal strip, small square fields empty or re-used, palm trees, ferries sailing from island to island all day. So our reward after all this privilege and accumulation is what we already had.

How did we get to this strange place, this interval, this island off Africa, so much more where we live than anything in the Express? But an opening in which a drama can be thought about disaster faced and brought under, about love fetched from the depths of our kind.

A little further up there is a bar. Looking out beyond the peaks and ravines to the sea with ferries and fishing boats passing across, it is possible to think calmly about the enemy and the enemy soul, how it seeks its increase endlessly and immediately, the cost deferred to others while above our heads the steady trade winds blow, forming mist at the summit from which the laurel forest draws water, and at night a star to steer us home on the edge of deep drops.

XXII

Two Poems Offered

A Prelude For W.S.G.

Very gently struck
the quay night bell.

Now

An ordinary and barely noticeable event
written into a free harmony, just as it was.
Hark! now I hear it, ding, just once.
        You see, Mr Graham,
I was gently struck when my father died,
"moving out past the islands" taking all his
unfinished business with him. I hear him now
saying, "I'm sorry. I shouldn't have died,
it upsets people, and there is enough
death in the world as it is." I'm sorry, I say
(and the bell moves slightly in the quay wind
without, I think, sounding) I didn't treat you better.
I was not free, I didn't know you on the open page
where all bells ring and songs sing themselves
over the sea, the gobbling sea waiting for us all.
I was still in my imaginary harbour. I remember
your departing incomprehension and help-
lessness that hangs in my speech now like
a bell barely rung. Language is never enough.
The bell so close to ringing, a tear, perhaps
an imaginary tear, falls on it from the real world,
the night of thought where when it rings it is heard.
And hearing it, we know. Well,
        I'll leave you now, Mr Sydney,
to your alcohol evening, coming home late
on the cliff path with the last star burning
by your foot, and in through your own front door.
And just then, when a closure is pending,
the quay night bell very gently tolls
and we know, we are all called out.

* * *

Note.
As well as several subsumed quotations from poems by W.S. Graham there is one from Matthew Francis's notes to New Collected Poems.

Henge As Verb
for Denise Riley

When I was a child I thought I was a thrush,
indeed the king of all thrushes, singing
circular songs in fear of the dark.

The songs grew and fanned out over the hillsides
tracing love's concealments and escapes,
the dark disintegrated. I shall defy

To the last of my days Blake's puritanical
cleaving of love. Water and stone, mud
and blood, love is strong in the clearing

And in the chorus, a harmony across the whole range
at which time hesitates, and comes to a sudden and
unexpected halt. The song was sung, a hawk hung

Over the centre of a vacated space, a turning
circle or record of love's defeat, where time
stayed and built a nest of inalienable experience.

We built an enclosure around it, a bank
to ring it in earth, a ditch to ring it in sky,
with an entrance and an exit and a night bell

So that it stayed, for time was exhausted
and slept as music. In all the harm a clearing
which would always be there, and always open.

I made all this up. Does it bear a resemblance
to any known reality? Did not the dead prince command
a certain stillness at the heart of an empty space?

A peace-making stillness. An absence of question,
an eye closed on sequence, θυμέλι, the inner protection
against theatre. For something had been lived here,

A bolt of grief, a shout of love, something that
opened the world and was forgotten, a clod of mud
sinking out of sight but maintaining its plea,

Le Tombeau de Mesdemoiselles de Visée at which
there is a great falling of small sharp pieces
asking to be erased. The changes fall together

Into the pit and, listen: the spirit is moving now,
in a trance music that ripens under the silence
and speaks to the darkness. Hold back your strides

Until these powers are matched and finally free.
Or as Beryl said observing Nina Simone's way of taking her bow
and striding off the stage, That totally uncompromising woman.

Studies in the reconciliation of world and fate
wrapped up and placed at the centre.
Take your bow and stride off-stage.

Appendix or refreshments
(dateless)

XV Pieces

Alstonefield 1995

In Dovedale a heron swoops into the updraught and sails away.

In the dining room at the George Inn it's very busy. There's a family here from one of the camp sites who find they haven't got enough money for a meal and are embarrassed, and the landlady says, "It's all right, if you can't pay you can't, order what you want and send a cheque later if you can." This should be the act of an entire economy. I don't just come here for the scenery.

I walk back to my lodgings through virtuoso bell-ringing.

The Stones

There are not so many questions.

What does constitute the good movement?

Picking an old man up off the stones is a movement of celestial scope. If it is not he might as well stay there. He'll end up there one day. Celestial moans. Fragile bones. And without picking old men up off stones no heavenly box is worth the postage on it. The stones are natural objects.

Floating Verse

Something very small happened. It was August 5th and I went to Brigg Fair. Nothing much happened but I ended saying that the green leaves would wither and the branches die before I proved false and that was about a quarter of what I meant.

What People Have

In the afternoon, walking across one of the town's big open spaces, we overtook a tall old man slowly pushing a supermarket trolley along the metalled path. He was bent steeply over it, his head twisted to the side, his step uneven and painful, and in a voice like a drainpipe he was saying two words over and over again in a continual drone, which at first I heard as French, "M'assister, m'assister, m'assister…" But what he was saying was, "My sister, my sister, my sister, my sister, my sister…"

51 Park Lane

The embanked wall against the waste land, the path through grass to the outdoor toilet.

The rickety wooden stairs up to the first floor back bedroom, where my mother nearly died of rheumatic fever in about 1925.

I come here to sleep in a wallpapered room with one small window.

A spider's sleep, a sleep of dandelion clocks and cloud.

A night-light standing in a saucer of water on an old wooden dresser.

A steady candle-flame in a small window, visible far across the rec.

Alpes Maritimes

The wine was dark at Hôtel Terminus, white ghost of a house across the road and a small falcon hovering over its garden, with one carnation. The façade pitted like weathered limestone. We ate sandwiches in dim light with the balcony window open, onto an island in a river of strategies for the future, swirling round us, small businesses, youth, pipings in the night. Sometimes the future is somebody else's future.

The stretching heights above us were a darkness, a past, nobody's. On the rock surfaces of the highest pastures are inscribed ancient cosmic fantasies, and desperate love yearning by 17th Century shepherds, catching floating verses from the bitter air.

In our hotel room in our cheap cocoon we scratched a meal together from the village shop in Saorge, long-term patience resulting from long-term patience.

Third Concert
for Jonathan Styles

That grows out of silence, that/

quiet building at night. Somebody in it? something stirs? somebody

tuning a rebab by candle-light

slow music for the sorting of bones

that grows out of measure, towards harmony
the small home between the hand and the string
the truths that are new and quiet
and grow out of each other.

* * *

Peter Hughes drove us up to Frascati, the cloudy evening heavy with warmth, the lights of Rome in the distance under a layer of cloud. We got *porchetta* sandwiches at the stalls and sat at long wooden tables with carafes of Frascati fresh from the autumn picking. Kings, I thought, made this possible, and we, not kings, made it continue.

Așa Beau Oamenii Buni

At some point during the course of the evening the musicians will go into this song, and that is when everybody starts weeping. It doesn't matter who they are – tourists, peasants, bank managers, gypsies, Communist dictators, airline hostesses... They'll all start swaying from side to side and nodding their heads and quietly join in the singing, sniffing.

The title can be loosely translated as "A good person is hard to find".

They are weeping in gratitude because the concept "good person" survives.

Lathkill, or, Putnik

It is never the end. We have string bands and bright plastic rings. These are major grips on the face of the universe.. The tear slides to the left of the eye, traverses a ridge, and evaporates. Leaving behind a footpath.

* * *

I used to dream of a university. I used to look at the older men queuing in the bus shelter in Mersey Square Stockport in the 1950s and see each one as a lecturer and imagine a subject for them: that one's Chemistry, that one's History, etc. They were middle-aged workers going home. I had to ignore their clothes but their faces offered no resistance to this exercise. Now I dream of there not being a university.

* * *

The
knowledge
we
pass on
to our
children
through
eight
languages
and
all
the
small
bones
of
the
left
hand.

!Kung Music

They close one eye
and sing about the food supply.
It is incredibly beautiful.

To a Grandchild

The song says "Don't ever leave me" but I shall,
I shall leave you, and so too eventually
will your mother and father, leave you,
to continue alone
with your dawn song.

* * *

Sitting on Ecton Hill next to a thistle
in the middle of the night, I realised
that I'm going to miss myself.

Sitting on Ecton Hill beside a thorn
in the middle of the night, I knew
that eventually I shall forget myself.

Afterword and Acknowledgements

My understanding of the way poetry was made public during the time of Sir Thomas Wyatt, is that poems were circulated in manuscript, generally without author's name attached, and persons who received them would, if they wished, recopy them into a personal collection. If, while doing this, they came across something they didn't like, they changed it. I have taken this liberty freely with my own poems, especially in the earlier parts of the book, mainly very lightly but occasionally amounting to a re-invention. It should not be assumed that the new versions necessary replace the old, though it is quite likely that they do. Anything herein which isn't poetry is included because of its contextual or sequential connection to that which is. I can only make a guess, but possibly between one-twelfth and one-tenth of the contents of this collection have never before been published in any form.

I am for ever indebted to those who have of their own free will published books and pamphlets by me, from the presses named in the list of sources below: Andrew Crozier, Tim Longville, Rosmarie Waldrop, Ian Patterson, Richard Downing, Andi Wachtel, Peter Larkin, Ian Robinson, John Welsh, Iain Sinclair, Richard Caddel, Randolph Healy, Michael Schmidt, Simon Smith, Alan Halsey, Ewan Smith, Rod Mengham, John Kinsella, Tony Frazer, Ken Edwards, Colin Whitworth, Jon Thompson, Peter Hughes, Brian Lewis, Alan Baker.

I am grateful to Carcanet Press, Manchester, for permission to reprint work collected in their publications, *Alstonefield* (2003) and *The Glacial Stairway* (2011); to Parlor Press, West Lafayette, IN, for permission to reprint work from *A Map of Faring* (2005); and to Longbarow Press, Sheffield, for permission to reprint work from *XV Pieces* (2012).

This collection would never have been assembled or published without the work and good sense contributed by Kelvin Corcoran and, of course, Tony Frazer of Shearsman Books.

Finally, I am very grateful to Keith Russ, for providing the schematic images of old Cornish mine workings for the covers of both volumes of this *Collected Poems*.

Sources

Love-Strife Machine. Ferry Press, 1969
The Canterbury Experimental Weekend. Arc Publications, 1971
The Whole Band. Sesheta Press, 1972
The Linear Journal. Grosseteste Review Books, 1973
Strange Family. Burning Deck Press, 1973
Following the Vein. Albion Village Press, 1975
The Musicians The Instruments. The Many Press, 1978
Preparations. Curiously Strong, 1979
Lines on the Liver. Ferry Press, 1981
Tracks and Mineshafts. Grosseteste Press, 1983
Ospita. Poetical Histories, 1987
Noon Province. Poetical Histories, 1989
[*Noon Province et autres poèmes*. Atelier La Feugraie, 1996]
Sea Watches. Prest Roots Press, 1991
Reader. Ewan Smith, 1992
Lecture. Equipage, 1993
Sea Watch Elegies. Poetical Histories, 1993
In Donegal. The Plague Press 1996
Between Harbours. Artist's Book by Colin Whitworth, Cambridge, 1996
Small Square Plots. Grille, 1996
Snow has settled... bury me here. Shearsman Books, 1997
Author. Folio (Salt), 1998
Untitled Sequence. Wild Honey Press, 2000
Passing Measures. Carcanet Press, 2000
Messenger Street. Poetical Histories, 2001
Aria With Small Lights. West House Books, 2003
Alstonefield. Carcanet Press, 2003
Excavations. Reality Street Editions, 2004
A Map of Faring. Parlor Press, 2005
The Llŷn Writings. Shearsman Books, 2007
The Day's Final Balance. Uncollected Writings 1965-2006, Shearsman Books, 2007
Best at Night Alone. Oystercatcher Press, 2008
Greek Passages. Shearsman Books, 2009
The Twelve Moons. Oystercatcher Press, 2009
The Derbyshire Poems. Shearsman Books, 2010
The Glacial Stairway. Carcanet Press, 2011
XV Pieces. Longbarrow Press, 2012
Chapters of Age. Open House Editions (Leafe Press), 2013
Due North. Shearsman Books, 2015

Index to Vol. 2

5:39 from Lyme Street	550	'Forgive these warriors…'	375
51 Park Lane	577	Four Transylvanian songs	379
A Cold Room in Granada	300	From an abandoned alley	309
A Prelude for W.S.G.	567	Front Room	16
'A step forward…'	310	Frustovento	296
Across Central Europe	304	Gropina / Leopardi / Gropina	24
After Mandelstam	19	Haydn at Csávás	386
After Terezín	302	Henge as Verb	569
Airs at Furthest Accord	350	'I'm out at night…'	549
Alpes Maritimes	578	'I shall fall…'	552
Alstonefield	149	'I used to dream…'	583
Alstonefield ('The light fills the ground…')	21	Kalotaszeg	293
		Kemptown	407
Alstonefield 1995	573	King's Cross to SOAS	391
Alstonefield Part VI	317	!Kung Music	585
Alstonefield, After Dinner	303	La Gomera	564
Argolid 2003	426	La Sologne 1991	18
Argolid 2004	438	Lancashire Graveyards	411
Aria with Small Lights	29	Lathkill, or, Putnik	582
Asa Beau Oaminii Buni	582	'Long since the stars…'	376
Ashlar Facings / Pink Rose	17	Loutro	346
Bardsey	554	Men of Destiny. The Stolen Picture	46
Best at Night Alone	353		
Bits and Pieces Picked Up in April 2007	347	Messenger Street	312
		Milia	547
Bukovina Song	385	Mull in the Rain	557
Castle Howard	20	Music in the Train	43
Chapters of Age	412	Music Night at the Old Slip Inn	47
Coda	292	Notre-Dame	15
Cuban Nights	371	Oh my Beauty!	44
Dioscuria	137	On Through Silent Lands	48
Distant Points	57	One Remains	45
Dreaming in La Habana	372	'Peter Hughes drove us…'	580
Drowsy Maggie	390	Pilliszántlaszlo	295
Due North	457	Place Dauphine	14
Essex Skies	408	Poems to Pictures by Jack B. Yeats	
ExoMani 2002 (10 Preludes)	423	Prelude: Night Shift	42
ExoMani 2005 (10 Postludes)	451	Pyrennean	343
First Sett	261	Room 40, Frühstückspension Caroline…	299
Floating Verse	575		
Food Bank	551	'Round the last corner…'	553

Sad Fates of the Songsters	373
Saint Louis' Island (first version)	13
Schiele	297
Second Sett	279
Shadowy Waters	399
Shining Cliff	401
'Sitting on Ecton Hill…'	587
Small Square Plots	25
'Stuck in Vienna…'	298
'Stumbling down the moors…'	552
Swavesey Lakes	419
Szászcsávás: the older stratum	378
Terezín	301
The Children of Maramureş	382
'The clue to the Neolithic…'	310
The Crowd Yelled Out for More	294
The Glacial Stairway, Part 1	327
The Glacial Stairway, Part 2	334
'The knowledge…'	584
The Lark in the Clear Air	389
The Little Watercolour at Sligo	50
'The man in Jack Yeats…'	311
The Road + Remix + Carol	396
The Songs	309
The Stones	574
The Towns along the Tisa	292
Third Concert	579
This Carol They Began	81
This Grand Conversation Was Under the Rose	51
This House…	344
Three Pastoral Poems	22
To a Grandchild	586
To the Memory of Frank Cassidy	388
Transylvanian Songs	381
Ultimul Drum	383
Vacated Thrones	95
Vertigo	377
Weddings of the Gypsy Flower Sellers	384
What People Have	576
Whistling Sands	410
'Write from henceforth…'	309
Zum Weißen Roß	305